101 WAYS TO SCORE HIGHER ON YOUR SERIES 7 EXAM

What You Need to Know Explained Simply

Revised 2nd Edition

First Edition by Claire Bradley

REVISED BY ATLANTIC PUBLISHING
EDITORIAL STAFF

101 WAYS TO SCORE HIGHER ON YOUR SERIES 7 EXAM:

What You Need to Know Explained Simply — REVISED 2nd EDITION

1405 SW 6th Ave. • Ocala, Florida 34471 • 352-622-1825• 352-622-1875–Fax
Web site: www.atlantic-pub.com • E-mail: sales@atlantic-pub.com
SAN Number: 268-1250

Library of Congress Cataloging-in-Publication Data

Names: Bradley, Claire, 1974- author.
Title: 101 ways to score higher on your series 7 exam : what you need to know explained simply / by Claire Bradley.
Other titles: One hundred one ways to score higher on your series 7 exam | One hundred and one ways to score higher on your series 7 exam
Description: Revised 2nd Edition. | Ocala : Atlantic Publishing Group, Inc., [2016] | Revised edition of the author's 101 ways to score higher on your series 7 exam, c2010. | Includes bibliographical references and index.
Identifiers: LCCN 2016040871 (print) | LCCN 2016049508 (ebook) | ISBN 9781620230572 (alk. paper) | ISBN 1620230577 (alk. paper) | ISBN 9781620230732 (ebook)
Subjects: LCSH: Stocks--Examinations, questions, etc. | Securities--Examinations, questions, etc.
Classification: LCC HG4661 .B67 2016 (print) | LCC HG4661 (ebook) | DDC 332.63--dc23
LC record available at https://lccn.loc.gov/2016040871

Printed in the United States

PROJECT MANAGER: Rebekah Sack • rsack@atlantic-pub.com
BOOK PRODUCTION DESIGN: T.L. Price • design@tlpricefreelance.com
JACKET DESIGN: Justin Oefelein • justin.o@spxmultimedia.com

Over the years, we have adopted a number of dogs from rescues and shelters. First there was Bear and after he passed, Ginger and Scout. Now, we have Kira, another rescue. They have brought immense joy and love not just into our lives, but into the lives of all who met them.

We want you to know a portion of the profits of this book will be donated in Bear, Ginger and Scout's memory to local animal shelters, parks, conservation organizations, and other individuals and nonprofit organizations in need of assistance.

– Douglas & Sherri Brown,
President & Vice-President of Atlantic Publishing

0.28
1.03
0.98
105.53
20.32
403.15
10.10
0.12
1.53
2.88

I would like to thank editors Amy Moczynski and Carrie Speight at Atlantic Publishing for their sharp eyes and great editing advice, all the participants in the case studies for sharing their experience, and my family for their patience and understanding while I was working.

TABLE OF CONTENTS

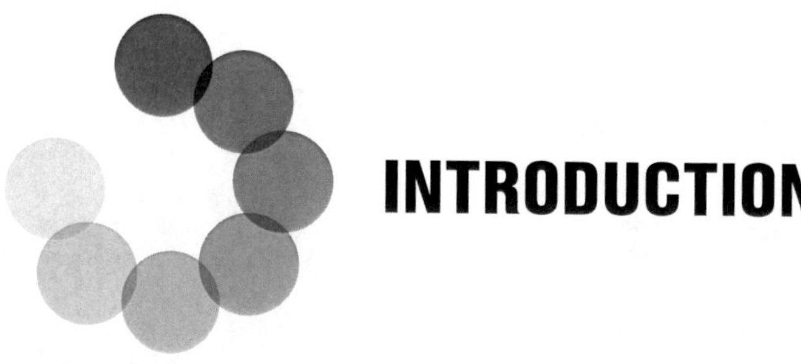

INTRODUCTION

Congratulations on your decision to take the Series 7 exam! Undoubtedly, you understand taking the exam will lead to a new career with new possibilities for the future and exciting new challenges.

The Series 7 exam qualifies you to hold the title of General Securities Registered Representative, or someone who works for a broker/dealer. Once you pass the exam, you are licensed to buy and sell securities, like bonds, stocks, options, and so on.

You have probably learned that taking the Series 7 exam is no easy task. The knowledge required to pass this exam can be daunting. Some people say that this exam is the hardest one they have ever taken.

This second edition of *101 Ways to Score Higher on Your Series 7 Exam* is now revised and updated to better guide you through your studies and includes insider tips to help you score higher on your exam. You will learn how to study more effectively and how to prepare for the exam with information in an easy-to-understand format.

You will prepare with practice questions at the end of each chapter, as well as with a full 260-question practice test, to ensure you have the knowledge needed on testing day. You will learn how to use your study time efficiently and how to use testing techniques to ensure you score as high as possible.

Studying for your Series 7 exam is your first step toward an exciting career as a registered representative. By using the time management tools and industry knowledge explained simply in this book, you are well on your way to facing the challenges ahead. With *101 Ways to Score Higher on Your Series 7 Exam: What You Need to Know Explained Simply* as your guide, you will be prepared come testing day.

HOW TO USE THIS BOOK IN YOUR STUDIES

Before you begin studying the test material in chapters 2 through 13, read the studying techniques listed in Chapter 1. With the amount of material you need to review, it is crucial you organize your time and efforts — just like you will once you become a registered representative. Chapter 1 will help you establish a studying schedule and reveal ways to avoid wasting time.

Even if you think you know how to study, read Chapter 1 to see if there might be new ways to save time and study more efficiently. You may discover new approaches to studying that better fit your undoubtedly busy schedule. Chapter 1 also explains what to expect on testing day — review this chapter carefully. With a strategic approach to your test, you will score higher and avoid making common mistakes new test-takers make. Throughout this book, you will see boxes, just like the one here:

TIP #1

These framed boxes include your 101 ways to score higher on your Series 7 exam.

These are insider tips; secrets that will help you outsmart the difficult Series 7 exam format. The 101 tips in this book are like having a mentor at your side, giving you the crucial information you need. These tips provide information on frequently tested subjects and will help you get past those unexpected questions so you can score higher. There are also terms you should know in bold to help you quickly scan each chapter after each studying session. Make sure you comprehend these terms, and how they relate to the material you will be tested on.

At the end of each chapter, you will find a checklist. The end-of-chapter checklist is a quick way to ensure you did not miss anything and prepares you for the sample questions. Once you feel you know all the material in the chapter, you can test your knowledge with the sample questions. Pay close attention to the questions you missed, and review what you did not grasp the first time in the corresponding chapter text.

TIP #2

Use the end-of-chapter checklist and sample questions to test your knowledge.

At the end of some chapters, you will find case studies full of insider advice from veteran registered representatives and other experts. These profiles of industry professionals will give you advice about your future career, explain what to expect once you start your career as a registered representative, and give you tips on how to avoid common pitfalls like not getting adequate rest, or failing to carefully read the questions on testing day and beyond.

To study the formulas all together, see Appendix A; it contains all the formulas you will find throughout this book. Take some time to practice your math skills, as your Series 7 exam will include a fair amount of calculations.

At the end of this book, you will find a full, 260-question Series 7 practice exam, reflecting questions you may find on testing day. Once you feel you are prepared and have finished studying, use this test as a mock exam. If possible, restrict your time so you are under the same time constraint as during your actual Series 7 exam. Find a quiet spot, set an alarm, and test your knowledge. The answer key at the back of this book will help you assess which areas are your weakest. By referring to the corresponding chapter listed with each answer in the answer key, you can review the material you missed.

With the 101 tips, clear and comprehensive information, and a practice test, *101 Ways to Score Higher on Your Series 7 Exam: What You Need to Know Explained Simply* is your no-nonsense, complete study guide to help busy professionals pass the Series 7 exam.

PURPOSE OF THE SERIES 7 EXAM

Before you begin studying, it is important to understand the purpose of the Series 7 exam. As the Financial Industry Regulatory Authority (FINRA; formerly the National Association of Securities Dealers, or NASD) states, the Series 7 examination is the qualification examination for General Securities Registered Representatives. The exam ensures registered representatives are competent to perform their jobs, which in turn protects investors.

So what does the exam expect from a registered representative? The Series 7 exam is based on five critical functions of a registered representative, each weighed differently by a number of questions.

The five critical functions are:

1. Find business for the broker/dealer: 68 questions
2. Perform a customer analysis, including financial situation, risk tolerance, and identification of investment objectives: 27 questions
3. Manage customer accounts, including opening accounts and transferring assets: 27 questions
4. Explain different investments to customers and make appropriate recommendations: 70 questions
5. Obtain and place customer orders and ensure transactions are completed properly: 58 questions

TIP #3

Know your test basics:

The Series 7 exam consists of 250 scored questions, plus 10 test questions that are not scored (you do not get to know which those are), for a total of 260 questions.

You have six hours, divided in two three-hour sessions, to complete the exam. You must score 72 percent or higher in order to pass.

The focus of the Series 7 is on your ability as a registered representative to give your customers the guidance they need to make investment decisions, within the laws and ethical rules. With each investment option this book discusses, it will add how this investment affects your client and what type of client is best suited for it.

Although you may be tempted to study these five critical functions in the order in which FINRA specifies, it is not the easiest way to break down the material. The markets and the securities traded in them are complex — the best way to understand how trading works is to start at the beginning. This book will begin by explaining the securities markets and will cover stocks, bonds, more complex securities like Direct Participation Programs (DPPs), and options. Each chapter builds off the knowledge you acquired in the previous chapter.

As you can see from the breakdown of FINRA's five critical functions of a registered representative, you will be most heavily tested on your knowledge of securities and how they apply to your customer recommendations. Expect to spend the bulk of your studying time on securities.

Your Series 7 will include many questions requiring you to make calculations. Use the sample questions to practice making these calculations and come up with your own scenarios. Your time at the exam is limited, so it is important you have practiced making calculations quickly to ensure you do not spend too much time on one question. The knowledge required for your Series 7 exam is vast, and many applicants get overwhelmed or do not prepare adequately. The Series 7 exam was created to protect registered representatives' customers; understanding this is the key to passing the exam.

TIP #4

The secret to being ready for you exam is to ask as you study: how does this apply to my future customers?

EXAM REQUIREMENTS: SPONSORSHIP AND SCHEDULING

Not just anyone can sign up for the Series 7 exam. In order to become a registered representative, an applicant must have a sponsoring securities firm submit an application along with required fees. This application form is called a U4. You can see an example of a U4 form on FINRA's Web site: **www.finra.org**. The form requires detailed information regarding your personal and professional background — make sure you fill it out accurately. Your firm will have a copy of this form on file.

You will also have to get your fingerprints taken as part of your registration. Ask your firm where their candidates go, or check your local police station for locations. Your firm will likely have procedures in place for their registered representatives.

Once you receive your confirmation of valid enrollment, you should register right away to take your Series 7 exam. To schedule your exam, contact your local testing center. It is possible your firm may schedule your exam for you; make sure you verify this. Look for contact information for your local testing center by visiting **www.prometric.com/finra**. You will have 120 days from the date you enroll for the Series 7 exam to take the test.

TIP #5

Make sure you are ready and arrive on time on testing day. If you do not show up, your firm will be charged the full testing fee (which would not reflect well on you). If for some reason you need to cancel or reschedule your exam, you need to do so by noon two business days before your test date.

CHECKLIST

- ☐ I understand the five critical functions of registered representatives, and how they should be the focus of my studies
- ☐ I know what type of questions the test contains
- ☐ I understand how to use the bold blocks of text to quickly review material
- ☐ I understand the purpose of the Series 7 exam and how to use it as a focus in my studies
- ☐ I have acquired sponsorship
- ☐ I have scheduled my exam

CHAPTER 1
Studying and Testing Strategies

For many applicants preparing to take the Series 7 exam, it has been a while since they had to study for a test. Series 7 requires complex knowledge that can overwhelm even the most practiced of students.

Many applicants, aside from studying for their Series 7 exam, are also studying for other exams or are learning their firm's practices to prepare for their job. Time management is critical. Even if you think you know how to approach your studies, consider some different techniques listed in this chapter. You may find a better way to study for the test.

WHAT KIND OF STUDENT ARE YOU?

Understanding how you learn best is an important component in devising your studying plan. Studying is not just reading and highlighting material along the way. There are many different ways you can retain material, and understanding each one can help you utilize your time most efficiently.

There are three different ways to learn:

- Auditory Learning: learning by listening
- Visual Learning: learning by watching, or creating graphs and worksheets that provide a visual learning aid
- Tactile or Kinesthetic Learning: learning by doing

Think about how you have learned things best in the past. Do you like to listen to a lecture? That makes you an auditory learner. Do you prefer to read? You must be a visual learner. Or do you learn best by doing something, like creating a customer profile? You are a tactile learner.

TIP #6

Adjust your studying techniques to the learning style that works best for you, so you use your time most effectively.

STUDYING TECHNIQUES

For many, a combination of these learning methods offers the best solution to learning new material. Mixing learning methods keeps you from burning out and can help you manage your studying time most effectively. Explore different learning methods and see what works best for you.

Try some of these techniques based on auditory, visual, and tactile learning:

Auditory Learning Techniques:

- Recite difficult-to-retain material; repetition can be a great tool in retaining formulas you will use to calculate answers on your exam.
- Recite material on a recording device. You can play it back on an MP3 player during a workout or listen to it during your commute home.
- Use rhymes or acronyms to memorize laws or formulas.

Visual Learning Techniques:

- Take notes or create graphs or checklists to sum up material in a visual way.
- Use highlighters to underline material as you read.

Tactile/Kinesthetic Learning Techniques:

- Create a mock customer profile and implement learned material during a mock counseling session. You can create this customer profile based on someone you know, or a fictional customer, if you like.
- Use the formulas in this book to apply theoretical concepts to practical scenarios. If you have difficulty following the text, use the sample questions and examples — they make more sense to tactile learners.
- Move around while studying.

Study Groups

Your firm may be hiring more people than just you to add to their team of registered representatives. If this is the case, you will find your fellow Series 7 applicants will be a great source of support. You may even want to team up and create a study group.

Study groups can be useful if you are a tactile learner. If you have difficulty comprehending certain material, help from fellow applicants may be useful. If you decide to create a study group, here are some tips to get the most out of your joint study time; they are also good tools when managing individual study time:

- Keep a schedule with a designated start and finish time.
- Use group texts to save time and stay in contact with the whole study group at once.
- Avoid distracting locations, like restaurants or other public places. If you need an auxiliary space, try reserving a meeting room at your library or coffee shop, if they have one.
- Have clear goals on what material you wish to cover during each meeting. Consider creating a study schedule (more on how to create one later in this chapter).
- Designate a group leader who will keep everyone on track; you can alternate between group members for each meeting.

For a study group to be successful, all group members need to be very focused on their goal. If you find one member to be particularly distracting, remind that person of your common goal: passing the exam. However, if you find you are part of a study group that is not the best use of your time, respectfully excuse yourself and continue your studies alone. Remember that your goal is to pass the exam, not to socialize.

A word of caution: Series 7 test studying does not lend itself well to studying in groups. The material is complex, theoretical, and since you are taking the test alone, you are best off studying alone to avoid wasting time. The risk of study groups is they become social gatherings, leading to time that could be better utilized by studying alone.

TIP #7

Think carefully before starting or joining a study group to prepare for your Series 7 exam.

Breaking It Down

As stated in the introduction, each of the five critical functions is weighed differently on the test by the number of questions — and you can use this to your advantage.

TIP #8

If you are in a time crunch, or have to decide which portions to review, study those items that carry the most weight. Look at the listings of the five critical functions in this book's introduction to see how the exam is weighted.

Other ways to break the study material into manageable chunks include:

- Using the checklists and bold text blocks in this book to test your knowledge. Once you have determined you know something, move on. There is no need to review something you already know; once is enough.
- Creating index cards on different subjects. You can use this book's bold words for condensed information. With these index cards, you

have small chunks of studying material ready for those 15 minutes in line at the DMV, those 10 minutes in the car waiting for your kids to get out of school, etc. This technique is great for applicants lacking big blocks of study time. Make sure you carry these index cards with you wherever you go.

- Ensuring you know how to make calculations. You can miss a question or two on theoretical knowledge and still pass, but you will have to be able to calculate numbers like how much a stock is in-the-money or the value of a stock after a split. If you are in a time crunch, focus on the formulas and make sure you know how to apply them.

TIME MANAGEMENT

As you will soon find as a registered representative, time management is a crucial component to any task. Whether you are studying or marketing to new customers, you will find managing your time wisely will benefit you in the long run.

The secret to successful studying is managing your time wisely. This book will guide you through all the subjects you will need to cover before taking the exam — look at the material in chapters 2 through 14 and break it down to fit your schedule.

How to Create a Studying Schedule

Before you dig into the studying material, make sure you have a plan of attack. Here is a simple way to create a schedule:

- Take your planner or a printed calendar (some computer softwares carry a calendar-printing function) and look at how many days you have from today until testing day.

- Using the breakdown you made of this book's chapters, divide the portions evenly among your calendar days, leaving the last two or three days for your practice test and review.

- Estimate how much time studying each portion will take, adding time for breaks if necessary.

- Decide when you will be studying. Schedule study time just like you would schedule an important meeting.

TIP #9

Your studying schedule is your tool to staying on track. If you follow your schedule, you will be ready on testing day.

Once you begin studying, keep track of how much time you studied and how much progress you made. Do you need more or less time than you thought? Adjust your schedule accordingly.

On the opposite page is an example of what your studying schedule might look like. Note how there is room to chart progress, to give a clear view of what was accomplished, and what still needs to be done.

Note how this schedule did not plan any study time for Sunday. Although it is important to take studying seriously, you should also schedule breaks and the occasional day off.

TIP #10

Allow time in your schedule for breaks and for days off if possible. Breaks give you a chance to recharge and be more productive when you sit down to study again.

QUICK STUDYING TIPS

Your new studying schedule may overwhelm you when you see all the hard work you have ahead. Here are some quick tips to make studying a little easier:

- If you have to forgo certain commitments, family or personal, explain to those involved that you are studying for an important exam. If you have children, reassure them that this imposition is only temporary. You can show them on a calendar when your test day is scheduled.

DAY	MONDAY	TUESDAY	WEDNESDAY	THURSDAY	FRIDAY	SATURDAY	SUNDAY
STUDY TIME	9-11 a.m. 7-10 p.m.	8-11 a.m.	7-11 p.m.	9-11 a.m.	12-4 p.m.	8-11 a.m.	None
TO DO	Study Chapter 2 with sample questions	Study Chapter 3, first half	Finish studying Chapter 3	Study Chapter 4, first half	Finish Chapter 4	Study Chapter 5, first half	None
ACTUAL	Finished Equity Securities	Chapter 3, first half	Finished Chapter 3, Chapter 2 questions	Chapter 4, first two-thirds	Finished Chapter 4, began Chapter 5	Chapter 5, first half	None
STILL TO FINISH	Sample Questions	Chapter 2 questions	None	None	None	None	None

Make sure you allow yourself time to enjoy some of your normal leisurely activities, to keep a balance with your rigorous studies.

- Find a quiet spot to study away from TV, Internet, or other distractions. If you live in a noisy house, consider playing soft music to drown out distracting sounds. And if you have trouble with procrastinating on your devices, try an app or browser extension that temporarily blocks internet access.
- Use the checklists and study plan in this book to chart your progress. Crossing off a subject as you finish it can be a very satisfying way to chart your progress.
- Eat well and get plenty of sleep. Your mind needs nourishment and rest to function at its best.
- If you are motivated by reward, consider promising yourself something nice when you pass the test, like a day out with the family or dinner at your favorite restaurant.

WHAT TO EXPECT ON TESTING DAY

Testing day does not have to be as stressful as you may think. The best way to study is to practice taking the exam using the mock exam in this book and to know what to expect on testing day.

TIP #11

Get a good night's rest, eat a healthy breakfast, and dress for comfort on testing day.

First, you need to make sure you bring everything you need to the testing center:

- ☐ A sack lunch and any snacks to eat during your break (try to keep these healthy to fuel your body)
- ☐ Government-issued ID; make sure your name matches the name you used to register for the exam
- ☐ Study material, like notes or index cards you made, so you can brush up on material while you wait
- ☐ A watch

You will not be allowed to bring in bags, purses, study materials, or electronic devices (like cell phones) into the test room. The exam center will give you a calculator, six pieces of letter-sized paper (or a whiteboard), and a pencil for use in each session.

The testing center employee will guide you to a cubicle where you will begin your test. Once the clock starts, you need to make sure you use your time wisely.

Owning Your Time

Your Series 7 exam divides the 260 questions between two three-hour blocks. There is a mandatory 30 to 60 minute break between the two blocks. Once you sign out after the first session, you cannot go back and change any answers.

You are allowed to take breaks during your exam, but your exam time is not paused for this. Avoid drinking a lot of water or other liquids so you are not wasting valuable time taking bathroom breaks.

Once you sit down to answer questions, it is important to break your allotted three hours into smaller segments. These segments will help you make sure you are on track.

TIP #12

To make sure you are on track on your test, try to complete at least 44 questions per hour, or one minute and 20 seconds on each question.

Series 7 exams are designed to give you ample time to finish each test portion. As long as you have studied and know the material, there is no reason for you not to finish your exam on time — provided you do not panic or make other mistakes that slow you down.

To move from question to question at a steady pace, there are a few test-taking tricks you can use:

- ☐ Read carefully. It is easy to miss a word (for example, "except"), and get the question wrong.
- ☐ Take your time to understand what is being asked.
- ☐ Do not get stuck on one question. If you are unsure of the answer, mark the question for review and move on.

- ☐ Use the process of elimination if you are unsure of the answer. Questions are usually designed to have two completely wrong answers and two that are close to correct.
- ☐ Every question is scored, so even if you have no idea what the answer is, guess. Unanswered questions are counted as a wrong answer.
- ☐ When in doubt, trust your gut. Your first choice is often the right one — do not make the mistake of over-thinking a question and changing a right answer to a wrong one.

TIP #13

The minute you start the test, use one sheet of scrap paper to write down any formulas you remember. This will relax your mind and allow you to focus on the questions.

Nerves can do a number on your mind, and it can be difficult to clear your mind enough to answer questions correctly. Releasing the stress of retaining information will allow you to focus on your test.

Types of Questions

Series 7 exam questions come in different types: closed-stem, open-stem, Roman numeral, and qualifying questions. This book will cover each type of question and how best to approach them to arrive at the correct answer.

A closed-stem question is the simplest and most common question type you will see on your exam. Here is an example of a closed-stem question:

1. A syndicate buys DEF Corporation shares at $100 a share. Their spread is $20, with a management fee of 15 percent. What is the price per share of DEF stock to the public?

   [A] $97
   [B] $120
   [C] $119.55
   [D] $132

An open-stemmed question expects you to finish a sentence or statement, like in this example:

1. GHI bonds are rated D by Standard and Poor's. This means the company

   [A] is in default
   [B] nothing; S&P does not have a D rating
   [C] is speculative
   [D] has just paid dividends

Roman numeral questions are the wordiest of question types and may confuse you with the options you have to choose from. You must read each question carefully; look at the example below to see what these questions look like:

1. Which of the following is true about Real Estate Investment Trusts (REITs)? REITs must:

   I. Invest in real estate or real estate-related securities
   II. Have at least 75 percent of assets invested in real estate
   III. Distribute 90 percent or more of income to investors to avoid corporate taxation
   IV. Only pass income to investors, not write-offs

   [A] I, II, and IV
   [B] II and III
   [C] None of the above
   [D] All of the above

TIP #14

Series 7 likes to include extraneous information in a question to confuse you. Focus on the information you need to answer these three types of questions and ignore the rest. Remember to read carefully; all the studying in the world will not help you if you rush through your exam.

Qualifying questions are variations on closed-stem, open-stem, and Roman numeral questions. These questions add a word like "most," "least," "except," or "only" — a qualifier that changes the answer. These questions are designed to test your ability to differentiate and will trip up careless readers. Here is an example of a qualifying question:

1. All of the following are common stockholder's stock rights, except:

   [A] Voting rights
   [B] Preemptive rights
   [C] Nomination rights
   [D] Dividend rights

CHECKLIST

- ☐ I have considered different studying techniques
- ☐ I have decided on a plan of action
- ☐ I have bought any supplies needed (notebook, index cards, recording device)
- ☐ I have made a studying schedule to ensure I will be ready on testing day
- ☐ I know what to bring on testing day and how to prepare by dressing comfortably
- ☐ I understand how to keep track of time during my test
- ☐ I can identify the different types of questions I can expect on the test
- ☐ I understand my best strategy is to read carefully

CASE STUDY: STEPHEN MERRITT

MasteringMultipleChoice.com
RR#4
Creemore, ON
Canada
(705) 466-6954
www.masteringmultiplechoice.com

Stephen Merritt is a former college instructor and the writer of *Mastering the Multiple Choice*. He sees the multiple-choice test format of the Series 7 exams as an opportunity rather than a disadvantage. "I always found that multiple choice exams were a gift — a test format that was easy to 'hack' and get better results on than you might on other test formats," he says.

Realizing that many other students are hindered by the multiple choice exam format, Merritt decided to share his experience with exam takers. "While working on my degrees, and later as a college instructor, I realized how much difficulty people had with the test format itself. Regardless of how much they studied, many people would perform horribly on the multiple choice question format."

Merritt says to pass a multiple choice exam, students must not just study the exam content, but the style as well. "You can't learn to drive a car simply by reading a book — you'll need to do some actual driving," he says. "Multiple choice exams are the same. To prepare for multiple choice question tests, you need to work in the format as much as possible."

To master multiple choice exams, he suggests students practice as much as possible. "Get old exams and sample exams. Put together a group and build your own multiple choice questions based on the course content," he suggests. "Every hour you spend working in the multiple choice format itself is going to deliver far more than simply staring at notes or textbooks."

"By mastering the format, students get points they would have otherwise left on the table, because of confusion, anxiety, or time issues," Merritt says, stressing that mastery of multiple choice is a skill that can be learned, even by those who have struggled with the test format in the past. "Once you develop some skills with multiple choice exams, you'll find your anxiety will drop dramatically, and your scores will rise as a result."

CHAPTER 2
Equity Securities

As discussed in the introduction, your first step in complying with the five critical functions is to understand different types of securities. This book builds each chapter off the previous one. If you begin studying here, you will build a solid understanding of different securities so you can explain them to your customers.

TIP #15

Understanding how equities work is the foundation to comprehending the more complex material on the test.

EQUITY BASICS

When a corporation needs to raise capital, it issues stocks. **Stock** is a form of ownership, or equity, in a company in the form of shares. Before covering types of stock, first you must understand the process involved in underwriting, or creating, equities. This section is about how a stock is born, the players involved, and some of the laws you as an applicant must know to pass the Series 7 exam.

There are a lot of fundamental concepts, laws, and functions to memorize within this portion of your preparation for the Series 7 exam. Take your time reviewing this material, and use the bold text to study. You will be tested on all of the subjects outlined in this section.

Functions

First, this book will discuss some of the people involved in the registration process. As a registered representative you could be working for any of the entities involved in the issuance of securities, so it is important you understand the roles of the players in the underwriting process.

When a stock is issued, the issuing corporation will hire an investment banking firm to manage the issuance of these equities. The investment banking firm will form a syndicate (group) of underwriters to sell the stock with a managing or lead underwriter at the head of this syndicate. A syndicate can hire a selling group if they feel they need help with the selling of securities.

The different entities involved in a stock issue are:

- **Investment banking firm**: this firm advises the issuing company and underwrites the issue
- **Managing or lead underwriter**: underwriter who puts a syndicate together
- **Syndicate**: group of underwriters, each responsible for selling a portion of the securities
- **Underwriter**: a broker-dealer who helps the issuer bring securities to prospective buyers
- **Selling Group**: brokerage firm the syndicate hires to help sell securities

To easily understand the hierarchy that exists between these different functions, look at diagram 2.1.

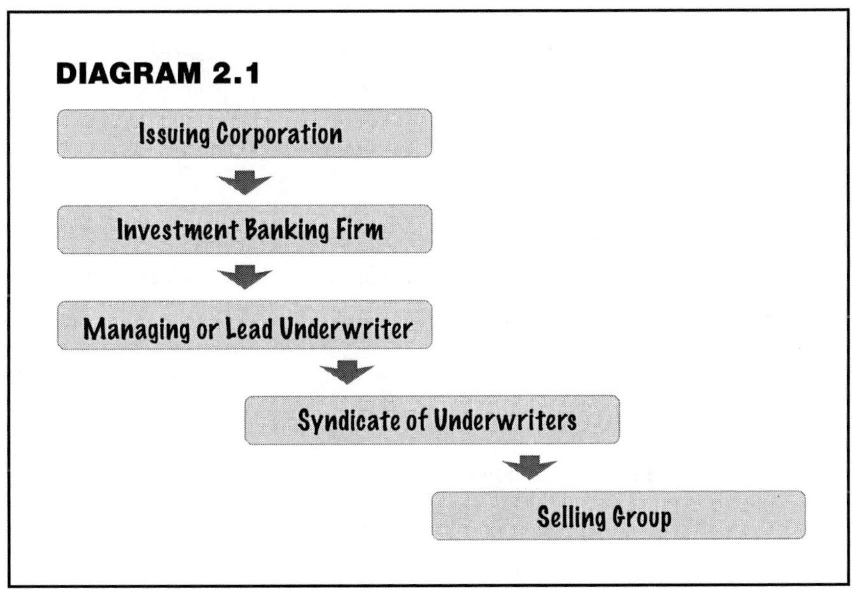

Where the Money Goes

Naturally, all these contributors to a securities sale want a part of the profits to make their efforts worthwhile. A syndicate will make a total profit, or spread, and pays the management fee from this, leaving them with a net profit called the takedown. Looking at the hierarchy chart will help you make sense of how the money trickles down. To understand how this profit is divvied up and how to calculate exact profits, look at this example.

EXAMPLE:

HOW TO CALCULATE **THE SYNDICATE'S SPREAD**:

Spread = public offering price – price paid to issuer
($12 – $10 = $2)

A syndicate buys shares of ABC Corporation at $10 a share. The price to the public is $12. This makes their spread, or total profit, $2.

HOW TO CALCULATE **THE SYNDICATE'S TAKEDOWN**:

Takedown = spread – management fee
($2 – $0.20 = $1.80)

Now all the salespeople will receive part of this $2 spread. First, there is the management fee for the managing or lead underwriter, say 10 percent. What is left will be divided among the syndicate and is known as the takedown.

HOW TO CALCULATE **ADDITIONAL TAKEDOWN**:

Additional takedown = takedown – concession
($1.80 – $0.50 = $1.30)

If the syndicate made use of a selling group, they will now have to share part of the takedown with the selling group members — this is called the concession. Profit the syndicate makes from securities that selling group members sell is called additional takedown.

As a continuation of our example, assume the selling group gets $0.50 a share.

This math can get a little confusing. Use the graph outlining the hierarchy in security sales to make sense of how profit trickles down and who gets paid first. Memorize these formulas, and practice your calculations with different scenarios to familiarize yourself with these terms — you will be expected to perform similar calculations during your Series 7 exam.

Once stocks are sold, records of holders need to be kept, which the issuing company assigns to a **transfer agent**. This transfer agent is usually a commercial bank, but sometimes an issuing corporation takes on these duties themselves. A **registrar** who works for the company ensures there is no over-issuance of stock. Once a stock certificate is issued, it can be transferred by **endorsement**, or signing the certificate over to its new holder.

TIP #16

Stock and bond (which will be covered later in this chapter, and in Chapter 3 on bonds) certificates act like a check: you can sign them over to someone else if you wish to do so.

Syndicate Agreements

When forming the syndicate, its members will come to a **syndicate agreement** on who gets paid what and the responsibility each member has to the shares the syndicate commits to as a whole. Syndicate agreements are either **Eastern Accounts**, where responsibility for sales is shared between members, or **Western Accounts**, where each member is only responsible for their portion of assigned syndicate shares. Syndicates decide the type of agreement based on preference; for Series 7, you simply need to identify how the type of agreement affects individual members' responsibilities.

EXAMPLE:

George Jones is part of a syndicate group of five underwriters. The group commits to 1,000,000 shares. He has sold his share of 200,000 shares. 100,000 shares remain unsold.

Under an Eastern Account, he would be responsible for selling another 20,000 shares (100,000 divided by five members). Under a Western Account, he would have met his obligation to the syndicate by selling his portion of the total shares, with no commitment to the unsold shares.

Six Steps to Registering Securities

When a corporation decides it wants to issue securities, it must go through six steps to register them.

The six steps in registering securities are:

1. Registering with Securities and Exchange Commission (SEC) with the name of the corporation, business description, officer information, and capitalization
2. Issuance of the preliminary prospectus, or red herring, to give potential investors more information about the upcoming offering
3. Forming the underwriting group or syndicate.
4. Issuing company and underwriters meet to formalize agreements regarding the issue. This is known as a due diligence meeting
5. Meeting "**Blue Sky Laws**" requirements. The corporation will register with the state(s)
6. Public Offering, with final prospectus

This is the most basic breakdown of the process involved. To expand on step five, Series 7 expects you to understand Blue Sky Laws and ways to register to comply.

In the 1929 stock market crash, many investors lost their money due to fraudulently represented investments — they were sold worthless investments (or pieces of blue sky, as one judge called them). In order to protect investors, many states require sellers to register the securities they are selling, providing financial data to aid in buyers' decision making. These registration requirements are known as Blue Sky Laws. For your exam, all you need to know is the how a company should register its securities to comply with these laws.

There are three ways a company can register with a state:

1. **Coordination**: the issuing company files with the SEC and the SEC helps the company file with the state
2. **Qualification**: when a security is exempt from filing with the SEC but must still file with the state
3. **Notification**: established companies who have filed with a state for previous securities offering(s) can simply renew their application

TIP #17

Series 7 will include questions about Blue Sky Laws because these laws focus on investor protection; make sure you understand their purpose and application.

COMMON STOCK

Now that you have an understanding of the basic process of underwriting securities, you will move on to different types of equity securities. Common stock is the most basic kind of share in equity, and gives its owner a right to vote and dividends if board members decide to distribute them.

Understanding Shares

When a corporation does its **initial public offering (IPO)**, it authorizes a number of shares to be issued to the public. **Authorized stock** is the total, maximum number of stock shares a corporation can issue, which is decided under its articles of corporation.

Companies usually do not want to issue all these shares at once to prevent low initial stock values. The company will hold back a portion of the authorized shares; the **issued shares** are stocks sold in the market as part of an IPO.

For various reasons, mostly to control the value of the stock, as well as taxes and expenses, companies will routinely buy some of these stocks back and hold on to them. Stocks the company buys back are called **treasury stock**. Remaining stocks in the marketplace are **outstanding stocks**. Look at diagram 2.2 to see how this issuing of shares works.

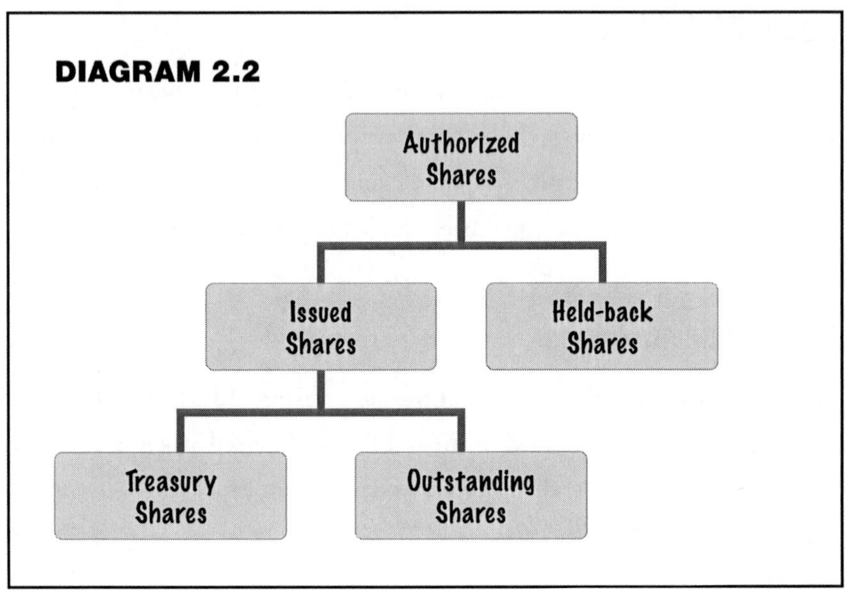

HOW TO CALCULATE **ISSUED STOCK**:

Issued stock = treasury stock + outstanding stock

The Series 7 exam will test your ability to calculate each of these types of shares, like in the following example:

EXAMPLE:

ABC Corporation has issued 1,000,000 stock shares. It has decided to keep 300,000 of treasury stock, leaving 700,000 shares in outstanding stocks.

Stockholder Rights

Because holding stock means owning a piece of a company, those stocks hold certain rights, which you are expected to know for your Series 7 exam. This book will cover calculations involved with some of these rights later in this chapter; for now, here are the rights you should know. Please note: these rights apply to common stock only. More information on preferred stock and corresponding rights will be discussed later in this chapter.

These are **common stockholder rights**:

1. Access to corporate books: a stockholder has the right to see a corporation's balance sheet and income statements
2. Voting: a common stockholder can vote on stock splits and dividends
3. Share in dividends: a common stockholder has a right to dividends if disbursed
4. Preemptive rights: right to buy shares before it is offered to others
5. Residual claims on corporate assets: common stockholders can hold claim to assets in case of the issuing company's liquidation.

Voting

Common stock comes with a stockholder's right to vote. Series 7 tests your understanding of these voting rights and how votes are allocated. A stockholder can vote in two ways: **statutory voting** and **cumulative voting**, which is determined in the stockholder agreement. The easiest way to understand statutory and cumulative voting is to use these terms in an example.

EXAMPLE:

Bill Smith owns 1,500 shares of ABC Corporation stock. It is time to vote for two board members. He has a total of 3,000 votes (1,500 shares × two board seats).

If he had a statutory vote, he would have to vote evenly, 1,500 for each position.

If he had a cumulative vote, he could spread his votes any way he pleased, using all 3,000 votes on one candidate if he chooses.

For your exam, all you need to know is how this voting process works for cumulative and statutory voting rights. When advising your clients on different investments, be sure to explain that stocks give ownership in a company and therefore the holder gets a say (or vote), a right not available in many other types of investments.

Stock Splits

When an issuing company wants to make a stock more interesting for an investor, it often chooses to split common stock. As companies grow and their stock prices increase, their stock is often too expensive for many investors. For example, a 2-for-1 forward stock split, which exchanges one stock share for two, would lower each share's price.

There are two kinds of stock splits with a forward split being the most common kind:

- **Forward split**: stock is split to create more shares with a decrease in price. This would make the stock cheaper and more accessible for some investors.

For instance, a 2-for-1 split of 100 shares of stock valued at $50 would give an investor 200 shares of $25 stock.

- **Reverse split**: stock is combined to increase price and decrease shares.

  For example, a 1-for-2 reverse split of 100 shares of $50 stock would result in 50 shares of $100 stock. This is a less common practice, often done if a stock has been devalued for some reason.

Although stock splits affect the number of votes an investor holds (because number of shares change), the percentage of votes and therefore the investor's voting power remains the same. For example, a shareholder of 50 shares of ABC common stock might receive 100 shares in a 2-for-1 stock split and end up with 100 votes. Although his or her number of votes has doubled, so have the rights of other investors. His or her percentage of voting power is therefore the same as before the split.

TIP #18

Stock splits can be confusing. Remember that the overall investment value does not change: if an investor had $10,000 invested before the split, that investor still has $10,000 total invested after a split.

Dividends

The main objective of an investor is to make a profit off their endeavors, which is where dividends, or earnings on stocks, come into play.

Companies will give their investors two kinds of dividends:

- **Stock dividend**: the investor receives their dividends in stocks, which is non-taxable.

The disbursement works like a forward stock split: shares increase and price decreases. For example, a 10 percent stock dividend of 500 stocks at $10 a share will result in ownership of 550 stocks at $9.09 a share: the 10 percent increase in shares resulted in a 10 percent decrease in stock price. Remember a stock split never affects the overall dollar value of the investment.

- **Cash dividend**: the investor receives dividend in cash, which is taxable and decreases the value of the stock.

For instance, a 10 percent cash dividend on $10 stock will give the investor $1 per share. The day after the dividend is distributed, called the **ex-dividend date**, stock is worth $9 a share.

Practice calculating dividends and stock values — you will be asked to do so in examples on your Series 7 exam.

Dividend Dates

When a customer considers buying a stock, you should be able to calculate whether that stock is about to pay dividends. Your exam may include questions regarding dividend pay-out; this book will cover how the dividend and stock purchase date relate in this section.

When a company declares dividends, it waits until the **record date** to create a list of investors who will receive dividends.

TIP #19

In order to receive dividends, an investor must buy the stock at least three business days before the record date because a purchase takes three days to settle.

EXAMPLE

XYZ Corporation has announced it will distribute dividends and set its record date on Tuesday, January 10. To receive dividends, an investor has to buy stock by end-of-trading Thursday, January 5. When you encounter questions like these on your exam, make sure you count business days, not calendar days to get to the right answer.

Value of Rights

For your Series 7 exam, you should assume common stock includes the right to buy stock at a discount, or subscription price. Just like some retailers use these types of discounts for loyal customers, stock issuers like to offer stock at a reduced price to entice their current stockholders to buy more stock. At time of issue the issuing company will determine the amount of rights needed to purchase a share at the subscription price.

Because this right is a value-added feature of stock, it needs to be reflected in the market value of a stock. A simple formula to calculate the value of this right is the **cum-rights** (cum is Latin for '"with") formula:

HOW TO CALCULATE **THE VALUE OF A RIGHT**:

Value of a right = (market price – subscription price)
÷ number of rights to purchase one share +1

Understanding the value of this right is important because the value of stock will drop by this amount once this right is used. The first day a stock trades without this right is called the **ex-date**.

TIP #20

For your Series 7 exam, you should know a company can choose to assign a **stated value** for bookkeeping purposes to protect stockholders in case of great losses. This is often done with a new stock issue to make investors feel more confident about purchasing the stock.

PREFERRED STOCK

Preferred stock works much like common stock in the sense it gives the investor ownership in a company. Preferred stock was created because investors often have different risk tolerance, tax needs, and financial objectives. Rights and dividends work differently for preferred stock, which you will learn in this section.

Rights

Preferred stock exists to give stockholders more rights and limit their risk in certain situations, mainly in a volatile market with greater risk of bankruptcy. A company's preferred stock will trade at a different price than common stock, depending on the value the market gives its right at the time.

A preferred stockholder's rights are:

1. Cash dividends regularly (either paid or owed, with exception of straight preferred stock—see "Types of Preferred Stock" for more details)
2. If the underlying company goes bankrupt, preferred stockholders will be paid back their investment before common stockholders

The second preferred stockholder right is most important. Preferred stockholders will be repaid their investment before common stockholders, should the issuing company go bankrupt. You should know that preferred stockholders have no voting rights.

TIP #21

Preferred stockholders' dividends are based on their par value, or face value, at issuance of the stock.

Types of Preferred Stock

To cater to different situations and stockholder preferences, issuers have created several types of preferred stock. These features sometimes benefit the investor, like senior preferred stock for an investor concerned about being repaid in case of bankruptcy. Sometimes the features benefit the issuer, like with callable preferred stock, where the issuer can control its stock price by having the option to buy it back. For your Series 7 exam, you should know the basic characteristics of all of these.

The different types of preferred stock are:

- **Straight preferred stock**: receives no accumulation of dividend if issuer does not pay dividend.
- **Cumulative preferred stock**: if dividend is not paid, it accumulates and is owed.
- **Convertible preferred stock**: can be traded for common stock at any time. Calculate by using conversion price decided at issue: **conversion ratio = par value/conversion price.**
- **Callable preferred stock**: gives issuer the right to buy back preferred stock at any time.
- **Participating preferred stock**: investor receives common stock dividend.

- **Prior or senior preferred stock**: investor receives money before other preferred stockholders in case of bankruptcy of issuer.
- **Adjustable or floating rate preferred stock**: dividend rate of stock is reset every six months in line with market interest rates.

OTHER EQUITY SECURITIES

Common and preferred stock are the two equity securities you will mostly be dealing with as a registered representative. To serve global investors, and to add benefits to the purchase of securities, the market offers **American depository receipts (ADRs)** and warrants. This book will briefly cover these here; Series 7 is unlikely to ask you about these equity investments, however.

American Depository Receipts (ADRs)

With the global economy of today, trading does not simply stop at the U.S. border. In order to administer foreign trades, there are ADRs, which are receipts for a foreign security traded in the U.S., as well as a way to buy foreign stock. It is negotiable, which means it can be transferred or sold. Because an ADR's dividends are paid in U.S. dollars, it carries applicable currency risk, due to the conversion of foreign currency at the market price.

TIP #22

Anytime Series 7 asks you a question about a security that deals with international currency or stock, like ADRs, immediately link this to currency risk.

Warrants

In its most basic definition, a **warrant** is the right to buy a stock at a set price stated in the warrant. Warrants are issued in certificate form and specify the amount (number) of stock the holder is entitled to use the warrant for, decided by the issuer of the corresponding stock. Warrants can be sold individually, or presented as part of a package to investors in conjunction with a stock sale. They are often used to make a stock purchase more attractive to buyers.

STOCKS AND YOUR CLIENT

In this chapter, you have learned about stock shares, dividends, rights, and other types of securities. Stocks give the investor a share of ownership in a company, which means the value of the stock is directly linked to the performance of the underlying company.

The potential gains of stock investing are unlimited, but so are the potential losses. If your client wishes to invest in stocks, you must explain that his or her gain is linked to the profit of the company. You must also advise your client that losses can mean loss of principal, or original investment. The risk involved in stock investment greatly depends on the underlying corporation's health. This book will discuss how to analyze corporate health in Chapter 11: Analyzing Securities.

The ideal client for stock investing is one who can bear the potential losses and understands that losses can erode principal.

CHECKLIST

- ☐ I understand equity basics, including the registering process for securities
- ☐ I know the functions of all participants in the securities sales process and how they are compensated within the hierarchy
- ☐ I understand common stock, rights, dividend, and stock splits
- ☐ I have reviewed preferred stock, different types of preferred stock, and how value is affected
- ☐ I understand American depository agreements (ADRs) and warrants

SAMPLE QUESTIONS

1. In compliance with Blue Sky Laws, XYZ Corporation has filed the appropriate documentation with its state. Because XYZ Corporation has issued securities before and filed with the state previously, it has filed by:

   [A] Notification
   [B] Qualification
   [C] Mail
   [D] Coordination

2. As a syndicate member, Bob Miller has sold his 10,000 shares of the 20-member syndicate's total 200,000 shares. The syndicate has 20,000 shares remaining and operates as an Eastern Account. How many shares does he still need to sell in order to fulfill his commitment to the syndicate?

   [A] 10,000 shares
   [B] None, he has met his obligation by selling his portion
   [C] 11,000
   [D] 1,000

3. A syndicate buys DEF Corporation shares at $100 a share. Their spread is $20 with a management fee of 15 percent. What is the price per share of DEF stock to the public?

   [A] $97
   [B] $120
   [C] $119.55
   [D] $132

4. DEF Corporation has issued 2,000,000 shares of common stock. In order to control the stock's value, DEF Corporation has decided to hold 500,000 shares. How many shares of treasury stock does DEF Corporation have?

   [A] 2,500,000
   [B] 1,500,000
   [C] 2,000,000
   [D] 500,000

5. Rosa Truman holds 1,000 common stock shares of XYZ stock with cumulative voting rights. It is time to vote for four board members and she feels strongly about voting for one particular member. She can:

[A] Put 500 votes per seat

[B] Put 4,000 votes toward that one seat

[C] Not vote at all; common stock does not hold voting rights for board seats

[D] Call XYZ Corporation to buy more votes

6. ABC Corporation is splitting their common stock with a forward, 2-for-1 split. Sam Richards holds 100 shares of ABC stock with each share valued at $20. How many shares does he hold after the split, and how much is each share worth?

   [A] 50 shares at $10 a share

   [B] 100 shares at $10 a share

   [C] 200 shares at $10 a share

   [D] 200 shares at $20 a share

7. DEF stock is trading at $30 a share. The Corporation has decided to issue its stockholders a 15 percent dividend. What is the value of DEF stock on the ex-dividend rate?

   [A] $30

   [B] $25.50

   [C] 34.50

   [D] $24

8. Anna Smith holds shares of preferred GHI stock. GHI Corporation has the right to buy back her preferred stock at any time. What type of preferred stock does she hold?

   [A] Straight preferred stock

   [B] Adjustable preferred stock

   [C] Company preferred stock

   [D] Callable preferred stock

9. Nina Waters holds an ADR for XYZ Corporation stock. The company is based in Germany and has just paid dividends. She will receive dividends in:

   [A] Deutschmarks

   [B] Euros

   [C] U.S. Dollars

   [D] No dividends; foreign investors do not receive stock dividends

CASE STUDY: SUZY RHOADES

TesTeachers, LLC
8655 E. Via De Ventura,
Suite E-175
Scottsdale, AZ 85258
(888) 422-7714
www.testeachers.com

Suzy Rhoades is an instructor for TesTeachers, LLC, an online pre-license and continuing education provider. TesTeachers specializes in offering pre-licensing lecture courses for insurance and securities in an online, streaming video format. The company also offers live lecture classes in Arizona and Colorado with Series 7 exam classes as part of their curriculum.

Rhoades feels strongly about making Series 7 material easy to understand for her students. "My main goal as a teacher is to make the information accessible to my students," Rhoades says about her focus when teaching the Series 7 course. "These courses can be like learning a foreign language. I never want to 'speak above' any student's head."

"The most successful Series 7 student is one with dedication and a desire to learn," Rhoades believes. "The student must carve time out every day to study for this exam," she says of this required dedication. The biggest mistake she has seen students make is to try to cram all the material at the last minute. "Don't do that!" she warns. "Students sometimes confuse memorizing questions with learning the concepts. It is the concepts that you must know, not that question ten has an answer of C."

Rhoades has some advice for testing day as well. "Do not forget to read the question," she says. "So many times, students miss the questions that upon review they really knew. They rushed through reading the question and missed a key word that made all the difference."

> During her classes, Rhoades welcomes students' questions and comments. "Don't be afraid to ask questions from your instructor, even those questions you think are stupid," she advises Series 7 course students. She adds that sometimes, asking the right question will cause "a light bulb to go off," which is her favorite part of teaching the Series 7 exam course. "That is why I teach: to see the light bulbs illuminate all over the nation."

CHAPTER 3
Debt Instruments

You have learned in the previous chapters stock gives the holder ownership in a company. When a company does not want to relinquish ownership, it can issue bonds. **Bonds** are debt instruments: they act as loans to the corporation to be repaid like debt. The holder of bonds is guaranteed payment of the principal, and receives interest on their investment. When investing in corporate bonds, the investor is a creditor rather than an owner of a part of a corporation.

Either a company or government institution issues a bond. Corporations use bonds to raise capital to operate or expand, and governments issue bonds to pay for public works projects. This book will discuss both in this chapter as part of the registered representative's required knowledge to perform critical function three: Explain different investments to customers and make appropriate recommendations.

TIP #23

Debt instruments, or bonds, are considered to carry less risk than stocks as there is no loss of principal investment.

CORPORATE BONDS

Although corporations issue stock to raise capital, most issue bonds as well. Bonds allow corporations to raise funds with a specific payoff date without relinquishing any ownership. This book will cover corporate bond types, risk, and features in this section.

Corporate Bond Basics

Bonds are legal agreements between the investor and issuing entity, just like any other investment. All bonds have an indenture agreement, much like a contract, usually printed on the back of the bond certificate. A bond's **indenture agreement** specifies **par value**, **coupon rate**, **maturity**, **collateral**, and **convertible** or **callable** features. This book will cover how all these features work in this chapter.

When a bond is issued, it has a par value much like stock does. But unlike stock, where the par value is simply a face-value starting point to the stock certificate, for bonds par value is a crucial value used in all calculations, such as dividend. A bond's par value is printed on the front of the bond certificate. Par value of a bond is the face value at issuance and acts as a benchmark in future trading. For example, if the stock market is volatile, and bonds are seen as a better and safer investment, bonds will increase in value. A bond with a $1,000 par value may now have a market value of $1,100, thus increasing the returns for the investor. Likewise, if the stock market is on the rise, a bond's returns may be seen as too low, devaluing the bond to a market value of $900. This book will discuss how to make calculations on market value later in this chapter; for now, simply understand that the par value is your starting point when making calculations for bonds.

TIP #24

Your Series 7 exam will assume a $1,000 par value for all bonds, if unstated. For example, if an exam question states: "John Miller holds a 6 percent bond," and nothing else, assume that bond has a $1,000 par value.

If a bond value is stated, it will state par at 100, like in this statement: "John bought a 6 percent XYZ bond at 100." The 100 stands for the $1,000 par value.

A bond has a maturation date, which is the date the bond's face or par value is due to the investor. Maturation dates vary per bond, and are determined by the issuer. Like a loan, this is when the debt must be repaid. As you can understand, this maturation date can be like a ticking time bomb for companies if they do not set money aside to pay investors their money back, which is why most companies create a sinking fund to prove their bonds are a stable investment. A **sinking fund** is a company's savings account to prepare to repay bonds.

Bonds with different types of maturation schedules are:

- **Series bonds**: these bonds are issued in different years, but all reach maturity at the same time.
- **Serial bonds**: bonds that carry different maturity dates.
- **Term bonds**: bonds that are issued at the same time and mature at the same time.

In return for their investment, investors receive interest, called the coupon rate. **Coupon rate** is the interest an investor receives on the par value of the bond. Later in this chapter this book will cover ways to calculate these basic bond features in examples, as part of your Series 7 exam requirements.

Types of Bonds

When covering different types of stock, this book discussed how each stock type catered to a different investor. Corporate bonds work in much the same way, accommodating investor needs with their features.

These are different types of bond certificates:

- **Fully registered bonds**: these most common kinds of bonds are registered in the investor's name and the investor received interest automatically, without having to submit any coupons.

- **Partially registered bonds**: these bonds only register the par value in the investor's name, not the interest. Also known as registered coupon bonds, these are no longer issued but still circulate in trading (and are therefore part of the Series 7 exam).
- **Bearer bonds**: these bonds are not registered in anyone's name to make trading easier, and have coupons physically attached that entitle the bearer to interest payments, which is why they are also known as coupon bonds. Like partially registered bonds, the risk of theft or loss is great, so they are no longer issued. Because bearer bonds still circulate, you must know them for your exam.
- **Book entry certificates**: bonds that are registered electronically, which are traded more easily due to the lack of paper trail.
- **Callable bonds**: bonds the issuer has a right to buy back, giving the issuer more control over its outstanding debt.
- **Put bonds**: bonds the holder has the right to redeem (or put back) with the issuer at par value, so the holder can liquidate his investment before maturation if desired.

TIP #25

Remember this: partially registered bonds and bearer bonds are both no longer issued, but still circulate in trading. They have been discontinued because earnings and ownership were too difficult to trace.

Risk Analysis: Secured and Unsecured Bonds

You will be advising your clients based on their risk tolerance, which is why Series 7 tests you on your understanding of secured and unsecured bonds. **Secured bonds**, as their names states, are secured by an asset the issuer owns, which is the easiest way to identify them.

Secured bonds and their collateral are:

- **Collateral trusts:** backed by financial assets the issuer owns and held by a trustee (a financial institution like a bank) in case of insolvency.
- **Guaranteed bonds**: backed by another firm like a parent company.
- **Mortgage bonds**: backed by property owned by the issuer.
- **Equipment trusts**: backed by equipment of the issuer (usually high-priced transportation equipment, like buses, trucks, or airplanes).

Unsecured bonds are a riskier investment because they are not backed by a security — a concept Series 7 expects you to apply to customer scenarios. Because of their high risk, these bonds generally carry a corresponding higher yield. For example, if you had a client who did not want to invest in stocks, but would like higher returns than a secured bond, an unsecured bond would be a recommendation you might want to make.

Unsecured bonds are:

- **Debentures**: by agreement, the bond holder receives interest when due at certain dates stated on the bond and principal at maturity.
- **Income bonds**: bonds where principal is paid at maturity but interest is only paid when the issuer's earnings are high enough, which is determined on the bond (very high risk).

Some bonds carry a protective covenant, requiring the issuing corporation to contribute money to an account specifically created to repay the bond obligation. This is called a sinking fund or defeasance provision. A corporate bond carrying a sinking fund provision is considered less risky, as there is a pool of money reserved to repay the obligation. If you were analyzing different bonds for your client, a bond with a sinking fund provision would be less risky, and would make a better recommendation for a client with lower risk tolerance.

TIP #26

For your Series 7 exam, remember this: the higher the risk, the greater the potential of return.

Bond Ratings

As part of critical function three, where you will be advising your customers on investments, you are expected to understand how a bond's rating can help you analyze risk. There are two rating institutions: Moody's and Standard and Poor's. Here is a chart showing how these institutions rate a bond's quality:

Quality	Standard and Poor's (S&P)	Moody's
Highest	AAA	Aaa
High	AA	Aa
Upper Medium	A	A
Lower Medium	BBB	Baa
Speculative	BB	Ba
Speculative (principal or interest payments missed	B	B
Speculative (no interest paid)	C	Caa
In Default	D	D

Once a bond reaches the speculative rating, it is considered higher in risk. Bonds in default are behind in payment obligation, and considered a bad investment. Standard and Poor's rating will break these ratings down further, by adding + and – signs, where Moody's will add 1, 2, or 3 (1 being highest,

3 lowest). Your Series 7 exam may ask you questions pertaining customer scenarios and risk, or how ratings work in relation to each other.

Yield

Like any investment, the objective of a bond investment is the return, or yield, on that investment. Because market value changes, so does yield. A bond carries nominal yield, reflecting the terms at the time of the bond's purchase, and current yield, which fluctuates with the market.

- **Nominal yield**: the interest of a bond at issuance, also called coupon rate.
- **Current yield**: the annual return of an investment based on the market price of the bond.

HOW TO CALCULATE **CURRENT YIELD**:

Current yield = annual interest ÷ market price

Current yield reflects the current market rate. For example if an investor carries a 9 percent bond, but market rates are at 10 percent, the bond's value will be less to reflect this difference. Your Series 7 exam will contain several questions where you will be expected to calculate the current yield based on different scenarios.

EXAMPLE:

George Jones bought a bond at $200, with a coupon rate of 7 percent. His annual interest comes to 0.07 times 200, equaling $14.

The bond now trades at $180. To calculate the current yield, you take the annual interest he receives ($14) and divide it by the market price of $180. This makes the current yield of the bond 7.78 percent ($14 ÷ $180).

TIP #27

Always remember that stocks receive dividend and bonds receive interest.

Accrued Interest

Just like the market rate affects a bond's value, so does the coupon date. The interest that accrues between coupon dates adds value to a bond, which you are expected to be able to calculate for your exam. To determine days of accrued interest, calculate the amount of days between the settlement date and the last coupon date.

HOW TO CALCULATE **ACCRUED INTEREST**:

(Days between coupon day and settlement day ÷ 360)
× annual interest

EXAMPLE:

XYZ corporate bond is a 5 percent bond, and has paid interest on May 31. Your client buys this bond, and the purchase settles on August 31. This bond receives $50 interest (5 percent of $1,000) annually. The accrued interest is for 90 days, so the math would look like this: (90 ÷ 360) × $50 = $12.50.

To calculate accrued interest, Series 7 assumes a 30-day month for all months of the year when calculating corporate and municipal bonds, and actual calendar days for government bonds.

Convertible Bonds

Some bonds carry the option of converting the bond into stocks, aptly named convertible bonds. An investor wishing to convert bonds to stocks would do so through their broker. Series 7, as part of a registered representative's duties to advise customers, will expect you to calculate the conversion ratio (or amount of shares a bond will give) of a convertible bond.

HOW TO CALCULATE **CONVERSION RATIOS**:

Conversion ratio = par value ÷ conversion price

EXAMPLE:

Joe Bennett bought an 8 percent ABC convertible bond at $100. His bond has a conversion price of $25. The conversion ratio is 4 (100/25), meaning he will receive 4 shares of stock for each bond he wants to convert to stock.

GOVERNMENT BONDS

The U.S. government issues bonds too, and most of the calculations you just learned for corporate bonds apply in the same way. Because the objective of the Series 7 exam is to test your ability to advise your clients on risk regarding investment, you should know this:

TIP #28

U.S. government bonds are the seen as the safest investment. Series 7 may give you customer scenarios, expecting you to choose between investment options for your client, based on the client's risk tolerance. U.S. government bonds are good investments for customers with low risk tolerance.

This is because, barring extremely unusual circumstances, the U.S. government will always be able to pay back your investment. Corporations can always go bankrupt, whereas the government is extremely unlikely to.

U.S. Treasury Securities

Because this book has already covered how to calculate interest, the rest of this section will simply cover types of government securities and their definitions. Make sure you know all of these, as Series 7 will test your knowledge, and not only in relation to interest and risk.

The different types of U.S. Treasury Securities are:

- **Treasury bills (T-bills)**: are issued at a discount to mature at par; carry an initial maturity of 4, 13, and 26 weeks.
- **Tax anticipation bills (TAB)**: geared toward corporate tax-paying investors, and issued at a discount to mature at par, usually a few days after corporate tax dates.
- **U.S. Treasury strips (T-strips)**: are issued at a discount to mature at par; mature after 6 months to 30 years.
- **Treasury notes (T-notes)**: pay interest every six months; mature at two, three, five, and ten years.
- **Treasury bonds (T-bonds)**: pay interest every six months; mature at 10 to 30 years.
- **Treasury inflation-indexed securities (TIPS)**: pay market interest every six months and par value adjusts to market inflation or deflation.
- **Non-marketable savings bonds**: non-negotiable, meaning they are not re-sold in the marketplace. **Series EE** bonds are issued at a discount to mature at par; at a denomination of at least $50; individuals cannot buy more than $50,000 in one year.

- **Series HH** bonds receive interest every six months; at a denomination of at least $500; one individual cannot hold more than $15,000 in this type of bond.

As previously mentioned, U.S. Government securities are seen as the safest investment. In Chapter 12, you will find out how to analyze risk for your customers; until then, remember U.S. Treasury securities are very low in risk.

U.S. GOVERNMENT AGENCY SECURITIES

Where the government directly backs U.S. Treasury securities, there are also other federal agencies that issue securities with government backing. In this section, this book will cover different types of bonds and the government agencies that back them. Government agencies issue these bonds to fund specific operations.

Collateralized Mortgage Obligations (CMOs)

Although you are unlikely to ever handle any of these for your customers, Series 7 still expects you to understand **collateralized mortgage obligations**, or CMOs, for your exam. CMOs are bonds backed by groups of mortgages that are issued by different agencies. These agencies use the bond issue to fund the mortgages, like Federal Housing Authority (FHA) or Veterans Assistance (VA) mortgages.

CMOs are issued by the following government agencies:

- **Federal National Mortgage Association** (FNMA, or Fannie Mae): owned by organizations that trade mortgages. Created to make home ownership more affordable, Fannie Mae purchases Federal Housing

Association (FHA) mortgages, Farmers Home Administration (FmHA), or Veterans Administration (VA) mortgages.

- **Government National Mortgage Association** (GNMA, or Ginnie Mae): an agency of the Department of Housing and Urban Development, Ginnie Mae backs FHA, VA, and FmHA mortgages traded by securities firms.
- **Federal Home Loan Mortgage Corporation** (FHLMC, or Freddie Mac): a subsidiary of the Federal Home Loan Bank (FHLB), packages different kinds of mortgages into mortgage securities, including but not limited to FHA, VA, and FmHA mortgages.

Investors get paid as homeowners make their mortgage payments or pay off their mortgage by either selling the house or refinancing their mortgage obligation. CMOs are split into different portions, or **tranches**, to diversify and limit risk for investors.

TIP #29

Remember this: CMOs do not carry a maturity date and carry extension and pre-payment risk.

To temper CMOs' risks, their tranches are broken down in different ways. Series 7 will test you on these.

The following CMO types are arranged from least risky to most risky:

- **Planned Amortization Class (PAC) tranches**: CMO tranche with the most certain amortization date and therefore the least risk (and corresponding return).

- **Targeted Amortization Class (TAC) tranches**: CMO tranche with less certain payment schedule (this can be for various reasons, like prepayment or higher risk mortgages) and higher risk and return.
- **Companion tranches**: these tranches are created to support the PAC and TAC CMOs and absorb prepayment risk.
- **Z-tranches**: these tranches are created as support until the CMO retires. Z-tranches are the last tranches remaining in a CMO. These tranches do not receive interest, but are bought at a discount and reach their full value at maturity.

Other Issuing Agencies

For your Series 7 exam, you will likely only be asked about Ginnie Mae, Freddie Mac, and Fannie Mae. Should you get a question regarding other government-backed securities, you will need to know the following agencies, as well as the securities they offer.

Other bond-issuing government agencies are:

- **Federal Farm Credit Bank**: Issues short-term discount notes and interest-bearing bonds with different maturities to fund Banks for Cooperative (COOPS), Federal Land Banks (FLB), and Federal Intermediate Credit Banks (FICB) to fund first mortgages on farm properties.
- **Federal Home Loan Bank**: Makes loans to banks to cover excess credit demand due to market fluctuations.
- **Student Loan Marketing Association (Sallie Mae)**: Owned by its participants, Sallie Mae guarantees student loans.

TIP #30

Expect regulations regarding mortgages to change following the 2008-2009 mortgage crisis. Be sure to keep up on the latest changes regarding mortgage-backed investments through **www.finra.org** to best advise your clients.

GOVERNMENT-BACKED MONEY MARKET INSTRUMENTS

Money market instruments are short-term debt instruments, generally carrying low risk for your customer. Money market investments usually carry a maturity of one year or less, providing liquidity should your client require it. They are generally issued at a discount, reaching par value at maturity.

Review the following government-backed money market securities; they will show up on your Series 7 exam as part of scenarios where you must identify their function or use to a client.

Federal Funds

Banks are required to carry a reserve (a percentage of deposits the bank holds). When banks are short on reserve funds, they borrow money from other banks at Federal Fund rates. These other banks tend to hold excess funds simply because their demand of funds was lower that day than the receiving Federal Funds bank. Federal Funds loans are usually only overnight loans, and happen daily as a common bank practice.

Federal Reserve Bank Repurchase Agreement (Repo)

A Federal Reserve Bank Repurchase Agreement is a contract where a seller agrees to repurchase an investment (often a T-bill) at a certain price and at a certain time. Repos are loans of $1,000,000 or more with a maturity of up to two weeks and are created to benefit short-term investment goals.

TIP #31

Remember Federal Funds and Repos are both short-term investments.

OTHER MONEY MARKET INSTRUMENTS

This is a short list of commercial money market instruments you are expected to know for your Series 7 exam, although you are unlikely to see many questions on these. As you will notice when reviewing these securities, they are mostly created to aid transactions in situations where short-term monies are required or need to be transacted in a safe and convenient way. Each will be briefly covered here.

Negotiable Certificates of Deposit (CDs)

Negotiable certificates of deposit are defined as negotiable time deposits with a higher interest rate due to the investment required ($100,000 is the minimum). These are very low-risk, negotiable investments — meaning they can be sold to other investors if the holder requires it.

Commercial Paper (CP)

Commercial paper is a corporate investment without collateral, making it a higher risk investment. The SEC does not require commercial paper to be registered. This investment is issued at a discount and matures at par, usually within 270 days, benefiting short-term investment goals.

Banker's Acceptances (BA)

Banker's acceptances are time-drafts (a short-term credit investment a bank backs). Companies utilize banker's acceptances (or banker's drafts, as they are also known as) when funding import or export transactions.

Eurodollars

Eurodollars are American dollars held at a foreign bank located outside the United States. The funds are the result of payments made to foreign corporations.

BONDS AND YOUR CLIENT

In this chapter, you have learned about both corporate and government bonds. As you now know, a bond's backing greatly decides the risk associated for your client. When you make bond recommendations, make sure you can adequately explain to your client how the repayment of the bond is guaranteed.

Of the bonds covered in this chapter, remember Treasury bonds are considered the safest investment. Risks associated with bond investment are market risk (because a bond's value fluctuates with the market) and inflation risk (because inflation might outpace returns).

The ideal client for bond investing has lower risk tolerance. Unlike stock investments, bonds maintain principal at a generally lower return than stock investing. Bonds are often used to balance out stock investments in a client's portfolio; see Chapter 12 on portfolio allocation for more information on this type of diversification.

CHECKLIST

This chapter covered a lot of different concepts, definitions, and government institutions and their role in investments. As government securities are an important component to advising your client of their investment options, Series 7 incorporates many questions regarding debt instruments. Use this checklist to make sure you are ready to answer any scenarios presented to you in the exam.

- ☐ I understand bond basics, like par value, maturation, and coupon rate, including how these components affect my customers' investment decisions.
- ☐ I can make appropriate risk analyses for my customers, advising on secured and unsecured bonds. I know how to use Standard and Poor's and Moody's ratings.
- ☐ I can calculate yield, including nominal yield and current yield.
- ☐ I can differentiate between government securities. I know U.S. Treasury securities, CMOs, and how tranches work.
- ☐ I understand both government-backed and other money market securities and how they work within the market.

SAMPLE QUESTIONS

1. XYZ Corporation wants to issue bonds. To ensure all bonds do not come due at the same time, the corporation needs the bonds to carry staggered maturity. XYZ Corporation will issue:

    [A] Staggered bonds
    [B] Term bonds
    [C] Serial bonds
    [D] Series bonds

2. John Griffin wants to buy DEF bonds, but only if he can redeem the bonds at par value whenever he wants. You will recommend:

    [A] Bearer bonds
    [B] Callable bonds
    [C] Redeemable bonds
    [D] Put bonds

3. XYZ has issued guaranteed bonds. This means the bonds are secured by:

    [A] Their own guarantee to repay
    [B] XYZ's property
    [C] Another firm, usually a parent company
    [D] The government

4. GHI bonds are rated D by Standard and Poor's. This means the company:

    [A] Is in default
    [B] Nothing; S&P does not have a D rating
    [C] Is speculative
    [D] Has just paid dividends

5. Bill Moore bought a bond at $1,000 with a coupon rate of 6 percent. The bond now trades at $1,200. What is the current yield of his bond?

    [A] 6 percent
    [B] $200
    [C] 8 percent
    [D] 5 percent

6. Dana Lewis bought a 7 percent convertible bond at $1,000. She wants to trade her bond of stock. Her bond carries a conversion price of $400. How many shares will she receive if she converts her bond?

   [A] 2,800
   [B] 2.5
   [C] 400
   [D] 70

7. What are the characteristics of a T-strip? They:

   [A] Are issued at a discount, and mature at par, usually maturing after 6 months to 30 years
   [B] Mature after tax season is over
   [C] Are issued at a discount to mature at par, usually maturing at 4, 13, or 26 weeks
   [D] Pay interest every 6 months, and par value adjusts to market rates

8. Bill Frank wants to invest in a CMO, but needs his exposure to risk to be as limited as possible. You will likely recommend a CMO with a:

   [A] Z-Tranche
   [B] Targeted Amortization Tranche
   [C] Deep Tranche
   [D] PAC Tranche

9. Chris Truman took out a student loan to pay for college. His loan is backed by:

   [A] Sallie Mae
   [B] Freddie Mac
   [C] Fannie Mae
   [D] Ginnie Mae

10. What is the Federal Fund rate?

    [A] 6 percent
    [B] The market interest rate of loans more than $1,000,000
    [C] The interest of Repo transactions
    [D] The rate of reserve requirement loans between banks

CASE STUDY: DONALD PURTILL

Purtill Financial, LLC
397 Sandhurst Drive
Highland Heights, OH 44143
(440) 449-1196
www.PurtillFinancial.com

Since establishing his company Purtill Financial in 2000, Donald Purtill has been offering investment management, financial planning, and tax preparation services to his clients. "We have $15 million in assets under management," Purtill says of the scope of his firm's responsibilities, "and we serve 56 client families. We are experts in investment analysis and help our clients achieve extraordinary returns."

During an average day, Purtill meets with prospective clients, analyzes current clients' portfolios, makes portfolio recommendations, as well as keeps up with e-mails and phone calls. Like other financial advisors, he believes strongly in putting the client's needs first. "A financial advisor should be a fiduciary whose first priority is doing what's best for his or her client," Purtill says. "Financial advisors should be highly skilled in investment, taxes, and financial planning."

"We enjoy helping clients save money on investing, and helping them grow their investment assets through good, low-cost, diversified investment choices," Purtill says when asked what he most enjoys about being a financial advisor. He takes a practical approach to explaining complex financial industry workings to his clients. "We explain things to them in simple language, using actual numerical, historical returns."

Purtill Financial built its business through client referrals and continues to grow this way. "We ask our clients to refer us to their friends and relatives," Purtill says. He keeps current on the industry by reading financial publications and receiving continuing education.

Purtill believes strongly the best way to be successful is to remain independent from bigger institutions, stating commission-only compensation as a reason. "Try to work with an experienced, independent, fee-only advisor."

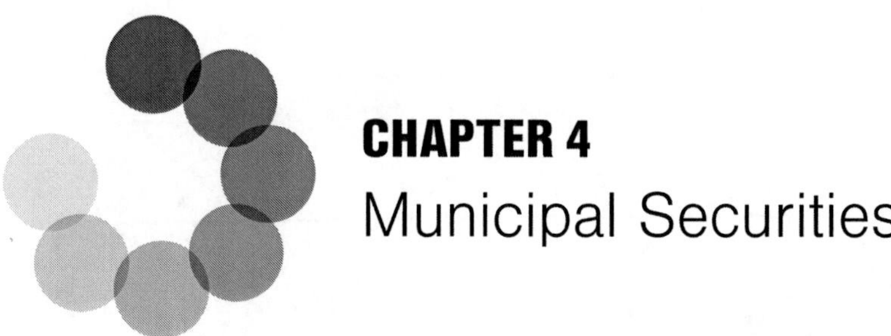

CHAPTER 4 Municipal Securities

Municipalities, such as state or local governments, need funding to build roads, hospitals, and other projects. To provide these needed funds, municipalities create municipal bonds. Although municipal bonds will not make up much of your clients' portfolios or come up often during your career as a registered representative, Series 7 tests relatively heavily on the subject. This chapter will cover municipalities to ensure you will be able to easily answer the questions on your exam.

MUNICIPAL SECURITIES: TYPES AND DEFINITIONS

When a municipality, like a county for instance, decides it wants to begin a project with bond funding, this municipality can choose **general obligation bonds** or **revenue bonds**. A municipality's taxes back general obligation bonds: the population's taxes will repay the bondholder. Expected revenue of the funded project will secure revenue bonds. The municipality will choose GO or Revenue bonds based on the type of project the bond is funding.

General Obligation (GO) Bonds

General obligation (GO) bonds are created to pay for projects that do not bring in revenue to repay the obligation. Projects a GO bond funds are bridges, roads (non-toll), schools, fire stations, police stations, etc. Instead of counting on revenue to back the obligation, GO bonds use the tax base of a municipality as a type of collateral. GO bonds need to get voter approval before they can be issued.

Because you, as a registered representative, will need to be able to assess risk for your customers, Series 7 expects you to analyze GO bonds for risk. Much like when assessing a corporation's ability to repay a debt, you can analyze a municipality the same way: by looking at past ability to repay debts. Because a municipality's taxing power backs a GO bond, it is considered a fairly safe investment with a corresponding lower yield. When assessing a municipality's taxing power, you must consider population, tax base, property values, and sales per capita (sales tax).

TIP #32

A note on property taxes: Series 7 may ask you to calculate property (or ad valorem) taxes, as part of a GO bond's backing. Make sure you use the assessed value, not the market value, as property taxes always use assessed value to determine taxes.

Although all these numbers are helpful in assessing taxing power, it can still be difficult to quantify risk for your customer. To create a concrete comparison between different GO bonds for a client, you should determine a municipality's debt per occupant: per capita debt.

HOW TO CALCULATE **PER-CAPITA DEBT**:

Per capita debt = (net direct debt + overlapping debt) ÷ municipality population

Net direct debt is the municipality's debt: the per-capita expenses of the municipality itself. Overlapping debt covers city, county, or state debt that an occupant of a municipality may also be responsible for. For example, an occupant of a city pays property taxes to the city, but is also liable for county taxes.

Series 7 exam questions will provide you with the necessary numbers to reach the right answer.

Revenue Bonds

Revenue bonds are created to fund projects that will generate the revenue to pay the obligation back. Examples of projects that a revenue bond might fund are utilities, airports, and toll roads.

TIP #33

Because revenue bonds are not funded by taxes, they do not need voter approval.

Because backing is inherent in the project, revenue bonds do not need to get voter consent, but the projects do need a feasibility study. For the study, the municipality hires consultants to project future revenue, as well as identify any engineering or community factors that could affect the municipality's decision to go ahead with the project. To protect the revenue bond holder, revenue bonds hold covenants, which are provisions written in the bondholder agreement, mandating the municipality to comply with certain rules.

Different types of revenue bond covenants are:

- **Maintenance covenants**: ensure the municipality takes care of the property (or facility and equipment).
- **Insurance covenants**: the municipality must insure the project.
- **Rate covenant**: the municipality must charge enough for use of facility to ensure principal and interest can be repaid to the investor.

Another important concept to factor into the risk involved in a revenue bond issue is that there is always the possibility there will be more bonds issued in the future. Because it can be difficult for a municipality to estimate cost, there may be a need to raise funds in the future. As a registered representative, you will want a **net revenue pledge** to be a part of the revenue bonds' issue to protect your customer. A net revenue pledge guarantees the municipality has the funds to repay bondholder obligations with generated revenue after paying operating expenses.

Determining the debt service ratio will help you assess for your clients how well a bond covers its debt obligation and your client as the investor.

HOW TO CALCULATE **DEBT SERVICE COVERAGE RATIO**:

Debt service coverage ratio: net revenue ÷ (principal + interest)

Industrial Revenue Bonds (IDRs)

Industrial revenue bonds (IDRs) require special treatment in this section because of the different nature of their backing. Even though municipalities issue IDRs, their repayment comes from corporate lease payment. Projects funded by an IDR are usually the construction of a building or space that will be leased out to a private corporation.

TIP #34

Remember IDRs are indirectly relying on a corporation's solvency and therefore carry higher risk.

Short-term Municipal Obligations: Notes

Just like corporations can issue short-term obligations to serve their purposes as well as the investors, so can municipalities. This section will cover types of notes, or debt obligations, as they function much like their corporate counterparts.

Different types of municipal notes are:

- **Tax anticipation notes (TAN)**: Notes a municipality's anticipated taxes will finance.
- **Bond anticipation notes (BAN)**: Notes issued to bridge time when long-term bonds will be issued.
- **Revenue anticipation notes (RAN)**: Notes issued to fund operations in anticipation of a municipality's expected revenue.

- **Construction loan notes (CLN)**: Notes issued to fund apartment buildings to provide funding for construction.
- **Project notes (PN)**: Notes used to fund low-income or subsidized housing projects.

You may notice from these listings that these notes provide interim funding (short-term finance solutions until long-term provisions are in place). These investments benefit short-term investment objectives for investors, with a low risk due to their backing.

Other Municipal Bonds

With so many public projects that a municipality may need to fund, there are just as many different types of bonds. This section includes a list of bond types you should know for your Series 7 exam.

Municipal bond types are:

- **Refunding bonds**: These bonds are issued to refund outstanding bonds, often if there has been a significant drop in market interest rates. The issuer saves money by issuing these lower-interest Refunding Bonds, to repay the higher cost of a callable bond. Sometimes called Advanced Refunding Bonds.
- **Pollution control**: Bonds issued to fund construction of pollution control facilities. Like with Industrial Revenue Bonds (IDRs), the value of the bond is rated by the solvency of the future lessee of the facility. This book will cover corporate assessment in Chapter 11.
- **Double-barreled**: When the good faith and credit of the issuer and the revenue of a project backs a bond, it is called double-barreled.
- **Moral obligations**: Issued when only a source outside the municipality's tax base or other revenue backs a bond. These bonds are

considered high risk, because they are backed solely by moral obligation, not monetary collateral.

- **Original issue discount (OID) Bonds**: These bonds are issued at a discount and reach par value at maturity. OID bonds also receive interest, which is non-taxable.

ISSUING PROCESS OF MUNICIPAL SECURITIES

As with any financial investment, there is a complex legal process for the issuer to navigate before issuing municipal securities. First, the bond counsel needs to approve the issue of the bond.

Bond Counsel

A municipality hires a law firm to navigate the legalities, such as the backing of a bond, involved in acquiring the funding needed for a project and the corresponding bond issue. This law firm, usually specialized in bond financing, becomes the bond counsel. This legal team will investigate the bond for its solvency and render an opinion on its issue.

Bond counsels have two types of opinions:

1. **Qualified**: the bond counsel sees issues, or qualifiers, that affect the bond issue.
2. **Unqualified**: the bond counsel sees no complications in the bond issue.

TIP #35

A bond can be issued without a legal opinion and needs to be stamped **ex-legal**. This can mean a bond is more risky for your client, as it has not received a legal opinion and therefore does not have the assurance of repayment that a legal bond does.

Selling Municipal Bonds

When it comes to selling municipalities, many of the same players and their roles apply as when selling securities. The municipality hires underwriters who form a syndicate. To review this hierarchy, read Chapter 2 on equity securities.

In order to have more money for the project the municipality seeks to fund, the underwriters try to keep the share of the underwriters and syndicate down. The cost of underwriters is added to the interest cost of the bond, which is a cost the municipality bears. Municipalities like to keep their Net Interest Cost as low as possible so there is more money to spend on the project and less cost to the bond.

These are a municipality's costs associated with the issue of a bond:

- **Net interest cost (NIC)**: total cost of interest payments a municipality will make to investors until a bond's maturity.
- **True interest cost (TIC)**: net interest cost (NIC) plus the time value of money. (This is the current rate of inflation.)

Remember the NIC and TIC look at a bond issue from the issuer's perspective. Although Series 7 may ask you a question related to NIC or TIC, you will be more likely to look at the buying process of municipal securities for your clients.

Buying Municipal Bonds

As a registered representative, you are expected to be able to compute the value of a municipal bond for your future customers. Because municipal bonds pay interest, the accrued interest factors into a bond's value. Most calculations for municipal bonds are the same as corporate bonds so review Chapter 3 to practice calculations like nominal yield, current yield, and yield to maturity.

TIP #36

For Series 7 exam questions on municipal bond calculations, assume a 30-day month for all months and a 360-day year (or 30/360, for a quick way to remember this rule).

A bond buyer needs to compensate the seller for the interest that has not yet been paid by the issuer, or **accrued interest**, as this adds value to the bond. To count the days of accrued interest, do not include the settlement date of the trade. Here is an example of a question you might see on your Series 7 exam:

EXAMPLE:

John Williams buys $10,000 of 6.5 percent municipal bonds on Monday, March 6. The bonds pay interest on March 1 and September 1. The settlement date of municipal bonds is on the third business day after the trade, so Thursday, March 9.

To calculate the accrued interest for the eight days (from March 1 to March 9), use this formula:

HOW TO CALCULATE **ACCRUED INTEREST**:

Accrued interest = principal × rate × time

For this example: $10,000 × 0.065 × 8 days ÷ 360 = $14.44. He would have to pay the seller of the municipal bonds $14.44 for accrued interest since the last payment date of March 1.

The Bond Buyer

The most well-known publication with primary market municipal bond issues in it is the *Bond Buyer*, a daily publication all municipal securities underwriters read. The *Bond Buyer* lists the visible supply of bonds, which are bonds issued in the upcoming 30 days. It also lists sales of the previous week called the **placement ratio.**

The *Bond Buyer* includes these indexes:

- **20 Bond Index**: an Index of 20 general obligation bonds with at least an A rating, maturing in 20 years.
- **11 Bond Index**: Index of 11 bonds of the 20 Bond Index, with at least an AA rating.
- **40 Bond Index**: Index of 40 GO and revenue bonds, listed by price.

- **REVDEX 25**: Index of 25 revenue bonds, rated A or better and maturing in 30 years, based on yield.

Other publications brokers use in municipal bond trading are the **Blue List**, which lists all municipal bond offerings alphabetically by state, and the **Dow Jones Municipal Index**, which lists weekly averages of state and city bond yields.

TIP #37

As a registered representative, you will use the *Bond Buyer*, the Blue List, and the Dow Jones Municipal Index to keep track of municipal securities daily (Series 7 will expect you to know this).

MUNICIPAL BONDS AND YOUR CLIENT

As you have learned in this chapter, municipal bonds offer another low-risk investment alternative to stock investing. When advising your client on different municipal bonds, make sure you can fully explain how the bond is backed. Like with corporate and government bonds, municipal bonds maintain principal investment, making them a far safer investment than stocks.

The ideal client for municipal bond investing has a lower risk tolerance and wishes to maintain principal. Municipal bonds can also offer tax benefits to some clients; to understand how investments affect taxes, see Chapter 8 on taxation. Consider contacting your client's tax advisor to fully understand how municipal bond investing may affect his or her state and local taxes.

CHECKLIST

- ☐ I know the different types of municipal securities, including general obligation (GO) bonds, revenue bonds, industrial revenue bonds (IDRs), and short-term municipal securities (notes)
- ☐ I understand how bonds are funded, and how their backing affects risk and yield
- ☐ I know how the issuing process of municipal securities works, including the role of the bond counsel
- ☐ I can identify the different indexes the *Bond Buyer* uses

SAMPLE QUESTIONS

1. Which of the following is true about general obligation (GO) Bonds?

    I. They are repaid by the revenue a project generates
    II. They are created to fulfill general obligations a municipality has
    III. They are created to fund non-revenue generating public projects
    IV. They are backed by the tax-base of a municipality

    [A] I and IV
    [B] I, II, and IV
    [C] III and IV
    [D] None of the above

2. Which of the following factors into assessing a municipality's taxing power?

    I. Market value of properties in the municipality
    II. Per capita debt
    III. Sales tax per capita
    IV. Tax base

    [A] I, III, and IV
    [B] II, III, and IV
    [C] All of the above
    [D] None of the above

3. XYZ municipality with a population of 500,000 has net direct debt of $1,000,000. There is overlapping debt from other counties of $1,000,000.

Your client is considering buying XYZ's bonds, and you need to assess the municipality's solvency. What is XYZ's per capita debt?

- [A] $1,000,000
- [B] $2
- [C] $4
- [D] $40

4. DEF's revenue bond funds a toll road and includes a rate covenant. What does this covenant do?

   - [A] It ensures the municipality will charge enough for use of the toll road to repay its bond investors
   - [B] It makes sure the bond's interest rates do not drop, so the bond is a safer investment for investors
   - [C] It makes sure the municipality carries insurance for the project
   - [D] It makes sure the municipality gives all bond holders the same interest rate

5. DEF municipality has finished its toll road, and the road has generated $1,000,000, with $500,000 in operating expenses. The municipality has $500,000 in 5 percent bonds outstanding. What is DEF's debt service coverage ratio?

   - [A] $500,000
   - [B] $95
   - [C] $100
   - [D] $200

6. Industrial revenue bonds are backed by:

   - [A] The leasing corporation
   - [B] The tax base of the municipality issuing the bond
   - [C] The industry's total revenue
   - [D] The municipality's promise to repay

7. **When is a BAN issued?**

   [A] When a municipality wants to fund a low-income housing project
   [B] When a municipality expects to receive revenue from a project
   [C] When a municipality wants to stop the issue of bonds
   [D] When a municipality needs to bridge time until long-term bonds are issued

8. **XYZ municipality is issuing a bond backed by their good faith, as well as the revenue of the airport the bond is funding. This bond is:**

   [A] A Moral Obligation Bond
   [B] A Project Note
   [C] A Double-Barreled Bond
   [D] A Transportation Bond

9. **ABC municipality wants to issue a bond. The bond counsel has rendered the bond issue unqualified. This means:**

   [A] The municipality is not qualified to issue the bond
   [B] The bond counsel sees no complications to the bond's issue
   [C] The bond counsel sees issues that would affect the bond's issue
   [D] The bond can be sold without a broker

10. **GHI municipality issues a three-year, 6 percent bond, with total bonds issued at 1,000,000. What is the bond's NIC?**

   [A] $180,000
   [B] $1,000,000
   [C] $1,060,000
   [D] $60,000

CASE STUDY: PAUL STAIB

Staib Financial Planning, LLC
10082 S. Fairgate Way
Highlands Ranch, CO 80126
(303) 346-5336
www.staibfinancialplanning.com

Paul Staib is the owner and operator of Staib Financial Planning, LLC, a fee-only financial planning and investment services provider in Highlands Ranch, Colorado. He believes very strongly in the importance of networking with other industry professionals. "As a self-employed business owner with no full-time employees, a large part of my day consists of networking with ancillary professionals like CPAs and estate attorneys." He focuses on customer service, too. "I enjoy helping my clients develop, implement, and manage financial plans to put them on course to reach their personal financial goals."

When Staib acquires a new customer, he first completes necessary paperwork and discusses financial goals. He then develops a financial plan based on the customer's risk tolerance. "I utilize a client questionnaire and discuss the client's responses to it with them in detail. We talk through their goals and investment duration, along with some hypothetical portfolios, to determine what is best for them."

When it comes to explaining the complex financial industry and how it works to his clients, Staib keeps it simple. "But provide the client with their desired level of knowledge or education on the specific topic," he advises. "You want to provide the client with the comfort that you know what you are doing while balancing that with the client's desire to discuss the details. Oftentimes, the client has engaged you as their expert because they don't want to get into the details."

He keeps current on the financial industry by reading both industry and non-industry items. "I self-study and research, attend conferences, seminars, and industry group meetings, and I network and socialize with complementary professionals like CPAs." His goal is to continue to grow Staib Financial Planning in the years to come.

Staib suggests those new to the industry find a mentor and dedicate themselves fully to building their business. "There are several success stories of folks who achieved their success in any number of ways — you need to select your own method, one you are comfortable with, and follow it with all your passion," he advises aspiring financial professionals. "What worked for one person may not necessarily work for you."

CHAPTER 5
Packaged Securities

Some investors have large resources and can spread their wealth among different securities as their goals dictate. As a registered representative you will advise your clients about how to use their wealth effectively. Rather than exposing your clients to undesirable risk that comes with investing in securities individually, the market has packaged securities to offer. Packaged securities take individual stocks, bonds, and money market instruments, like the ones covered in the previous chapters, and group them together by type, industry, or investment objectives.

Real estate investment trusts (REITs) are an example of grouped securities by type (in this case real estate investments); annuities and mutual funds are grouped by objective (in this case retirement).

To understand packaged securities, you must first understand the companies that manage these securities and how they operate.

TIP #38

Series 7 likes to include a relatively large amount of questions on management investment companies — make sure you are ready to answer them.

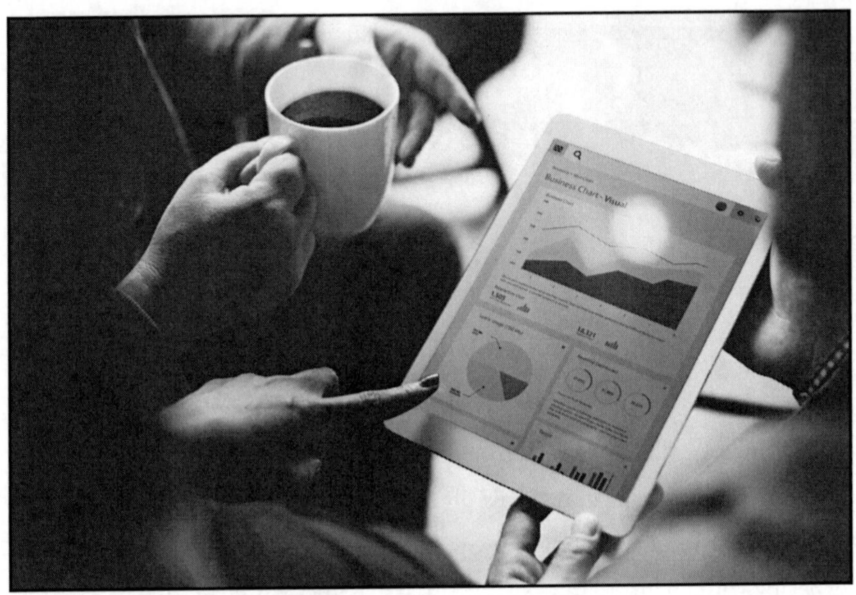

MANAGEMENT INVESTMENT COMPANIES

The main duties of a management company (better known as a mutual fund management company) are to take this pool of monies and decide on appropriate investments, in line with the packaged security's goal. The management company also makes portfolio decisions, aiming to diversify the investment choices. Packaged securities allow investors to benefit from professional investment strategies while making small investments. A management company makes investment and portfolio decisions for a fee (usually 0.5 to 1 percent), and investors pay a sales charge, or load, when they buy shares. This sales charge depends on the fund.

An important law regarding management investment companies is the Investment Company Act of 1940. It was created as the result of misleading practices (like overcharging for stocks bought, and charging high fees) that led to great investor loss. This act was passed by Congress, requiring investment companies to register with the SEC and follow their policies, demanding full disclosure to investors. For your exam, you should know the Investment Company Act of 1940 makes sure companies do not overcharge investors, investments are diversified to reduce risk, and returns on investment are disclosed.

TIP #39

Investment Company Act of 1940: this act regulates investment companies' pricing policies, promotion, and allocation of investments.

Investment Companies Defined

Management investment companies are either diversified or non-diversified. Non-diversified companies will have a narrow investment pool, exposing your client to market risks associated with the type of investment. By knowing an investment company is diversified you as a registered representative know your customer is protected from some investment risks. A diversified management company must have no more than 5 percent invested in one company and cannot buy more than 10 percent of voting stock in one company.

At their most basic organizational level, management companies' funds are either open-ended or closed-ended:

- **Open-ended funds**: best known as a mutual fund, these funds have an unlimited amount of shares available — new investors are always welcome. A prospectus needs to be available to investors. The make-up of these funds will change as the number of investors increases.
- **Closed-ended funds**: also called publicly traded funds, these funds carry a fixed amount of shares, which are sold to investors and consequently traded in the market. These funds are designed to fix the

investments included in the fund, for investors who do not like the fluctuations in make-up associated with open-ended funds.

TIP #40

Remember closed-ended funds are a one-time offering of securities and open-ended funds offer securities continuously.

Because investors have different objectives, management investment companies have created different types of funds. This book has compiled a basic list of funds, but you should remember the market always changes.

The most important understanding you should have as a registered representative is how different funds affect risk. Series 7 will likely give you customer scenarios in which you will have to recommend investments based on risk tolerance. Some funds are compiled, like growth and income funds, so keep this in mind when analyzing best choices for your customer. You should be familiar with the funds listed below and how to apply them to different Series 7 exam scenarios.

Different types of funds are:

- **Balanced funds**: funds that balance investments between bonds and common and preferred stocks to tamper risk.
- **Bond funds**: invest in bonds; low risk.
- **Common stock funds**: invest in common stock. These funds are often specialized by goal, like growth funds, or stock type, like blue chip funds (investing in blue chip stocks.
- **Dual-purpose bonds**: invest in two types of stock to serve combined goals, like income and capital.

- **Exchange traded funds**: funds where stocks are not bought from the issuer, but traded at various exchanges and NASDAQ.
- **Government bond funds**: invest in Treasury securities only.
- **Growth funds**: funds that have capital appreciation (growth) as a goal.
- **Income funds**: funds that invest in bonds, often higher risk or "junk" bonds, to increase income.
- **Index funds**: invest in funds that mirror an index, like Standard and Poor's. The fund's objective is to have earnings in line with the market.
- **International funds**: invest in foreign securities. These funds are often used to diversify investment portfolios.
- **Money market funds**: invest in short-term money market investments.
- **Municipal bond funds**: invest in municipal bonds only, often limited by state.
- **Specialized funds**: invest in a particular industry, companies in the same area, etc. These funds are speculating on out of the ordinary growth in a particular investment segment.

TIP #41

A fund's investment objective is the most important factor in deciding if a fund is right for your customer: the fund's objective needs to match the customer's goal.

A note on rules of conduct: as a registered representative, you should be aware of certain rules of conduct on your part, as well as on the part of the underwriter of mutual funds shares.

The underwriter is not allowed to offer you "perks," like vacations or other in-kind monetary compensation for buying shares. In turn, a registered representative is prohibited from re-selling investment company shares for a profit.

Ways to Invest

To buy into mutual funds, or open-ended funds, a customer can buy shares in different ways, depending on goals and resources. With a **regular account**, the investor simply buys a certain amount of shares. A customer agrees to buy shares regularly with a **voluntary accumulation plan**, or signs a **letter of intent (LOI)** if buying a large amount of shares at a discounted sales charge, or load.

Here is what you should know for the Series 7 exam about ways a customer can purchase shares:

- **Letter of Intent (LOI)**: The investor has to meet the share requirement stated in the LOI within 13 months, the agreement can be backdated up to 90 days, and shares are kept in an escrow account until the LOI obligation is met.
- **Voluntary accumulation plan**: the investor limits price fluctuation risk by investing periodically, or using **dollar cost averaging**.

Dollar cost averaging is an investment approach often used in mutual fund investing. When an investor buys shares periodically (say once a month), he or she hopes to balance out market fluctuation by averaging his or her cost out. Series 7 will likely test you with a scenario where an investor uses a voluntary accumulation plan, so you will need to know how to calculate **average cost per share**.

EXAMPLE:

Trish Williams deposits a total of $600 in ABC Fund over three months, making her monthly investment $200. The price of shares was:

Month 1: $50
Month 2: $60
Month 3: $55

To calculate the average cost per share, you must first determine how many shares she owns.

Month 1: $200/$50= 4 shares
Month 2: $200/$60= 3.33 shares
Month 3: $200/$55= 3.64 shares
Total shares held: 4 + 3.33 + 3.64 = 10.97 shares

To calculate average price per share, you must now divide total amount invested by the amount of shares: $600 ÷ 10.97 = $54.69

HOW TO CALCULATE **AVERAGE COST PER SHARE**:

Average cost per share = total dollars invested ÷ shares bought

Although the formula is simple, make sure you take each step shown in the example to arrive at the right amount. Series 7 will try to trip you up by inserting answers that are close to the correct answer.

To entice investors with more resources, investment companies often offer discounts on sales charges (say at 1 percent) at different levels in investment: the higher the investment amount, the lower the sales charge. For instance, an investment company may decide investors of more than $10,000 get a discount in sales charge (say 0.75 percent). When an investor hits this pre-arranged level disclosed by the investment company, it is called hitting the **breakpoint.**

TIP #42

Breakpoints are available to individual investors or corporations but not to investment clubs and must be disclosed in the fund prospectus.

Calculating Sales Charge

Series 7 will expect you to be able to make some calculations based on the value of the trading fund, including public offering price (POP) and net asset value (NAV). To correctly answer some of the exam questions, you should know how to compute the percentage of sales charge that is part of the public offering price.

HOW TO CALCULATE **SALES CHARGE**:

Net Asset Value (NAV): value of fund's assets ÷ outstanding shares

Public Offering Price (POP): Net Asset Value (NAV) + broker's commission

Sales Charge (percent): (POP-NAV) ÷ POP

EXAMPLE:

XYZ mutual fund has a net asset value of $18 and a public offering price of $20.

The sales charge is ($20 - $18)/$20 = 0.1, or 10 percent

This is an easy calculation; remember sales charge is always computed as a percentage of the public offering price.

UNIT INVESTMENT TRUSTS (UITS)

In a unit investment trust (UIT), the registered company holds income-producing investments in a trust for investors. The company issues shares, or units, and investors receive dividends and other income regularly.

Unit investment trusts come in two types:

1. **Fixed investment trust**: trust terminates when the investments (usually bonds) mature.
2. **Participating trust**: trust invests in set mutual funds shares, with no set maturation.

TIP #43

Unit investment trusts, unlike mutual funds, have a fixed portfolio investment allocation, and they do not employ investment managers. UITs have no management fees.

FACE AMOUNT CERTIFICATES

In this rare type of investment, investors buy certificates at a discount; the face amount is to be paid when the certificate matures. Face amount certificates are often backed by assets such as real estate. You will not see many questions on this type of investment as part of your Series 7 exam. Simply know what face amount certificates are, should they come up as an investment choice.

ANNUITY CONTRACTS

Insurance companies sell annuities with the intent of paying investors during their retirement years. Annuities come in fixed form and variable. Because only variable annuities count as securities, Series 7 will likely only test you on variable annuity contracts.

Fixed Annuities

The only thing you should know about fixed annuities is they have a fixed rate of return. The investor is guaranteed a dollar amount for his or her lifetime — he or she will not sell this investment.

Fixed annuities are a safe investment due to guaranteed payout, but they hold purchasing power risk. Because these contracts are made years, often decades, ahead of their payout, they carry great inflation risk (for example, $500 in 1980 will buy more than $500 in 2010).

Variable Annuities

To leverage against inflation, insurance companies issue variable annuities. Variable annuities work like mutual funds and must be sold with a prospectus. The insurance company will keep funds separate from their other business. Most companies use annuity funds to turn around and invest in stocks and bonds to ensure they make a profit and keep up with inflation.

TIP #44

Variable annuities carry investment risk and are considered securities.

The funds in this separate account will have a target interest rate, or **assumed interest rate (AIR)**. AIR is an estimated return to give investors an idea of what returns may be. Profits and losses are passed on to the investor.

Here are different types of annuities you should know about on your Series 7 exam:

- **Life annuity**: this investment pays out only for the life of the investor and stops paying when the investor dies.
- **Joint life with last survivor annuity**: this annuity pays two investors for both their lifetimes; pays both portions to the survivor (usually a spouse) until their death.
- **Life annuity with period certain**: this annuity gives a payout for a specified time (20 years for example) with survivor benefits should the investor die before the term is up.

REAL ESTATE INVESTMENT TRUSTS (REITS)

Real estate investment trusts (REITs) are investments in real estate projects. An REIT can invest in mortgages, properties, and construction loans.

REITs must have at least 75 percent of all assets and income derived from investments in real estate, government securities, or cash, and must distribute 90 percent or more of income to investors to avoid corporate taxation.

TIP #45

Unlike real estate limited partnerships (see Chapter 6), REITs only pass income to their investors, not write-offs, or deductions.

PACKAGED SECURITIES AND YOUR CLIENT

Packaged securities offer your client the ability to avoid the risk of investing in one particular company, which is a type of diversification. There are still significant risks involved in packaged securities investment. Your client can lose principal investment if investing in stock. There is also an added risk for particular industries: if your client invests in REITs and the real estate market goes down, you client will see a loss.

Some packaged securities offer significant protection against losses, however. There are mutual funds that package stocks, bonds, and money market instruments for certain target investment dates. To fully understand the risks associated with a packaged security, you must look at the underlying investment and its risks.

The ideal client for a packaged security varies depending on the underlying securities. To best advise your client on packaged securities, try to match the client's investment goal with the packaged security's objective.

CHECKLIST

- ☐ I understand how management companies use open-ended and closed-ended funds
- ☐ I can identify different fund types and their risk
- ☐ I know how breakpoints apply to investors, and how to calculate cost-per-share and sales charge
- ☐ I can define a unit investment trust (UIT) and a face amount certificate company
- ☐ I know how fixed and variable annuities work.
- ☐ I know what a real estate investment trust (REIT) is

SAMPLE QUESTIONS

1. What are the qualifications of a diversified management company?

   I. It has to be open-ended
   II. It cannot hold more than 5 percent of voting stock in one company
   III. It cannot hold more than 10 percent of voting stock in one company
   IV. It must not have more than 5 percent of its assets invested in one company

   [A] I and II
   [B] Only IV
   [C] III and IV
   [D] All of the above

2. ABC fund carries a fixed amount of shares, which are sold to investors and then traded in the market. ABC fund is a:

   [A] Closed-ended fund
   [B] Fixed fund
   [C] Open-ended fund
   [D] Mutual fund

3. XYZ fund invests in two types of stock to serve combined goals. XYZ fund is a

   [A] Specialized fund
   [B] Index fund
   [C] Combined fund
   [D] Dual-purpose fund

4. Dan James deposits $50 a month into GHI fund for 4 months. Price per share has fluctuated each month:

   January: $10 a share
   February: $11 a share
   March: $12 a share
   April: $10 a share

   What is his average cost per share?

   [A] $11
   [B] $50

[C] $10.68
[D] $10.89

5. DEF mutual fund has a total asset value of $2,000,000, with 500,000 shares outstanding. The public offering price of one share of DEF fund is $4.30. What is the broker's commission for this fund?

[A] $0.70 per share
[B] Unknown; you need to read the prospectus to know this
[C] 7 percent
[D] 7.5 percent

6. Jennifer Jones invests in a unit investment trust. Her shares have no maturation date. She invests in a:

[A] Fixed investment trust
[B] Open-ended investment trust
[C] Variable investment trust
[D] Participating trust

7. Bob Patterson has invested in an annuity and has just passed away. His wife will receive the payout of this annuity for another ten years. This annuity investment is a:

[A] Life annuity
[B] Life annuity with period certain
[C] Family annuity
[D] Joint life with last survivor annuity

8. Which of the following is true about real estate investment trusts (REITs)? REITs must:

I. Invest in real estate or real estate related securities
II. Have at least 75 percent of assets invested in real estate
III. Distribute 90 percent or more of income to investors to avoid corporate taxation
IV. Only pass income to investors, not write-offs

[A] I, II, and IV
[B] II and III
[C] None of the above
[D] All of the above

6.500
6.000
7
8
9
5
6
3

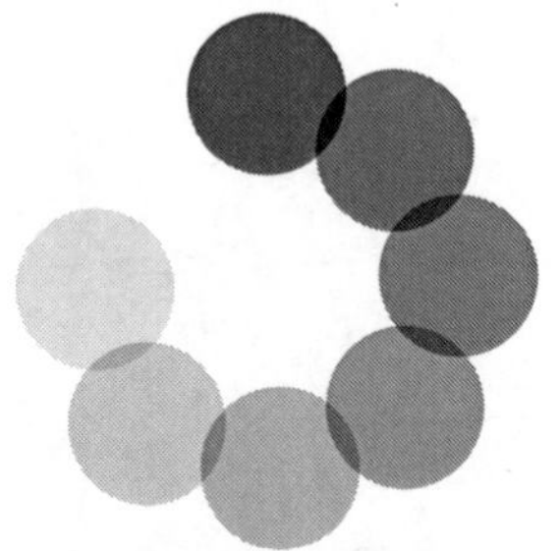

CHAPTER 6
Direct Participation Programs (DPPs)

Direct participation programs (DPPs) were created to form tax shelters by investing in real estate, equipment leasing, and oil and gas programs. Although those shelters have largely been eroded by the Internal Revenue Service (IRS) due to overuse by investors and DPPs are not a popular investment choice due to the associated risk, Series 7 still includes them on your exam. This chapter will cover the basic characteristics of a DPP, as well as different types of DPPs as Series 7 exam-required knowledge.

BASIC CHARACTERISTICS

Participants or investors in a DPP are long-term investors and directly affect cash flow and investments of a corporation. The partnership does not pay taxes, and all profits and losses flow directly to the investors.

TIP #46

Series 7 considers all DPPs limited partnerships so consider the two terms interchangeable.

To differentiate between corporations, which have greater tax liabilities, and limited partnerships, the IRS has imposed requirements on limited partnerships investment organizations to avoid misuse of tax benefits.

A limited partnership must have:

- A **general partner**, or manager, and a **limited partner**, or investor, at a minimum.
- **Limited life**: where a corporation aims to exist forever, a limited partnership must have a maturity date or goal determined in the partnership agreement (generally more than a year).
- **Locked investment**: limited partners cannot sell or transfer their investments like stock, to avoid misuse of tax benefits.

Formation

Limited partnerships demand great investor commitment and participation, much like managing a company, which is why a limited partnership's members complete an agreement upon formation. This agreement outlines the basic rights and obligations of investors, or limited partners, and is called a **certificate of limited partnership**. The certificate of limited partnership is filed with the home state of the limited corporation and works like a contract, obligating its members to keep in compliance with the agreed terms.

The following is detailed in the certificate of limited partnership:

- Partnership name, or names, titles, and addresses of all partners
- Current investments and conditions of future investment by the original partners
- Distributions of profits and losses
- Length of the life term
- Rules regarding sale or re-assignment of shares
- Dissolution provisions

Because investors play such an active role as limited partners, limited partnerships require new investors, or partners, fill out a **subscription agreement**, detailing annual income and net worth, much like credit application. As a registered representative of a potential investor in a limited partnership, you will review this subscription agreement for accuracy. This signed agreement does not hold any significance or grant any authority beyond being part of the application process.

TIP #47

Remember limited partners do not hold authority within a limited partnership; only general managers do.

OIL AND GAS PROGRAMS

Oil and gas limited partnerships invest in oil or gas by buying rights to existing, income-producing wells, or by investing in drilling programs with hopes of discovering oil and gas. Investments in drilling programs are, for imaginable reasons, the more risky of the two types.

Tax Advantages

As most oil and gas limited partnerships are created in part to provide tax advantages, it is important you know the IRS allowable deductions, particular to only oil and gas programs, for your Series 7 exam.

Oil and gas limited partnerships benefit from tax write-offs particular to the industry:

- **Depletion**: limited partnerships are allowed deductions for depletion of resources (the oil and/or gas wells) as a percentage of resources sold.
- **Tangible drilling costs (TDCs)**: deductions allowed for depreciation of salvageable assets (like equipment) over several years.
- **Intangible drilling costs (IDCs)**: a limited partnership is allowed to write off non-tangible expenses, like employee wages and fuel costs.

TIP #48

Oil and gas direct participation programs are considered very high risk: not only is the DPP investment form risky, but the oil/gas industry is high risk as well.

REAL ESTATE PROGRAMS

Real estate limited partnerships invest in government-assisted housing, land, construction, and existing properties. Investing in real estate can provide investors with long-term rental income, sales profit, or appreciation. Although these programs all have real estate investment in common, they each carry a wide variety of risk, and serve very different investment objectives.

Types of real estate limited partnerships are:

- **Public or government-assisted housing**: This limited partnership investment derives its income from rental payments and tax credits. This is the least risky of real estate investments because the government backing these programs compensates for any payments tenants miss.
- **Existing real estate**: The goal of existing real estate investments is for the limited partnership to gain immediate rental income. Although

this is still a lower-risk real estate investment, maintenance and repair costs can eat into the partnership's profits.

- **New construction**: The limited partnership purchases land, builds homes, and then hopes to sell the homes and land at a profit. New construction is considered less risky than land investment.
- **Land**: Investing in land has the simplest of goals for a limited partnership: to wait for the land to appreciate. Because there is no rental income or return on investment, this is considered a high-risk investment.

EQUIPMENT LEASING PROGRAMS

The goal of equipment leasing limited partnerships is to receive income and use write-offs as the equipment depreciates. Unlike other limited partnerships, investors in equipment leasing programs look for a mix of income and tax advantages, with no expectation of long-term appreciation (as the equipment depreciates). Series 7 will not ask you much about equipment leasing programs, but you should know the two types of equipment leasing programs for your exam.

The two equipment leasing limited partnerships are:

- **Full pay-out lease**: In this scenario, the limited partnership purchases equipment anticipating to lease on a **long-term** basis, usually to only **one user**. One contract pays for the equipment.
- **Operating lease**: The limited partnership leases equipment for a **short term**. The partnership needs **several lease contracts** before the equipment and financing is paid for.

DPPS AND YOUR CLIENT

As DPP investors, your clients can be liable beyond their principal investment as companies can operate at a loss and accrue debt — meaning losses can be unlimited. The best approach when advising your client on limited partnership investing is to explain in detail the risks involved.

The ideal client for DPPs has a very high risk tolerance, the ability to commit to the DPP long-term, and an advanced understanding of investments and the market. DPPs are often used as a way to reduce taxes, so before representing your client in DPP investing, you will want to confer with his or her tax advisor.

CHECKLIST

- ☐ I understand how direct participation programs (DPPs), or limited partnerships, work
- ☐ I know the IRS qualifiers that define limited partnerships
- ☐ I know the different steps required in the formation of a limited partnership and the registered representative's role in the investor's submission of the subscription agreement
- ☐ I can differentiate between the different types of limited partnerships, including oil and gas programs, real estate programs, and equipment leasing programs
- ☐ I understand the different types of risk attached to each of these programs

SAMPLE QUESTIONS

1. Which of the following is true about direct participation programs? DPPs:

   I. Pay taxes as a partnership
   II. Investors only receive profits and do not share any losses
   III. Are usually a short-term investment
   IV. Are a safe investment for any investor

   [A] II
   [B] I and IV
   [C] I, II, and III
   [D] None of the above

2. Your client wants to invest in a limited partnership. Your duty as a registered representative is to:

   [A] Do nothing; limited partnerships are not part of a broker's business
   [B] Review the subscription agreement to ensure its accuracy
   [C] Fill out and sign the subscription agreement
   [D] Sell the shares if your client requests it

3. An oil DPP has incurred fuel expenses while running their operation. Can the limited partnership deduct this expense?

   [A] Yes, this is an intangible drilling cost deduction
   [B] Yes, this is a tangible drilling cost deduction
   [C] No, limited partnerships are not permitted by the IRS to deduct expenses
   [D] No, this expense does not qualify as a tax deduction

4. A limited partnership receives income from leasing trucks. Their leases are short-term with a steady turnover of equipment. This is a(n):

   [A] Short-term lease
   [B] Operating lease
   [C] Full pay-out lease
   [D] Truck lease

CASE STUDY: JAMES MANKTELOW

MindTools.com
2nd Floor, 144-157 St. John Street
London EC1V 4PY
United Kingdom
+44-20-7788-7978
www.mindtools.com

MindTools is an international organization that teaches more than ten million people each year how to be more effective in their careers. James Manktelow is an instructor at MindTools. "Students and members develop rich and sophisticated skills in areas such as leadership, team management, problem solving, decision making, time management, and communication and business creativity," Manktelow says of the organization's comprehensive teachings.

Manktelow teaches a time management course for MindTools, which takes a lifestyle-oriented approach to the subject. "We help people to think about what they want to achieve with their lives, and then teach them the organizational skills that will help them achieve their life goals," he says. Manktelow believes time management skills are crucial for career as well as life success. "Time management skills are vitally important because these are the skills that help people live a life that is truly meaningful and fulfilling," he explains. "With poor time management skills, you are an unhappy, stressed, overworked victim in the workplace. Time management skills help you take control and shape your life into a form that matters to you."

Part of MindTools's time management course is about teaching students the far-reaching implications of effective time management. "People think time management skills are all about saving a minute here or a minute there," Manktelow says of this common misconception. "Of course they do this, but they do so much more."

"Our time management approach teaches people to go through the process of examining the things that are important to them, and from this develop their life goals," Manktelow says. He explains students go on to convert those life goals into actionable goals, which professionals can track as part of their own day-to-day self-organization system. "The course then teaches a variety of strategies for prioritizing work, managing distractions, and delegating work where appropriate."

"Take the time to think your life goals through in detail," Manktelow advises registered representatives starting their new careers. "Once you have developed these goals, adopt an organizational system that helps you realize them. Yes, this does take time, but this investment will yield huge returns and life happiness."

CHAPTER 7
Derivatives

As investments go, derivatives are more complex and therefore difficult to understand. Derivatives, or derivative instruments, are contracts based on the value of an underlying investment, most often a company's stock. Investors use derivatives to speculate and profit on the direction of a particular stock or the market as a whole. Derivatives are more widely known as **options** — a term this book will use for the rest of this chapter.

TIP #49

Your Series 7 exam will include up to 40 questions on derivatives.

BASIC FUNCTIONS

At their most elemental, options give an investor the right to buy or sell an investment at a certain price. A simple way to look at options is as insurance policies against missing out on buying or selling a stock at a set price. The investor can either use, or exercise, the option, or sell it on the open market.

These are the two option types:

- **Call:** this option allows the investor to buy a stock at a price determined by the seller of the option
- **Put**: this option allows the investor to sell a stock at a price determined by the seller of the option

Types of options on a certain stock make up a class, for example puts on XYZ Stock are a class. All options have a striking price, which is the price when an option is exercised.

TIP #50

The buyer of an option is the holder; the seller is the writer.

When someone wants to buy or sell an option, they place an order. All of the components of an option order or contract are specified by the **Options**

Clearing Corporation (OCC). The OCC issues all options contracts, is co-owned by the exchanges, and regulated by the SEC. It keeps track of sellers and buyers, ensuring both meet the options contract obligations.

There are definitions you must know before moving on to more complex option concepts and calculations, some you have just covered in reading an option order. Make sure you understand these basics, as you will need to know them for the sections to come.

Options definitions you must know:

- **Class**: options of the same type (call or put) of the same underlying security.
- **Series**: options of the same strike price, same class, and same expiration month.
- **Strike price**: also called **exercise price**, this is the price at which the option is exercised.
- **Expiration date**: the month an option expires.

You will need to understand how to read an option order on your Series 7 exam, which is best explained in this example.

EXAMPLE:

This is how an option order ticket might appear; below it is what each component means:

Sell 2 ABC Mar 50 call at 4

Sell: The investor is selling this option

2: Amount of batches of 100 stocks, in this case 200

ABC: The underlying security, ABC stock

Mar: this is the month the option expires, March in this case
50: this is the strike price: the price when an investor can exercise the option
Call: this option is a call, meaning to buy a stock at a certain price
4: the premium attached to the option, in this case $4 times 200 shares, so $800

This book will look at more examples, and what these numbers mean to your clients, later in this chapter.

Calls and puts work like insurance, protecting the holder against getting stuck with a stock that drops quickly, or losing out when that stock rises. You will learn more about this in the section on option strategies.

TRADING PROCEDURES AND OFFICIALS

You already know the OCC acts as an overseeing organization in the options process. This book will now review the options process, and all the organizations and players involved.

Options are traded on the following exchanges:

- **American Stock Exchange (Amex)**
- **Chicago Board Options Exchange (CBOE)**
- **New York Stock Exchange (NYSE)**
- **Pacific Stock Exchange (PSE)**
- **Philadelphia Stock Exchange (PHLX)**

These exchanges all use different but similar procedures when it comes to trading options. Generally, the exchanges trade this way, with some minor variances on each exchange:

When a customer wants to place an order, the broker will fill out an order ticket for the brokerage firm's **floor broker**, the broker whose job is to take orders to the trading floor. If the order can be filled immediately, it will go to the option's **market maker** for execution. The market maker is a broker registered to trade specific options for their own account.

If an order cannot be executed immediately due to market conditions, the public order will go to the **order book official** (OBO), who holds the order until market conditions are right. Once the order becomes active, the OBO can make use of a **board broker**, who helps with trades for the most active options.

To simplify this trading procedure, look at the below chart. Once a broker fills out an order ticket for his customer, it goes through the following steps:

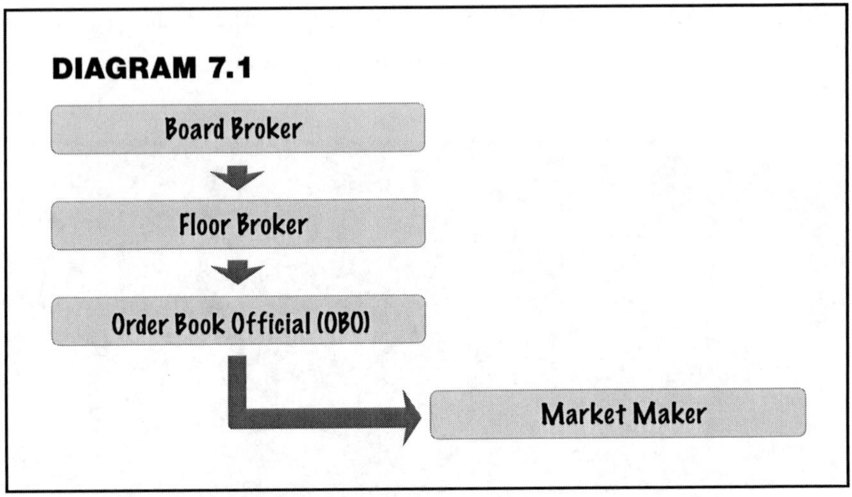

The New York Stock Exchange uses **specialists** instead of market makers for account execution — their titles are different, but their functions are the same. For your Series 7 exam, assume that the Pacific Stock Exchange (PSE), American Stock Exchange (Amex), and the Philadelphia Stock Exchange (PHLX) all use the same procedures as the New York Stock Exchange.

CALL AND PUT OPTIONS

Calls are options that give the holder or buyer the right to buy the security at a certain price, where the seller is obligated to sell at that price. The buyer of a call option is betting on the stock's price is increasing, whereas the seller is betting that the stock will decrease.

In market terms, when you are speculating a stock will grow, you are bullish; when you are speculating a stock will fall, you are bearish. Conversely, puts allow the buyer to sell at a certain price, holding the seller of the option obligated to buy at that price.

TIP #51

Buyers of calls are bullish, sellers of calls are bearish. Buyers of puts are bearish, sellers of puts are bullish.

If you are having trouble grasping these concepts, look at options from the seller's perspective. Much like an insurance company collects premiums, hoping the insured do not come to collect on the policy, so does the seller of options. Option sellers hope the stock will do the opposite of what the option protects the buyer from.

In-the-Money and Out-of-the-Money

To understand where an option stands in the marketplace, it is important to understand how to calculate the call or put's worth in relation to the trading price.

Understand these terms in relation to the value of an option:

- **In-the-money**: when an option is profitable for the holder. For a call, it means the stock is trading higher than the strike price; for a put, it means the stock is trading lower than the strike price. If an option is trading in-the-money, it has **intrinsic value**, meaning there is a profit to be made if the option is exercised.
- **Out-of-the-money**: when an option is not profitable for the holder. For a call, it means the stock is trading lower than the exercise price; for a put, it means a stock is trading higher than the strike price.
- **At-the-money**: when an option's strike price and the stock market price are the same.

TIP #52

An option premium does NOT factor into in-the-money and out-of-the-money calculations.

Series 7 will give you questions expecting you to calculate how much an option is in-the-money or out-of-the-money. To arrive at this number, simply calculate the difference between market and strike price.

EXAMPLE:

XYZ Stock is trading at 60. Trish Bailey is holding a call option of this stock with a strike price at 55. This option is in-the-money, with an intrinsic value of 5 (60 - 55).

For this same XYZ stock trading at 60, an investor who held a put option at 55 would be out-of-the-money at 5: the stock is trading $5 too high to make it interesting for him to exercise his option to sell his XYZ stock at 55.

In the preceding example, she can now exercise her call option, or trade it for its intrinsic value. As you can imagine, an option's value does not just depend on this intrinsic value, but also on how long it is still useable — its **time value.** Series 7 may test you on calculating the time value of an option, which is easy to do with this formula:

HOW TO CALCULATE **TIME VALUE**:

Time value = premium – intrinsic value

The exam will likely give you two numbers: the premium and intrinsic value of an option scenario. Figuring out the time value is then a matter of simple math, like in the example above. Premiums are affected by this time value and also by the state of the underlying security and general perception in the market about that security's future.

Calculating Break-Even, Maximum Loss, and Maximum Gain

To best advise your future customers, you need to be able to give the best or worst case scenario of buying a call or put: you need to be able to calculate the maximum gain or loss attached to an option. Likewise, you need to know the break-even point of an option.

When calculating the profitability of an option, you can get lost in the math and related formulas. The easiest way is to understand what is happening in different scenarios, which this book will cover in the following scenarios, resembling questions on your exam.

EXAMPLE:

Barry Walker buys a call for ABC stock at a premium of $5; the order ticket would read: **Buy 1 ABC Oct 50 call at 5**. Logically, his maximum loss is his premium. If ABC stock goes down, and his call is out-of-the-money, he will simply let his option expire, having lost only his premium of $5, or $500 (remember that the 1 in the call option stands for 100, the smallest possible value of an option).

In this same scenario, his maximum gain is unlimited. If ABC stock soars, and he exercises his call, his gain can continue along with ABC stock gains.

To find his break-even point, you need to figure out when he has recouped all his cost related to the call. If he exercises his call and buys ABC stock at 50, he still needs to add his cost of 5 to break even. His break-even point is 55, or $5,500.

WHEN BUYING A CALL:

Maximum gain: unlimited
Maximum loss: premium

HOW TO CALCULATE **THE BREAK-EVEN POINT FOR BUYING A CALL**:

Break-even point = strike price + premium

Now look at this same scenario, but change it to the sale of a call. Calvin Jones **sells 1 ABC Oct 50 call at 5**. In selling this call, he is speculating ABC stock will not gain past $50 a share, so he can simply collect his premium. His maximum gain is the call premium.

If ABC stock, against his bearish expectations, soars and the buyer of the call exercises their option, his maximum loss is unlimited. ABC stock could go through the roof, leaving him with the strike price and premium while the call buyer pockets the gains.

He has already collected his premium by selling the call. To break even, he needs to sell ABC stock at the strike price, minus the premium he collected for the call, so 45, or $4,500 in this case.

WHEN SELLING A CALL:

Maximum gain: premium
Maximum loss: unlimited

HOW TO CALCULATE **THE BREAK-EVEN POINT FOR SELLING A CALL**:

Break-even point = strike price - premium

Likewise, you can apply this reasoning process to calculate maximum gain, maximum loss, and break-even point for puts.

EXAMPLE:

Mandy Carter buys a put: Buy 1 DEF Oct 40 put at 4. Her maximum loss is her premium: if DEF stock drops and she does not exercise her option, her premium is all she will lose, which in this case is $400.

Her maximum gain is realized if she exercises her option to sell her DEF stock at 40. Because she has paid a premium for the option, you will have to deduct this expense from her sale. In this example, her maximum gain is 40 - 4 equaling 36, or $3,600.

To break even, she needs to recoup the expense of the put premium. If she exercises her put option at the strike price, she still needs to deduct her premium to break even. In this case, that means 40 - 4, so 36, or $3,600.

WHEN BUYING A PUT:

Maximum gain: strike price – premium
Maximum loss: premium

HOW TO CALCULATE **THE BREAK-EVEN POINT FOR BUYING A PUT**

Break-even point = strike price – premium

Using this same example, Greg Miller is the seller of this option, so Sell 1 DEF Oct 40 put at 4. His maximum gain is realized if the put is not exercised, and he can pocket the premium.

His maximum loss is realized if DEF stock tanks and he is left with the worthless stock he is forced to buy through the sale of this put option. Therefore, his maximum loss is the strike price, minus the premium he collected, so 36, or $3,600.

In a break-even scenario, the put would be exercised by the buyer, and he would then have to turn around and sell the DEF stock at the strike price minus the premium, so 36, or $3,600.

WHEN SELLING A PUT:

Maximum gain: premium

Maximum loss: strike price – premium

HOW TO CALCULATE **BREAK-EVEN FOR SELLING A PUT**:

Break-even = strike price – premium

TIP #53

Instead of memorizing formulas and plugging in numbers, try to reason your way to the right answer.

The sample questions at the end of this chapter will provide you with more opportunity to practice options math. If you find you have difficulty with the concepts, try creating your own scenarios like the ones used throughout this chapter.

Opening and Closing Transactions

Up until now, you have only seen individual call and put purchases and sales. Investors trade options as they do other securities, which means they sometimes counter options to close them out. Series 7 expects you to be able to identify transactions as opening or closing, as well as calculate gain and loss. Like in the calculations above, you will focus on reasoning your way to the right answer by using an example.

When an investor first buys a call or put, this is called an **opening purchase**. Likewise, when an investor sells a call or put, this is an **opening sale**. For various reasons relating to their investment objective, investors can decide to close out this position. This is done by a transaction opposite to the investor's current position: if an investor bought an option, they will have to sell it, and vice versa. This is called a **closing purchase** or **closing sale.** These definitions by themselves are confusing, so look at an example to logically reason your way to the right answer on your Series 7 exam.

EXAMPLE:

Tom Peters bought a call: Buy 1 GHI Oct 50 call at 5. This is his opening purchase. GHI stock price has changed, and he would like to close out his position. He would have to sell this same option, so Sell 1 GHI Oct 50 call at 5. This is a closing sale.

Series 7 will ask you to calculate gains and losses, based on different scenarios of opening and closing transactions. Look at this example to see which steps to take to arrive at these numbers.

EXAMPLE:

Jenny Brown bought 100 shares of ABC stock at $100 a share. She decides to sell 1 ABC Oct 110 call at 5. She held this position for two months and sold her ABC stock at 109. She closed the ABC Oct 110 call at 4.

To calculate her gain or loss, go through each of the purchases and sales step-by-step. First, she spent $10,000 on ABC stock. She collected a premium for the call she sold, which was $500, reducing her expense to $9,500. She then sold her stock for $10,900, gaining $1,400. To close out the calls she sold, she had to spend $400 to buy closing purchase call. This leaves her gain at $1,000.

Notice in this example, you simply went through each purchase and sale, step by step to arrive at the gain. Approach your Series 7 exam with this same methodical tactic and you will get these seemingly complex options questions right every time.

OPTIONS STRATEGIES

Using calls and puts, investors can speculate on a stock's performance. Beyond the simple call and put purchase, there are options strategies used in the market you will need to know about as a registered representative. This section will cover different options strategies and explain the reason the investor might use them.

TIP #54

Options strategies are all based on the investor's expectation of a particular stock in the marketplace.

Neutral Strategies

When an investor uses neutral options strategies, he or she positions himself or herself to make a profit if he or she expects the stock to stay stagnant or near-stagnant. The investor essentially hopes the options will not be exercised, so he or she can just collect the premium, There are many neutral options strategies; for your Series 7 exam, you should know the covered call and covered put, as well as the short straddle.

The most simple of neutral options strategies is a **covered call**. In case of a covered call position, the investor sells call options backed by a holding of the underlying stock. Expecting stock to remain stagnant, or close enough to stagnant for the call not to be exercised, the investor simply collects his or her premium on the call options.

In case of a **covered put**, the investor sells put options on stock held, expecting the stock to remain (near) stagnant again so he or she can collect the premiums.

When an investor uses a **short straddle** strategy, he or she sells both a call and a put option at the same strike price and with the same expiration date. Expecting the underlying stock to remain stagnant, the investor aims for neither option to be exercised so he or she can collect both premiums.

TIP #55

A neutral strategy is no less risky than a bullish or bearish strategy — just because an investor expects the market to stay neutral does not mean he or she is less exposed to risk.

Bearish Strategies

As you may have concluded after learning investor motivation on neutral strategies, a bearish options strategy is used when the investor expects the underlying stock to fall. Bearish strategies include put purchase, bear put spread, selling a "naked" call, and a bear call spread.

As explained in this chapter's put options, a **put purchase** is a simple way for an investor to protect himself or herself against a drop in stock. If the stock drops, the investor can sell it to the writer of the put option at the strike price.

In case of a **bear put spread** (also called a debit spread because the investor has to pay more in premium initially), the investor buys and sells put options with the same expiration month. By buying a put option with a strike price of 60, for example, and selling a put option with a strike price of 40, the investor insures his or her ability to sell a dropping stock at 60. The investor in this example hopes the put option sold is not exercised so he or she can simply collect the premium.

A **bear call spread** works similar to the bear put spread: the investor buys and sells call options with a different strike price, but with the same expiration month. Expecting the stock to drop, this investor would have bought a call option at 60, for example, and sold a call at 50. If the stock drops below 50, as expected when taking this strategy, the investor simply collects the net premium of the call transactions. For this strategy to be profitable, the premium of the call purchase needs to be lower than the premium of the call sale.

Selling a "naked" call happens when an investor sells a call without holding the underlying security. The investor expects the stock to drop (bearish expectations), and therefore speculates the call is never exercised so he or she can collect the premium. Naked positions like these are very risky, as the investor is forced to buy the stock to comply with the option, should it be exercised.

TIP #56

"Naked" (or uncovered) writers of calls or puts speculate that the option they sold will never be exercised because "naked" writers do not hold the underlying securities. This strategy is extremely high in risk.

Bullish Strategies

When an investor expects a certain stock to rise, he or she can assume a bullish strategy. Bullish strategies are a call purchase, bull call spread, selling a "naked" put, and a bull put spread. Most of these strategies are simply opposites of the bearish strategies just explained.

Buying a call, or a **call purchase**, is a simple way to ensure when a stock rises, you are able to buy it at the option strike price, so your loss is limited.

When an investor takes a **bull call spread** position, he or she buys and sells call options with the same expiration month. To make a bull call spread strategy profitable, an investor would buy a call at a lower strike price (say 50), and would sell a call at a higher strike price (say 65). This way, he or she ensures

not to be left out should the stock rise as the investor expects, and he or she collects a profit if the call sold is exercised.

A **bull put spread** involves an investor selling and buying a put with the same expiration month. The investor will sell a put at a lower strike price and buy a put at a higher strike price, expecting the stock to rise high enough to exercise his put. This allows him to make a greater profit.

An investor can **sell a "naked" put** if he or she expects the underlying security to rise. Even though the investor does not hold the stock, he or she expects the stock to rise and the option not to be exercised. The investor will collect the option premium as profit but risks having to buy the stock should it drop low enough for the option to be exercised.

OPTION TYPES

Just as there are different types of securities, as detailed in the preceding chapters of this book, the market trades corresponding options on these securities. The next section will briefly cover each of these and their characteristics you should know for your exam questions.

Index Options

Index options are options based on the performance of an exchange or industry segment, allowing investors to speculate on market movement in these industries or indexes. These options can be based on exchange indexes, like the NYSE, or on industry sectors, like retail. The movement of this index, calculated by the underlying securities' value, decides the value of the index options traded. Calculations for index options work the same way as for stock options.

TIP #57

When index options are exercised, they always pay out in cash.

To limit the potential loss for the seller, index options are sometimes **capped**, or limited, at certain points in-the-money. You can tell an option is capped when it has CAPS in front of the strike price, like this: **Buy 1 XYZ CAPS 300 call at 5**. Only S&P 100 and S&P 500 trade capped index options.

Debt Options

Debt options are options based on debt instruments, like government or corporate bonds. These options speculate on the interest rate and value of the underlying debt instrument. Although debt options speculate on low-risk debt instruments, they are not considered less risky than stock options.

Foreign Currency Options

Foreign currency options speculate on the value of an underlying currency, like the Japanese Yen or Euro. Foreign Currency Options work like stock options, giving the holder the option to buy or sell the currency at a certain strike price. Calculations work like stock options.

Long-Term Equity Anticipation Securities (LEAPS)

The options discussed so far all have a short life span and make speculations on the short-term performance of the underlying security. To accommodate an investor's long-term speculations, investors can use **long-term equity anticipation securities (LEAPS)**.

LEAPS speculate on the long-term, two-to-five year performance of an underlying security, and are traded on NYSE, Amex, and NASDAQ. They work the same as the options you have already covered, but cover a longer term.

OPTIONS AND YOUR CLIENT

Options are used to speculate on a stock's performance in the market and carry great risk. Losses can span beyond principal investment, especially when your client uses a margin account to buy or sell options; more on this in Chapter 14 on margins.

The ideal client for options investing is highly knowledgeable on investing and the markets and can tolerate a great deal of risk. Options usually require a larger amount of start-up capital to be effective, so take a close look at your client's available investment capital if he or she is interested in entering the options market. When advising your client on options investing, impress upon him or her the risks involved. Options are only suitable for clients with the highest of risk tolerance.

CHECKLIST

- ☐ I understand calls and puts and how to read an order
- ☐ I know the options trading process and the individuals involved
- ☐ I can calculate in-the-money and out-of-the-money for an option, as well as the investor's maximum loss or gain
- ☐ I understand how opening and closing transactions work
- ☐ I can identify neutral, bearish, and bullish options strategies
- ☐ I understand how index options, debt options, LEAPS, and foreign currency options work

SAMPLE QUESTIONS

1. **John Gregory sold a call to XYZ stock on the securities market. He is the:**

   [A] Writer of the call
   [B] Manager of XYZ Corporation
   [C] Holder of the call
   [D] Securities broker

2. **On the order ticket Sell 2 GHI Dec 90 call at 5, 5 stands for the:**

   [A] Strike price
   [B] Amount of days the holder has to exercise the option
   [C] Premium the buyer pays for the option
   [D] Premium the seller pays to the buyer should the call be exercised

3. **What is the role of the order book official (OBO)?**

   [A] He orders books for registered representative
   [B] He is the exchange bookkeeper
   [C] He executes orders immediately
   [D] He holds orders that cannot executed immediately until market conditions are right

4. **The seller of a put is:**

   [A] Bearish
   [B] Neutral
   [C] Unsure of market direction
   [D] Bullish

5. **Sarah Jones holds a put option for XYZ stock at 60. XYZ stock is trading at 70. Her option is:**

   [A] In-the-money at 10
   [B] Out-of-the-money at 10
   [C] Breaking even
   [D] Unsure; you need to know the premium she paid for the option to calculate this

6. Karen James has bought 1 EFG Dec 80 call at 6. What is her break-even point?

   [A] 74
   [B] $7,400
   [C] $8,600
   [D] 6

7. Doug Smith sold 1 ABC Feb 100 put at 4. What is his maximum loss?

   [A] $140
   [B] $400
   [C] $9,600
   [D] $10,400

8. Frank Moon bought 1 XYZ Mar 50 call at 4. This is a(n):

   [A] Opening purchase
   [B] Opening sale
   [C] Closing sale
   [D] Call sale

9. Mark Leonard bought 500 shares of GHI stock at $80 a share. He sells 1 GHI Mar 100 call at 6. He held this position for a month and then sold his GHI stock at $85 a share. He closed the outstanding call at 5. What is his gain or loss?

   [A] Gain of $1,000
   [B] Gain of $2,600
   [C] Gain of $5 a share
   [D] Loss of $1,000

10. Mary Jones sold a call for XYZ stock. She does not hold any XYZ stock. She is:

    [A] Neutral
    [B] Bullish
    [C] A "naked" call writer
    [D] A "naked" put holder

11. Bob Miller sold a call for DEF stock at 40 and bought a call for DEF at 60. His strategy is a:

    [A] Bull call spread
    [B] Bear call spread
    [C] Neutral strategy
    [D] "Naked" strategy

12. When index options are exercised, they are paid out in:

    [A] Stock
    [B] Interest in the underlying security
    [C] Cash
    [D] Bonds

13. Which of the following is true about LEAPS? LEAPS:

    I. Are long-term options
    II. Are based on the two-to-five-year performance of the underlying security
    III. Are traded on NYSE, Amex, and NASDAQ
    IV. Are always capped to protect investors

    [A] I and IV
    [B] I, II, and III
    [C] All of the above
    [D] None of the above

CASE STUDY: DAVID NILSSEN, CEO

Guidant Financial Group
13122 NE 20th Street, Suite 100
Bellevue, WA 98005
(888) 472-4455
www.guidantfinancial.com

In 2003, David Nilssen co-founded Guidant Financial Group, specializing in guiding clients with self-directed IRAs. "We offer a self-directed IRA/ LLC structure to our clients that allows for investments into both traditional and non-traditional assets inside their IRAs," he explains. Guidant Financial Group works with clients and financial advisors, offering self-directed IRAs as alternative investment vehicles. "The most popular investments we see are real estate related."

Like many other financial professionals, Nilssen most enjoys working with customers. "Each person is unique, and we love understanding what their goals are and what investments get them excited."

Nilssen believes it is important for financial advisors to be open to alternative investments for their clients, like the kind of investments Guidant Financial group offers. "Many of our clients sever the relationship with their financial advisors because they are not open to the concept of owning non-traditional assets within their IRAs. This is really a loss for both the client and the advisor." Nilssen believes financial advisors should have their client's best interest in mind, "even if it means losing a portion of their portfolio to an outside asset. It is beneficial in the long run for both parties involved."

Guidant Financial Group requires prospective clients to go through a pre-qualification process to determine if the investments they are considering are viable and allowable within an IRA. "After this pre-qualification, we hold one-on-one consultations with each client, before they even decide to utilize our services or pay us a fee," Nilssen says. He explains this process ensures the investments are right for the client before any agreements are signed.

Nilssen advises prospective financial advisors to hold the client's peace-of-mind and financial security paramount to any personal objective an advisor may have. "People do business with people they like," he says simply, warning that clients will walk away if they suspect an advisor does not have their best interest in mind. "If you can put aside your potential personal gain and focus on your client's objectives, you will come out on top in the end."

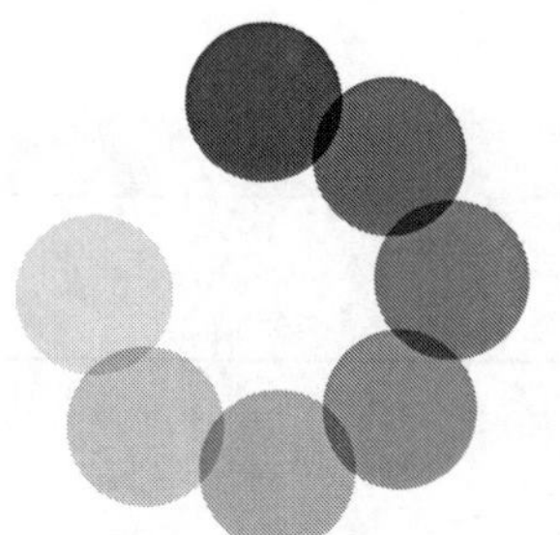

CHAPTER 8
Investment Information: Taxation

As part of your duties as a registered representative, you need to be able to advise your customers on the tax implications of different investments. In this chapter, you will learn how the IRS treats investment income and how this affects your clients' investment decisions. Not only will you be tested on taxation, but you will also be applying these in your portfolio analysis.

This does not mean you need to be a tax expert, however. This chapter will cover what you need to know to pass the Series 7 exam, nothing more.

HOW TAXES AFFECT DIFFERENT INVESTMENTS

When it comes to investments, the IRS treats dividends, capital gains, and interest in different ways. At its most basic, there are progressive and regressive taxes. **Progressive taxes** cover income tax and gift and estate taxes — progressive taxes affect higher-income customers more. **Regressive taxes** are set taxes on payroll, sales, property, etc. Regressive taxes are set at the same rate for everyone, regardless of income.

Defining Income

The IRS differentiates between three types of income: passive, active, and portfolio income. Passive income is derived from activities in which an individual is not actively involved, like DPPs (or limited partnerships). You can only write off passive income against passive losses. Active (or earned) income (like a person's paycheck), as its definition states, covers all income earned from an individual's activities. This income is taxed in that person's tax bracket. Portfolio income includes all income derived from securities investments; this book will cover this in detail in the next section.

TIP #58

When Series 7 mentions passive income, it will expect you to link this to DPPs, or limited partnerships. Make sure you understand that passive income can only be written off against passive loss.

Portfolio Income Tax

Portfolio income can be derived from dividends, interest, and capital gain (or loss.) This book will cover tax implications of these three in this section.

Dividends can be received in stock or cash. Stock dividends are not taxed, but this reduced value of the individual stock share resulting from the stock dividend does affect capital gains or losses.

TIP #59

Series 7 likes to ask questions about taxes on cash dividends.

Cash dividends are taxed in two ways: if held fewer than 61 days, they are taxed at the recipient's tax bracket; if held more than 61 days, at no more than 15 percent.

Interest income comes from bonds, either corporate, municipal, or U.S. government securities bonds. Corporate bond interest is fully taxed. Municipal bonds are tax-free for federal filings, but may be taxed at the state level. U.S. government bond interest is taxed federally, but tax-free in state filing.

Mutual Funds and Taxes

Mutual funds and their distribution of gains come in many different sizes and the IRS treats mutual funds based on their investment type, as well as their objective.

Because of their investment in corporations, corporate bond funds income is taxed as income. Stock funds' income, as well as short-term capital gains, are capped at 15 percent for tax purposes. Municipal bonds funds income and long-term capital gains are not taxed by the federal government.

As you can see from the tax-free classification of long-term capital gains on mutual funds, the IRS favors long-term investments. Even if dividends received from an investment are added to the fund, the investor is still liable for taxes.

TIP #60

The longer the term of the investment, the lower the taxes.

Capital Gain/Loss and Taxes

While dividend and interest is acquired throughout the investment holding period, there are no capital gains or losses unless that investment is sold. The IRS distinguishes between long- and short-term holdings when setting tax rates.

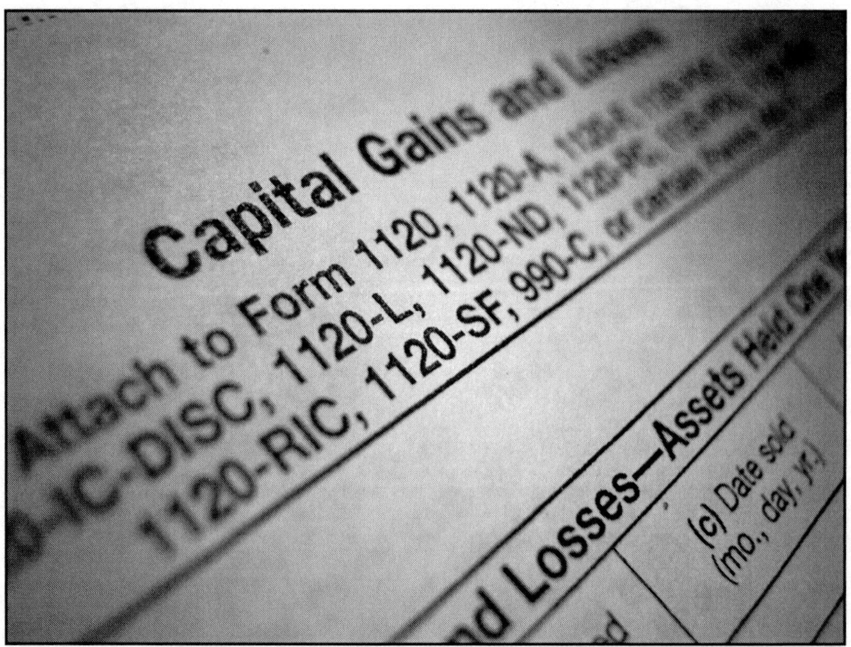

When an investor holds a security for less than one year before selling, the capital gain is taxed at their tax bracket and the capital loss can be used to offset capital gain on other investments. When an investor holds a security for longer than a year before selling, the IRS considers this investment long-term. Long-term capital gains taxes are capped at 15 percent; long-term capital loss can be offset by long-term capital gain on other investments. If there is a net capital loss, the investor can write up to $3,000 off against his income.

TIP #61

An investor must sell his investment to be taxed for capital gains.

Wash Sale Rule

Because savvy investors might sell a security at a loss, claim the capital gains loss, and then repurchase that same security, the IRS came up with the Wash Sale Rule. Prior to 1984, when the rule was applied to individual investors, investors could create artificial market activity by buying and selling stock. **The Wash Sale Rule** states investors cannot buy or sell the same security 30 days before or after claiming a loss on the sale of that same security.

Investors can still make those sales or purchases; they just cannot claim a loss on them. Series 7 may give you a scenario in which to apply the 30-day Wash Sale Rule, so make sure you understand how this works.

Accretion and Amortization for Bonds

Because bonds are often issued at a discount to mature at par, the gains an investor makes from holding the bond (or **accretion**) is income. Look at the preceding section on portfolio taxes to see how different bonds are taxed. For Series 7, you will need to be able to calculate accretion to find taxable value in different question scenarios. You will look an example to see how you might calculate annual income related to bonds.

EXAMPLE

Karen Williams bought a 5 percent corporate bond at 75, maturing after 10 years. For bonds, assume a par value at maturation of $1,000; she bought her bond for $750. To calculate her annual income for this bond, you will need to add her annual interest income, as well as the gains made annually toward the par value. Her interest is 5 percent, so $50 a year. Her total accretion is $250 ($1,000 - $750), which makes $25 for each of the 10 years to the bond's maturity. Her annual income is $25 + $50 = $75.

Not all bonds are issued at a discount, however. If a bond is bought at a premium, the holder can amortize the cost of this the premium over the life of the bond. Simply put, the holder can deduct the loss incurred by paying a premium from the interest (or gain) he or she receives from the bond. In the following example, you can see how **amortization** of the premium is calculated.

EXAMPLE

John Griffin bought an 8 percent 10-year bond at 105. To amortize the $50 premium he paid for this bond, you divide it by 10 to reach the annual cost, so $5. He receives $80 a year in interest (8 percent on a $1,000 bond), making his annual income after amortization $80 - $5 = $75.

RETIREMENT PLANS

Retirement plans are an important part of an investment portfolio as saving for retirement is a goal of virtually every investor. Understanding the investor's tax bracket is very important in making investment recommendations, as the need to reduce taxes is greater for clients in higher tax brackets than those with lower income. Series 7 will test your understanding of the tax implications of different plans.

TIP #62

The **Employee Retirement Income Securities Act (ERISA)** was signed into law in 1974 to loosen prior retirement plan eligibility and regulate how pension plans are managed.

Tax Qualifications

To best advise your customers as a registered representative, you need to know which retirement plans allow for before-tax or after-tax contributions: which plans are tax-qualified plans and which are non-qualified plans.

Tax-qualified plans allow the investor to use pre-tax dollars to invest, therefore deducting the contributions from his income. Under a tax-qualified plan, both contributions and gains are tax-deferred, meaning the investor does not pay taxes until he or she withdraws from the account, presumably in retirement.

Non-qualified plans take contributions from after-tax dollars. Gains are tax-deferred under non-qualified plans and when the investor draws from the account at retirement, the contributions are not taxed again.

TIP #63

For Series 7 exam scenario questions about retirement, look for the customer's tax objectives: Traditional IRAs are best for those wishing to reduce taxes now and Roth IRAs are for individuals in lower tax brackets.

Individual Retirement Accounts (IRAs)

The IRS has set rules and limits for contributions to retirement account, as explained on the **www.irs.gov** Web site. As the tax code changes often, make sure you keep tabs on these changes as a registered representative. It is helpful to consult a tax professional regularly, as he or she will be up-to-date on tax code changes. For your Series 7 exam, you can assume the following rules regarding IRAs.

The most common type of IRA account is the tax-qualified **traditional IRA**. IRAs are only funded by contributions the individual holder makes. For your exam, you should know the following rules:

- Each account has a maximum contribution of $5,000 per person, $1,000 more if the contributor is over 50.
- Contributions are tax-deductible (if not covered by an employer pension plan).
- Contributions up to April 15 can count toward the previous tax year.
- Withdrawals are fully taxed as income.
- Holders cannot withdraw funds until age 59½, or they will incur a 10 percent penalty added to their income tax bracket. Exclusions to this penalty are withdrawals used for disability, first-time home purchase, or higher education expenses. Penalty is waved for estate distributions (when those distributions come from a deceased individual).
- Investor must begin withdrawals by April 15 after he or she turns 70½ (there is a 50 percent tax penalty on withdrawals that are not taken).

Investors who do not wish to take the tax deduction of contributions may choose to invest in a **Roth IRA**. Clients in low tax brackets, for instance, may prefer to take advantage of the tax-free withdrawals at retirement a Roth IRA offers. Roth IRAs have fewer qualifiers than Traditional IRAs.

Here is what should know about Roth IRAs for your exam:

- The maximum contribution per person is $5,000, $1,000 more if the contributor is over age 50.
- Contributions are not deductable.
- Withdrawals are entirely tax-free.
- Contributors may withdraw when older than 59½, provided they have held the account at least 5 years.
- Investors may not earn more than $110,000 ($160,000 jointly for married couples) annually to be allowed to make contributions.

Simplified Employee Pensions (SEP)-IRAs are retirement plans for self-employed individuals, or those working for small-business employers without traditional retirement plans. An SEP-IRA allows the employer to make tax-deductable contributions of up to 25 percent of the employee's annual income (up to $45,000; adjusted to cost of living) to the account.

Coverdell IRAs are not retirement accounts at all, but since they began as Education IRAs, this book will briefly cover them here should you get a question covering these accounts on your exam. **Also known as Coverdell Education Savings Accounts, these accounts are savings vehicles for the education of children under 18**. Contributions of up to $2,000 of after-tax dollars annually are permitted, and gains and withdrawals are tax-free, provided the money is used for higher education. This book will cover procedures regarding the opening and closing of these accounts, and what happens when the child reaches age of majority in Chapter 13, in the section on custodial accounts.

Other Retirement Plans

You will briefly cover other retirement plans here, although it is unlikely Series 7 will ask much about these plans.

An **Employee Stock Ownership Plan (ESOP)** allows an employee to invest in his or her employing company's stock. The company gets a tax deduction at the market value of the stock. This is a risky investment, as this investment is not diversified. If the company goes bankrupt, for instance, the employee does not only lose his or her job, the stock owned in the employee's ESOP is also worthless.

A **403(b) Plan** allows an employee working for a non-profit with 501(c)(3) classification to make tax-deductable contributions to their retirement account. These plans are also known as Tax Deferred Annuities (TDAs), or Tax Sheltered Annuities (TSAs).

Like with a Coverdell Education Savings Account, **Section 529 Plans** allow investors to save for higher education. Section 529 Plans are state-run and sometimes allow for contributions to be deductable from state taxes. Contributions are federally taxable.

TIP #64

Coverdell Education Savings Accounts have federal tax benefits, and Section 529 Plans have state tax benefits.

GIFTS AND ESTATE TAXES

You are not studying to be a tax accountant or attorney, but for your exam, you do need to understand the tax implications of securities a customer may receive as a gift or estate distribution. This book will cover the basics here; do not spend too much time on these as Series 7 does not test you in detail on these.

Gifts

The best way to comprehend the tax implication of a gift of securities is to look at the transaction logically from the perspective of the IRS. With its tax ruling, the IRS aims to keep people from taking advantage of the rules: the government does not want people to claim losses by giving a gift of securities.

To understand the value of a gift for tax purposes, you must determine its **cost basis**. The IRS assumes the donor (or giver) of the securities' cost if there is a gain; the market value at the time of the gift if there is a loss in the value of the securities.

Series 7 will ask you questions using different scenarios where you will be expected to calculate the tax implications of a gift of securities. Determine the cost basis of the gift first and you will easily be able to come to the right answer.

Estate Taxes

In case of the inheritance of securities, the estate pays any taxes incurred by the transfer of assets. All you should know for your exam is the cost basis of estate-distributed securities is the market value on the day of the original owner's passing.

TAXATION AND YOUR CLIENT

Although you are not your client's tax advisor, your investment recommendations will greatly affect your client's tax returns now and in the future. A thorough understanding of your client's tax situation is vital in making the right recommendation, particularly when it comes to retirement investing.

Make sure you discuss your client's wishes when it comes to taxation now and in the future before starting any investment activity. Consider meeting with the client's tax preparer or requesting several years' worth of tax returns to get a picture of their tax situation. For estate implications, make sure you are aware of your client's distribution of assets in his will.

CHECKLIST

- ☐ I understand the difference between progressive and regressive taxes
- ☐ I know IRS income classifications of passive, active, and portfolio income
- ☐ I understand the tax code regarding interest and dividend
- ☐ I know how mutual fund capital gains are taxed
- ☐ I know what the Wash Sale Rule is and how it is applied
- ☐ I can calculate accretion and amortization to determine annual bond income
- ☐ I can identify different retirement plans and know the IRS qualifiers for Traditional and Roth IRAs
- ☐ I can determine the cost basis for estate distributions and gifts of securities

SAMPLE QUESTIONS

1. John just bought a stereo and he paid 8 percent sales tax. John paid:

    [A] Excise tax
    [B] Progressive tax
    [C] Aggregate tax
    [D] Regressive tax

2. Mona Simmons invests in a limited partnership, which has given her returns for the year of $20,000. The limited partnership carried a loss of $5,000. What is her income from this investment?

    [A] $10,000
    [B] $15,000
    [C] $20,000
    [D] $25,000

3. In January, Gregory Smith bought a 7 percent corporate bond for $4,000, and sold it 9 months later for $6,000. Which of the following is true?

    [A] He will not be taxed more than 15 percent on the profit he made because he held the bond longer than 61 days
    [B] He can deduct up to $3,000 from his income
    [C] He will be taxed at his bracket for both the interest income, and the capital gains from the sale of the bond
    [D] He will not be taxed because he invested in a bond

4. Jim Long bought a 6 percent corporate bond at 70, maturing after 10 years. What is his annual income?

    [A] $90
    [B] $60
    [C] $360
    [D] $13

5. Max Miller bought a 10-year, 10 percent corporate bond at 120. What is his annual income?

    [A] $10
    [B] $100

[C] $120
[D] $80

6. **Chris Williams wants to invest in an IRA, but needs for his withdrawals at retirement to be tax-free. You would recommend a:**

    [A] Roth IRA
    [B] Traditional IRA
    [C] SEP-IRA
    [D] Coverdell IRA

7. **Hannah Jones bought 100 shares of ABC stock at 60. She passes away, and leaves her stock to her niece Ashley Jones. The stock now trades at 100. Ashley Jones has to pay:**

    [A] The price her aunt paid for the stock, which was $6,000
    [B] The difference between the price her aunt paid and the current market value: $4,000
    [C] The market value of the stock at the time of her aunt's death: $10,000
    [D] Nothing; the estate will pay any taxes incurred by the transfer of assets

CHAPTER 9
Explaining Security Markets and Functions

As a future registered representative, Series 7 expects you to understand how the securities market works so you can explain it to your customers. You have covered stocks, bonds, government securities, as well as various ways these securities are packaged. Now that you understand the characteristics of securities, you will cover how they trade in the marketplace. This chapter will discuss Self-Regulatory Organizations (SROs), the primary and secondary marketplace, and controlling factors. The information here is kept brief, and focuses only on what you may be tested on during your Series 7 exam.

First, you should know Congress created the Securities and Exchange Commission (SEC) to oversee market activity. The SEC's job is to regulate the market, protect consumers, and enforce several acts.

The SEC enforces:

- **The Securities Act of 1933** (also known as the Truth in Securities Act): requires registration and disclosure of securities in a prospectus.
- **The Securities and Exchange Act of 1934**: assigned enforcement responsibilities of the 1933 act.

- **The Trust Indenture Act of 1939**: required all securities issued must be filed with an indenture agreement, specifying a trustee free of conflict-of-interest.
- **Investment Advisers Act of 1940**: requires all investment advisors to register with the SEC.
- **Investment Company Act of 1940**: requires all investment companies to register with the SEC and comply with SEC regulation.

Because of its sizable task, the SEC counts on Self-Regulatory Organizations (SROs) to police the marketplace.

SELF-REGULATORY ORGANIZATIONS (SROS)

Although membership is voluntary, most brokers are members of at least one **self-regulatory organization (SRO).** SROs can enforce their rules by fining, reprimanding, or suspending violating members; SROs do not have the authority to criminally prosecute violators of its rules. This section will explain the four SROs you need to know for your Series 7 exam: FINRA, NYSE, MSRB, and CBOE.

Financial Industry Regulatory Authority (FINRA)

FINRA is an SRO that regulates and operates NASDAQ and the Over-the-Counter (OTC) market. FINRA does not only enforce its own rules, but also the SEC's. FINRA also handles complaints and administers your Series 7 exam.

TIP #65

FINRA used to be known as the National Association of Securities Dealers (NASD). Older reference books, as well as your exam, may refer to FINRA as NASD. Make sure you understand these organizations are one and the same; NASD and NYSE were combined to form FINRA.

New York Stock Exchange (NYSE)

As the largest and oldest exchange market in the United States, the NYSE lists securities, sets exchange policies, and enforces them. Like FINRA, NYSE has the authority to reprimand, fine, and expel non-compliant members (firms or registered representatives).

Municipal Securities Rulemaking Board (MSRB)

The MSRB was created to develop regulation regarding municipal securities transactions by banks. MSRB makes rules for these transactions, but does not actually enforce them — nor does it enforce SEC rules. Although these rules are not enforced, issuers of municipal securities comply, to make sure they can raise the capital needed with the bond issue.

Chicago Board Options Exchange (CBOE)

For your Series 7, all you need to know about the CBOE is it regulates options trading and enforces its rules.

Tip for your exam: Series 7 likes to trip you up with its questions by suggestion these SROs back securities in some way. Any time a questions or answer implies one of these SROs guarantees or approves securities, make sure you know this is not within the capacity of any SRO.

WORKING IN THE PRIMARY MARKETPLACE

Chapter 2 covered the players in the underwriting of a security involving the creation of a new issue. These new issues of securities make up the **primary marketplace**, which consists of two types of new issues: **initial public offerings (IPOs)**, and **primary offerings**.

When a company compiles its first securities offering, it is "going public" with its IPO. As you know from Chapter 2, companies usually hold some stock back (their Treasury Stock). When this Treasury Stock is then sold to the public, it is called a Primary Offering.

TIP #66

A broker or syndicate member is not allowed to hold back stock from an initial public offering or primary offering (to sell later at a higher price). This is a practice known as free riding, prohibited by SEC regulations.

THE SECONDARY MARKETPLACE

Trading does not cease after these first sales, which brings us to the secondary marketplace. The **secondary marketplace** (or **aftermarket**) has four components: **the first (or auction) market, second (or OTC) market, third market, and fourth market**.

The first market trades listed securities on the floor (like on the NYSE). The second market involves the OTC trading of securities not listed with the SEC. The third market trades exchange-listed securities OTC by phone or computer orders from traders.

The fourth market trades securities between institutions without a brokerage firm. These fourth market trades are tracked on Institutional Networks' (or Instinet) computerized system for institutional traders.

OVER-THE-COUNTER (OTC) MARKET ORDERS

As mentioned in the previous section, securities are either traded on an exchange floor as registered securities, or traded OTC as unlisted securities. This book will cover the process for both security types in this section.

TIP #67

U.S. Government Securities and Municipal Bonds only trade OTC.

Dealers and Brokers

A securities firm can act either as a dealer or a broker in the sale of securities. Their role (and corresponding commission) has to be disclosed on the confirmation of the trade. If a firm sells securities from its own account, it is acting as a **dealer**. If a firm makes a trade on securities not in inventory, the firm is the **broker.**

When a dealer buys securities for a customer, it charges a **mark-up** (sales charge) to the customer. When this same dealer sells securities for a customer, it charges a **mark-down**, taken out of the customer's profit. When a firm acts as a broker, it charges a **commission** to act as a middle-man.

TIP #68

A firm can never be both dealer and broker in a transaction as it violates trading rules.

NASDAQ

To track the most actively traded OTC stocks, traders use NASD's Automated Quotation service (NASDAQ). NASDAQ tracks asking prices, bids of stock, and quotes on convertible bonds, preferred stock, and warrants.

NASDAQ is comprised of its national market (NNM) stock listings and capital market stocks. To meet the listing requirement of NASDAQ's NNM, a stock must list for at least $5 and have at least 400 round lot shares (100 shares make up a round lot), so 40,000 shares. NNM issues can be bought on margin (see Chapter 12). Capital market stocks of the NASDAQ (also known as small cap stocks) are stocks that did not meet NNM requirements.

NASDAQ has different types, or **access levels**, of information on its trades.

Here are the NASDAQ access to information levels you should know:

- **Level I**: Created for registered representatives, this computer screen displays bid and ask prices for several hundred NASDAQ stocks.
- **Level II**: For traders, this screen displays asking prices of each market maker (principal or dealer).
- **Level III**: Most complete information for market makers, allowing them to enter and change quotes.

PLACING ORDERS

As a registered representative, you will be placing orders for your customers, adding desired features, as well as reading ticker tape. Market order placing procedure is covering in this section.

Market Orders

Market orders are orders of securities that are executed immediately and at the best price. Market orders come as buy orders, sell orders, or selling short orders.

When an investor is **short** a stock, this means he or she does not hold it. When an investor is **long** a stock, this means he or she owns the stock.

Buy and sell orders are self-explanatory: a customer simply wants to buy or sell a security right away and at the best price available at that moment. When a customer sells short, he or she is selling securities not held by borrowing them from a lender. Selling short is a way to profit from a downward market: the seller borrows stock from the lender, then repays that stock debt at a later date, profiting from the drop in stock price. Selling short is a bearish strategy.

TIP #69

All short sales must go through a margin account (see Chapter 12) to ensure the seller can pay even if great losses are incurred.

Stop and Limit Orders

A **stop order** is a conditional order: the customer wants to buy or sell a security should it reach a certain market price to limit losses.

A **buy stop order** is used to protect a customer who is short a stock but sold a call; when the stock goes up, against expectations, the customer buys it to prevent greater loss. A **sell stop order** is used to protect a customer who is long a stock; by selling before the stock drops too much, the customer limits losses.

TIP #70

A stop order is placed to stop losses.

A **limit order** is also a conditional order: the customer wants to buy or sell a security at a certain market price, to increase profit.

A **buy limit order** is used if stock is at a price that a customer deems too high, but will be executed if that stock drops to a desired market price. A **sell limit order** is used by a customer who holds a stock and wants to sell it once it reaches a certain market price or higher.

A combination of the stop and limit order is the **stop limit order**. These orders protect the seller or buyer of stock from a too-significant drop or rise in market price. A stop to sell a stock at 50, for instance, may include a limit provision at 49. This would ensure the order to sell is triggered at 50, but will only be executed if the seller can still get at least 49 for his stock. This order would look like this: sell 100 XYZ at 50, 49 limit.

Series 7 will ask you questions regarding stop and limit orders, giving you scenarios. Here is an example:

EXAMPLE

Joe Miller places an order to sell XYZ at 60 stop. The ticker shows these stock prices: 60.70, 60.50, 60.30, 60.05, 59.50, 60.50, 60.45, 60.30, 60.45.

In this case, the order was triggered at 59.50 (when it first dropped below 60), and executed at 60.50 (the next stock price on the list).

TIP #71

When you get a question on stop and limit orders, look at the situation from the customer's perspective: is the customer trying to prevent loss or maximize profit?

Order Features

To fit different customer wishes, there are order features that can be added to the regular orders you just covered. Many of them are self-explanatory, but make sure you know what each one does, as you are sure to receive at least one question on these on your Series 7 exam.

These are order features you should know:

- **All or none (AON)**: order must be filled entirely (can be done in segments) or not at all.
- **At the open**: order must be filled at the opening price of a security (can be all or part of the order).
- **At the close**: order must be filled as close to closing price as possible or is canceled.
- **Day**: order that is only good for that trading day.
- **Fill or kill (FOK)**: order must be filled immediately or is canceled.
- **Good until canceled (GTC)**: orders can stay open until filled; specialist will clear his books in April and October so the order would have to be re-entered then.
- **Immediate or cancel (IOC)**: order like FOK, but can be partially filled.

- **Not held (NH)**: order allowing broker to fill it later if a better market price is expected.

TIP #72

Fill or kill (FOK) and all or none (AON) orders are no longer accepted by FINRA, but your exam may still include these order types in questions.

Ticker Tape

As a registered representative, you should be able to read ticker tape, which is the most up-to-date report of stock trades. Ticker tape used to be printed on actual strips of paper, now it is disclosed on television (like your finance programs). You will look at an example and dissect its features so you are ready should these come up in Series 7 exam questions.

EXAMPLE

XYZ.P 3K = 44.20^0.25

> XYZ.P: the company stock, XYZ; the P stands for preferred stock
> 3K: the amount of shares
> 44.20: price of the trade
> ^0.25: how much the stock went up (or down, if a different scenario) since the previous trading day

As you may have noticed, the stock name carried an extra letter to indicate this was a sale of preferred stock. When it comes to ticker tape, there are as many symbols as the alphabet has letters. For Series 7, you only need to be able to identify the most common ones.

Here are the ticker symbols you should know for your exam:

- **.P**: Preferred Stock
- **.X**: Mutual Funds
- **.R**: Rights
- **.W**: Warrants

SECURITIES MARKETS AND YOUR CLIENT

It is likely your client has hired you for your knowledge of the market and how to place orders so he or she does not have to worry about the logistics. Your knowledge of order types and how to place them is important to your client. Share the implications of a day order, for example, or a not held order. Although your client may not ask you for details, it is your duty to share any knowledge you have on the possible ramifications of certain orders.

The ideal client for the direct market orders you have just covered varies by the type of security you are buying or selling for the client. Frequent trading is more suitable for a client who understands the market and can bear the risk associated with the security you are trading. Clients not as versed in the market workings would be better advised not to incur the risk of frequent trading. Sharing your knowledge regarding particular securities and order types is key to a successful experience for your client.

CHECKLIST

- ☐ I know the four SROs and the capacity in which they act when it comes to their regulations and SEC regulation

- ☐ I understand the functions of the primary and secondary marketplace
- ☐ I know what a broker's and dealer's functions are
- ☐ I understand NASDAQ and its listings, as well as the three levels of disclosed information
- ☐ I know what selling short is
- ☐ I understand how stop and limit orders work with a customer's objectives
- ☐ I can identify different order features
- ☐ I can read ticker tape

SAMPLE QUESTIONS

1. Which of the following is an SRO?

    I. FINRA
    II. SEC
    III. CBOE
    IV. NASDAQ
    V. IPO

    [A] I, II, and III
    [B] I and III
    [C] I, IV, and V
    [D] I, II, III, and IV

2. John James is a broker assigned to handle the IPO of DEF stock. He decides to hold back 25,000 shares to sell when the stock price of DEF has stabilized and to make sure he gets the best price. He:

    [A] Is acting as a broker
    [B] Is holding Treasury Stock, a common practice for IPOs
    [C] Is bullish
    [D] Is free riding, an illegal practice according to SEC rules

3. A broker is buying ABC stock by phone. ABC stock is an exchange-listed security. This is an OTC transaction in:

    [A] The first market
    [B] The second market
    [C] The third market
    [D] The fourth market

4. Kevin Brown is selling XYZ stock to a client. His firm has the stock in inventory. He:

    [A] Acts as a broker and will charge a commission
    [B] Acts as a dealer and will charge a mark-up
    [C] Acts as a broker/dealer, violating SEC rules
    [D] Acts as a dealer and will charge a mark-down

5. As a registered representative, you are looking at an information screen on your computer. It displays bid and ask prices of NASDAQ stock. This is:

[A] NASDAQ Level I information
[B] NASDAQ Level II information
[C] NASDAQ Level III information
[D] NASDAQ Level IV information

6. **Harry Smith is placing a sell order for ABC stock. He does not actually own the stock. He is:**

   [A] Bullish, and selling long
   [B] Bullish, and selling short
   [C] Bearish, and selling long
   [D] Bearish, and selling short

7. **Carrie Williams is short XYZ stock and wants to limit her losses should the market take an undesirable direction. She will likely buy:**

   [A] XYZ stock to cover her short position
   [B] A buy stop order
   [C] A sell stop order
   [D] A call

8. **Bob Henderson holds DEF stock and wants to make sure he does not incur significant losses, should DEF stock suddenly drop. He places a stop limit order: sell 100 DEF at 80, 79 limit. The ticker shows the following stock prices:**

   85, 84.75, 82.50, 80.25, 79.75, 80.50, 79.50, 79.25

   When was the order triggered, and what was the execution price?

   [A] Triggered at 80.25, executed at 79.25
   [B] Triggered at 79.75, executed at 80.50
   [C] Triggered at 79.75, executed at 79.50
   [D] Triggered at 79.75, executed at 82.50

9. **Frank Miller places an order with his broker to buy 100 shares of ABC stock with an IOC order feature. This means his broker:**

   [A] Needs to fill his order by the end of the trading day
   [B] Can fill the order later, when the market price could be better
   [C] Needs to fill the entire order of 100 shares or abandon it altogether

[D] Needs to fill the order immediately, whole or in part, or it is canceled

10. This ticker tape comes across your desk: DEF.W 5K= 52.25^0.50. This is a report of the trade of:

    [A] DEF stock
    [B] DEF mutual funds
    [C] A put of DEF stock
    [D] DEF warrants

CHAPTER 10
Economics, Securities, and the Business Cycle

Although you are not studying to be an economist, Series 7 expects you to understand economic theories, the role of the Federal Reserve in the securities market, and business cycles. Understanding this bigger picture will help you explain the reasons for your advice to your customers and make you a more knowledgeable registered representative.

You have covered many rules, definitions, and calculations; this chapter will be more about general theory. I recommend you read it in one sitting, let it sink in, and review the basic definitions should some of these elude you. Expect this chapter to be more about comprehending than about studying.

TIP #73

For your exam, you should understand economic theory, but do not spend too much time on it.

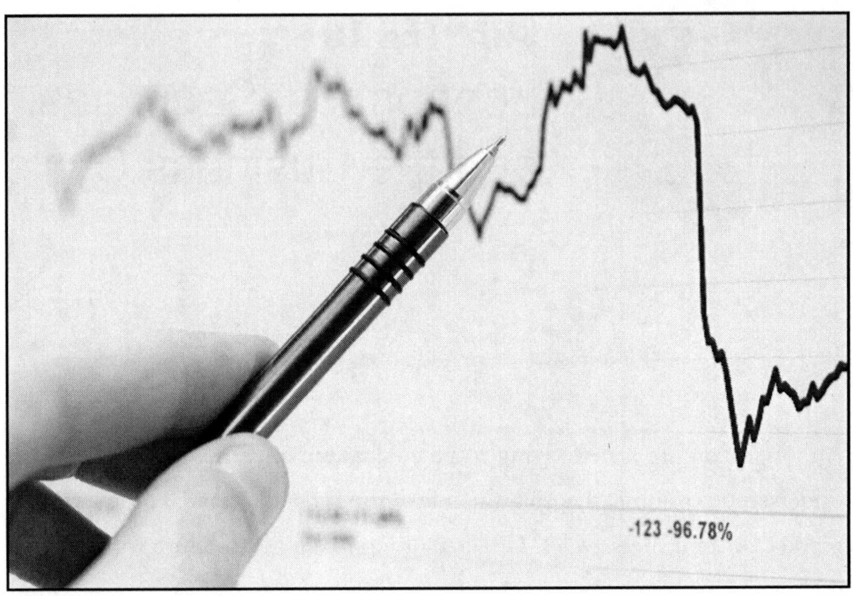

ECONOMIC THEORIES

There are many economic theories. For your Series 7 exam, you should know the two overarching theories: Keynesian theory and Monetary theory. This book will briefly cover both theories and how they interpret the market.

Keynesian Theory

Keynesian theory is based on British economist and government advisor John Maynard Keynes' *The General Theory of Employment, Interest, and Money,* which was published in 1935. Up until then, classical economist believed an economy worked best if left alone. Keynes argued excessive demand led to inflation and insufficient demand to deflation. Keynesian Theory believes governments should intervene by controlling the money supply (you will cover this later in this chapter) for an economy to remain balanced.

In his work, Keynes argued that as a result of reduced consumption, businesses made lower investments, which lead to unemployment. People were worried about not having their jobs, which led to a lower propensity to consume and an increase in savings. This is an example of a domino effect called **the multiplier effect**, which Keynesian theorists believe leads to a recession, or even depression in an economic cycle.

Monetarist Theory

Monetarist theory states the key to a healthy economy is a steady money supply. Monetarists state a gradual growth in money supply (which is the result of the natural growth of an economy), not government intervention, leads to a stable economy. This book will cover the different types of money supply later in this chapter when you look at the Federal Reserve's role in money supply.

BUSINESS CYCLE

The business cycle is a reflection of the **gross domestic product (GDP)**. Decades of study have proven there is a cyclical nature to our economy and to business. By studying the five stages of a business cycle, as well as economic indicators, economists (and registered representatives) can make predictions as to where an economy is headed.

TIP #74

If a Series 7 exam question mentions gross domestic product, it will expect you to relate the number to the business cycle.

Five Stages of a Business Cycle

More than a century of economic data has led economists to identify a cycle in the state of the markets. As you look at these five stages of a **business cycle**, imagine moving from the base of a bell curve up to the peak and back down again.

The five stages of a business cycle are:

1. **Early expansion**: during this first stage, interest rates and inflation are low; consumer confidence, spending, and growth are rising.
2. **Late expansion**: as a continuation of the first stage, demand grows and begins to outpace supply, causing inflation and a rise in interest rates.
3. **Peak**: growth is at its highest and begins to decline. Reduced spending by businesses and consumer follows.
4. **Recession**: once an economy's GDP has declined for two consecutive quarters, it is in a recession. Reduced consumer demand, unemployment, and lowering inflation are all signs of this stage in the business cycle. If this downturn continues beyond 18 months, it is called a depression.
5. **Recovery**: after hitting its low, the economy begins to recover. This last stage is indicated by a rise in consumer and/or business spending, which leads to the beginning of a new business cycle.

Although this business cycle seems to make predictions of economic events simple, this is hardly the case. Duration of cycle stages, as well as the sheer complexity of an economic system, makes prediction difficult. To aid in identifying these stages, economists and investors look for economic indicators.

Economic Indicators

Economic indicators are quantifiable ways to identify the state of the economy. Every month, independent economic organization **The Conference Board** publishes a report on the state of the most important economic indicators. Indicators are either leading, coincident, or lagging.

Leading indicators are numbers that change before the economy as a whole — they give us a taste of what is to come. Examples are first filings for unemployment, new building permits issued, and the index of consumer expectation.

Coincident indicators give us a picture of the present state of the economy. Examples of coincident indicators are industrial industry production, individual income, and retail sales.

Lagging indicators change after the economy has already moved to the next stage in the business cycle. Lagging indicators are prime interest rates, ratio of consumer debt to income, and the **consumer price index (CPI),** which is an indicator of inflation or deflation.

TIP #75

The two most important economic indicators are the country's gross domestic product (GDP) and consumer price index (CPI). These numbers show how the production of the entire economy fares, as well as how stable prices are.

Business Cycle and Markets

The interaction between the business cycle and investments is complex; too complex to cover completely here. For your Series 7 exam, you should know **investments with a fixed return (like bonds and fixed annuity) are adversely affected by inflation.** Because returns do not rise with inflation, the investment is in essence worth less.

Stocks will rise right along with inflation, as inflation is the by-product of an upward market. There are certain stocks that are more prone to being affected by the economy than others.

Cyclical stocks are investments in industries that are heavily affected by an economic up- or downswing. Examples of cyclical industries are the auto industry, construction, and retail. When consumers cut back their expenditures, it is in cyclical industries like these.

Defensive stocks deal in assets that are more immune to the effects of an economic cycle. These stocks are in industries like food and energy — the necessities of life.

TIP #76

To remember the difference between cyclical and defensive stocks, imagine a cyclical stock moving with the market and a defensive stock defending itself against it.

THE FEDERAL RESERVE

The Federal Reserve System (or **the Fed**, as it is commonly known) works as the central bank of the United States. It is comprised of a network of 12 regional Federal Reserve banks, 24 branches, as well as many member banks. The **Federal Reserve Board** supervises this network and sets and executes

monetary policy for the country. The Fed controls the supply of credit and money; to understand how this works, you must first look at the different types of money supply.

Money Supply

Money supply is broken into categories named M1, M2, M3, and L. Each of these categories is separated by their ease of use: how easy it is to access this money supply and spend it.

M1 is the most liquid kind of money supply, like cash-in-hand, demand deposits (money that can be drawn from banks without notice), and traveler's checks. M2 and M3 decrease in liquidity; below is an exact listing of what each category is comprised of.

- **M1**: most liquid: cash in circulation, demand deposits, and traveler's checks.
- **M2**: M1, plus time deposits < $100k, individual money market accounts, overnight repurchase agreements, and overnight Eurodollars.
- **M3**: M2, plus time deposits >$100k, institutional money market accounts, and term repurchase agreements.
- **L:** M3, plus T-Bills, savings bonds, commercial paper, banker's acceptances, and U.S.-held term Eurodollars.

TIP #77

For your Series 7 exam, remember M1 is most liquid; the other money supply categories simply degrade in liquidity.

The Fed and the Market

In its effort to control money supply to regulate the economy, the Fed has several tools to its disposal. First, the Fed controls the **Fed Fund Rate** — the rate at which banks loan/borrow money to meet **reserve requirements**. Reserve requirement are the minimum amount of cash a bank must hold to cover customer withdrawals.

Furthermore, the Fed can choose the **discount rate** — the rate at which banks can borrow money from the Fed. Investors watch changes in the discount rate very closely as it sends a message about where the Fed is expecting the economy to go.

The Federal Reserve Bank of New York buys and sells U.S. Treasury securities in open market operations using **repurchase agreements**. Simply put, the Fed buys Treasury securities so it can temporarily inject money into the system, only to agree to sell them again according to the agreement. Conversely, the Fed can sell Treasury securities to reduce the money supply, called a **reverse repurchase agreement** (also called a matched sale). The Fed's open market operations are supervised by the Federal Open Market Committee (FOMC).

TIP #78

Remember this: the Federal Reserve uses the Fed Funds Rate, reserve requirements, the discount rate, and open market operations to guide the economy through its business cycles.

To understand the desired effect of the Fed's actions, look at whether it increases or decreases money supply. Decreased money supply slows an overheated economy, where increased money supply stimulates an economy.

INTERNATIONAL MARKETS

With increasing globalization of our markets, each country's securities investments are affected by its trading partners. The exchange rate of currencies and the interest rate in foreign countries versus these rates in the United States are both important components of international trading.

An important tool in analyzing a nation's economic health is its **balance of payments.** The balance of payments contains the balance between import and export activities (**current account**), as well as the amount of investment either country makes in each other's economy (**capital account**).

ECONOMICS AND YOUR CLIENT

As you have learned in this chapter, economics and the business cycle affect all investments. The risk associated with economics and the business cycle is market risk, and this risk is carried by all investments, whether bonds, stocks, or options.

When you discuss particular investments with your client, make sure you at least briefly touch upon economics and how market risks affects the market as a whole and the client's investments. During market decline, you can use a simplified explanation of the business cycle to reassure your client that even though times are bad now, the market will pick back up as part of the business cycle's recovery.

CHECKLIST

- ☐ I understand the difference between Keynesian theory and Monetary theory
- ☐ I know the five stages of a business cycle
- ☐ I can identify economic indicators as leading, coincident, and lagging
- ☐ I know what cyclical and defensive stocks are
- ☐ I understand how the Federal Reserve controls the money supply
- ☐ I know how to analyze an international market's balance of payment, including the current and capital account

SAMPLE QUESTIONS

1. **Which of the following is true about Monetarist theory?**

   [A] Monetarists believe inflation should be avoided at all cost.
   [B] Monetarists believe in Keynes' theories.
   [C] Monetarists believe the key to a healthy economy is a steady growth in money supply.
   [D] Monetarists believe a government should control the money supply.

2. **When an economy's GDP has been decreasing for two consecutive quarters, this is called a:**

   [A] Recession
   [B] Depression
   [C] Recovery
   [D] Peak

3. **Retail sales are up, according to The Conference Board's report. This is an example of a:**

   [A] Leading Indicator
   [B] Lagging Indicator
   [C] Coincident Indicator
   [D] Recovery Indicator

4. When it comes to impact by the business cycle, stock in restaurants is considered

   [A] Defensive
   [B] Cyclical
   [C] Recessive
   [D] Leading

5. John Truman has a money market account. Within the market, this falls under:

   [A] M1
   [B] M2
   [C] M3
   [D] L

6. The Fed is selling Treasury securities with a promise to buy them back again at a later date. This is called a:

   [A] Put
   [B] T-Sale
   [C] Repurchase agreement
   [D] Reverse repurchase agreement

CASE STUDY: DAVID FRIEDMAN

Telephone Doctor, Inc.
30 Hollenberg Court
St. Louis, MO 63044
(314) 291-1012
www.telephonedoctor.com

Effective customer service skills are an important attribute for registered representatives who are building their customer list. David Friedman, general manager for Telephone Doctor Customer Service Training, believes customer service training can teach professionals skills that are often assumed but not mastered. "Many feel our techniques are too basic," he says of his on-site and DVD customer training course. "The reality is common sense is not as common as people think."

"Most front line service providers lack basic skills," he continues. Friedman explains with customer service training, professionals are better equipped to do their jobs, as well as gain more customers. "Better training translates to higher customer satisfaction and reduced stress on the service provider."

The customer service course Friedman provides uses real world examples. He stresses how important attitude is when it comes to effective customer service. "Once someone has the right attitude, we can help them with the proper wording, skills, and techniques."

"Either you have a passion for serving the customer or should consider another line of work," Friedman says, matter-of-factly. "Great customer service is difficult to fake."

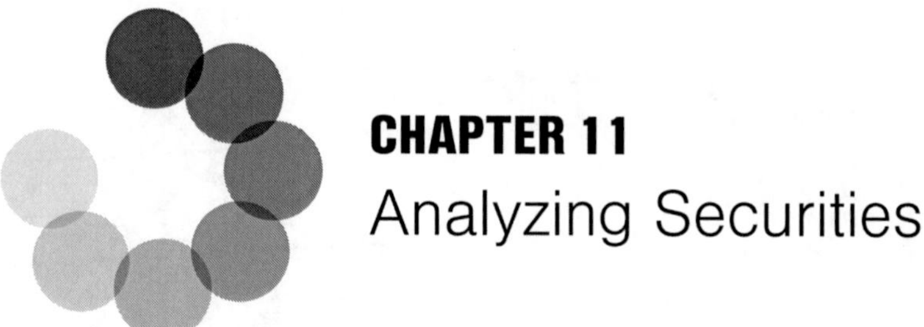

CHAPTER 11
Analyzing Securities

In order to make securities recommendations to your customers, you must first know how to compare one investment to another: you need to analyze investments based on data. As a registered representative, you will make two types of analyses: fundamental and technical. You will likely use both types in conjunction, but Series 7 expects you to identify one separate from the other.

FUNDAMENTAL SECURITIES ANALYSIS

For a fundamental analysis, you will look at different companies, comparing their state to determine risk. A **fundamental analysis** is an industry risk analysis, which means you will analyze company management, balance sheets, income statements, and any other data on the health of the corporation. A fundamental analysis also looks at the state of the industry as a whole (see Chapter 10 on defensive and cyclical stock and how they are affected by the business cycle).

Balance Sheet

Just like you did when you created a customer profile, you will look at assets versus liabilities on the company's **balance sheet**. Series 7 expects you to identify how different expenditures affect a company's balance sheet; this book will explain those components below.

The components of a balance sheet are:

- **Assets:** Include fixed assets (like property and equipment), current assets (like cash, accounts receivable — the more liquid assets), and intangible assets (like copyrights, goodwill, etc.).
- **Liabilities:** Long-term liabilities (payable later than 1 year), and current liabilities (due within a year).

HOW TO CALCULATE **NET WORKING CAPITAL:**

Net working capital = asset - liabilities (also known as net worth or stockholders' equity

The stockholders' equity or net worth of a company is of particular interest to your client as it shows the quality of investment the stock is.

Valuating inventory is an important component of determining assets. The value of inventory depends on if a company uses a last-in-first-out (LIFO) method, or a first-in-first-out (FIFO) method. With LIFO, inventory most recently bought will be sold first; with FIFO, a company rotates inventory so the longest-held items are sold first. If you encounter a question regarding valuation of inventory, you will determine value by looking at inventory method.

TIP #79

It is unlikely Series 7 will ask many questions regarding balance sheets, but you may be given a scenario where you need to identify what a change in assets will do to net worth. Make sure you understand how changes in assets and liabilities affect net working capital and you will be able to move right along on your test.

Income Statements

A company's income statement is another tool in analyzing its health. An income statement calculates a company's sales income (net sales), and deducts expenses like cost of goods sold, and depreciation to determine profit.

For Series 7, you should be able to identify **earnings before interest and taxes (EBIT)**, **earnings before taxes (EBT)**, and **net earnings after taxes (EAT)**.

These are income statement formulas you should be familiar with:

- **EBIT** = net sales - cost of goods sold - operating expenses - depreciation
- **EBT** = EBIT - bond interest expense
- **EAT** (or net income) = EBT - Taxes

Ratios

To compare two or more different companies and the risk involved when investing in their stocks, there are ratios Series 7 expects you to be able to calculate. This book will list them here; your exam questions will give you the values to use when computing your answers.

First, you must understand liquidity ratios. Determining a company's liquidity is important as liquidity affects growth, profitability, and credit rating.

These are liquidity ratio formulas you should be familiar with:

- **Current ratio**: current assets/current liabilities
- **Quick asset ratio**: (current assets - inventory)/current liabilities
- **Acid test ratio**: (cash + marketable securities)/current liabilities

Next, you need to determine the capitalization of a company to determine risk of bankruptcy. These ratios allow you to compare companies based on their ability to repay debt by measuring obligations (or debt) against assets.

These are capitalization ratio formulas you should be familiar with:

- **Long-term capital** = long-term liabilities + stockholders' equity
- **Bond ratio** = bonds par value/long-term capital
- **Debt-to-equity ratio** = (bonds + preferred stock)/equity

Measuring a company's profitability is another way to determine its health. Comparing different companies' profitability will give you a quick picture of their ability to generate profit.

These are profitability ratio formulas you should be familiar with:

- **Operating profit margin** = operating income/net sales
- **Net profit ratio** = net income/net sales

To determine if a company is in good shape to repay debts, you must also determine if the company is not holding too much debt, or "spread too thin," by assessing its asset coverage.

These are asset coverage ratio formulas you should be familiar with:

- **Net asset value per bond** = net worth/bonds shares outstanding
- **Bond interest coverage** = EBT/bond shares outstanding
- **Book value per share** = (assets - liabilities)/bond shares outstanding

To relate these numbers per share and make them easier to interpret for investors, there are several earnings per share ratios.

These are earnings per share formulas you should be familiar with:

- **Earnings per common share (EPS)** = (net worth - preferred stock)/ common shares outstanding (if convertible bonds are included, this is fully diluted EPS)
- **Price-earnings ratio (P/E)** = market price/earnings per share
- **Dividend payout ratio**: common dividend/earnings per share

One last way to compare investments is the simplest and most commonly used: comparing returns in the marketplace. Returns and market value are the cumulative effect of all these ratios and the easiest measure of profitability.

These ratios can easily take up hours of studying time. Although they are important when analyzing securities, Series 7 only asks a few questions regarding this section.

TIP #80

If crunched for time, make sure you know these formulas, as they are most likely to show up on a question:

Acid test ratio: (cash + marketable securities)/current liabilities

P/E ratio: market price/earnings per share

TECHNICAL SECURITIES ANALYSIS

Technical securities analysis involves the study of past movement of a security. Investors who use technical analysis believe just like a business cycle has a predictable pattern, so does a security's market value. Where fundamental analysis is a study of individual stocks, technical analysis bases its trading decision on the market as a whole.

Technical analysis uses three sources of information: market theories, indexes, and charts.

Market Theories

Market theories study different segments of the market. **The Dow theory** looks at the market from a long-, intermediate-, and short-term perspective to identify trends. This theory argues if the market as a whole declines, so will individual stocks, regardless of their position or rating.

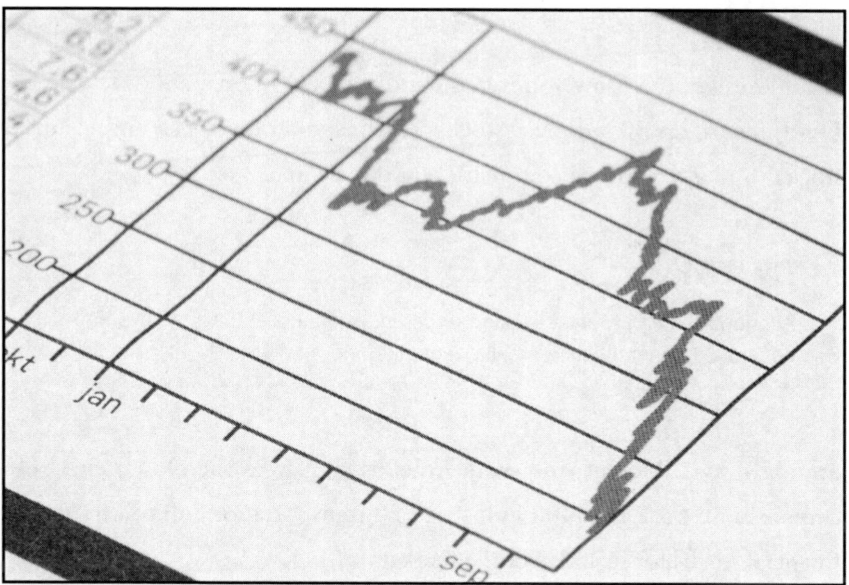

The **advance-decline theory** compares rising stocks to falling stocks daily to interpret market direction. According to this theory, it is more accurate to look at individual stocks than the market as a whole to see trends. Applying the advance-decline theory, an investor can interpret a market that is **oversold**: when the index is declining, but individual stocks show an uptrend. Conversely, an **undersold** market will show an index incline but decline in individually sold stocks.

The **odd-lot theory** looks at customers trading in odd-lot (or small) numbers of stocks (1-99 shares), with the assumption these customers are usually wrong. This theory is also called the **contrarian theory** as it takes the opposite position of a market segment.

The **short-interest (or cushion) theory** looks at short sellers' actions to determine market direction. It also takes a contrarian position: this theory assumes a rise in short sales actually means the market will rise.

Indexes

As indexes go, the **Dow Jones** is the most widely known and tracked. The Dow Jones tracks 30 industrial stocks, 20 transportation stocks, and 15 utility stocks — plus a 65-stock compilation of those three.

TIP #81

Although the Dow Jones is listed under indexes, it is actually an average because it only reflects a small segment of the market.

Standard and Poor's Composite Index is similar to the Dow Jones in its composition. S&P uses 400 industrial, 20 transportation, 40 utility, and 40 financial stocks for its index of the market.

There are many other indexes, but since Series 7 will not question you on these, this book will leave them for now. Once you have passed the exam, however, you may find it useful to study these indexes to understand how they indicate market direction.

Charts and Patterns

Now that you understand market theories and know how indexes can provide data, you will next study how charting this data can help anticipate market direction. Charting is also called **creating a trendline**.

When a stock is trading within a relatively narrow price range, it is called **consolidation**. The bracket the stock trades in has a **support** (lowest trading price), and **resistance level** (highest trading price). When there is consolidation in a stock's market price, it is said to trade stable. Once this same stock breaks through the support or resistance level, it is called a **breakout**.

Over the long term, a stock can move up (an **uptrend**) or down (a **downtrend**.) These trends can show up in charts as **saucers**, or inverted saucers, as seen in figures 11.A and 11.B, and **head-and-shoulders** configurations, as seen in figures 11.C and 11.D.

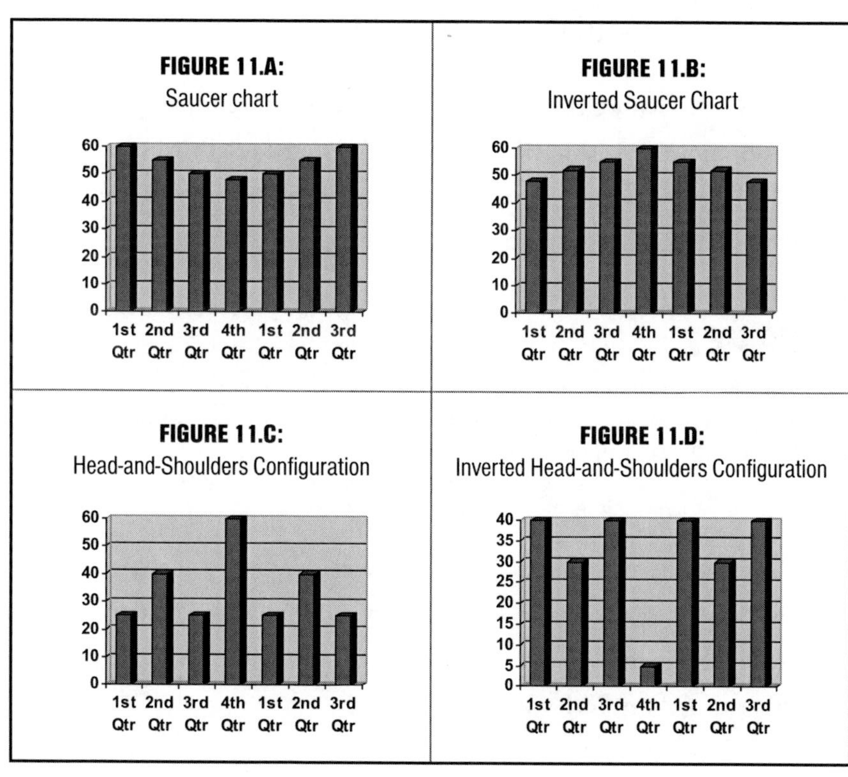

Municipal securities and mutual funds can be compared by applying the above theories. When you compare them for your customers, make sure you look at factors like repayment (for municipal securities), loads, fees, and asset allocation (for mutual funds). Review Chapter 4 on municipal securities and Chapter 5 on packaged securities to ensure you understand what factors apply when making comparisons for your clients.

PORTFOLIO THEORY

When it comes to making decisions regarding your customer's portfolio, there are several theories you can apply. These portfolio theories are:

- **Portfolio diversification**
- **Capital asset pricing theory (CAPT)**

A simple way to reduce risk incurred from individual securities' performance is diversification. Diversification, as this book covered briefly when discussing portfolio allocation based on customer profiles, means investing in stocks, bonds, and money-market instruments.

TIP #82

Diversification cannot protect a customer against market risk: when the market as a whole declines, the individual stocks will go down with it (see Chapter 10's section on business cycles).

To try to quantify the risk associated with a certain stock, analysts created a formula called the capital asset pricing theory (CAPT). This equation finds the expected rate of return on a stock by relating it to T-bills, which are risk-free, and the return of the S&P's 500.

In Chapter 10, you identified cyclical stocks and defensive stocks. By determining a stock's Beta value, you can quantify how closely this stock will adhere to the S&P's 500. Stocks that follow the market have a beta value of 1.0; stocks less-affected by the market (like defensive stocks) have a lower value, versus a higher value for cyclical stocks. Review Chapter 10 on the business cycle for defensive and cyclical stocks, and considerations for your client.

IN FORMULA FORM, THE CAPT PRINCIPAL LOOKS LIKE THIS:

r = rf + B

r = return of stock

rf = risk-free rate of T-Bills

B = Beta value of stock

It is unlikely you will have to use this formula on your exam; simply be aware it exists. It is important you understand portfolio diversification, as it applies to portfolio management, both on your exam and while working with your future clients.

SECURITIES ANALYSIS AND YOUR CLIENT

Securities analysis is an important skill you need as a registered representative in order to best advise your client on investment choices. Your client has hired you to give him or her insights and analyses he or she is not knowledgeable enough to make.

Before discussing securities analysis in detail, consider your client's knowledge regarding investments. Investment-savvy clients will appreciate your explanation of securities analysis, but less-knowledgeable investors will be content just knowing you are on the job. Adjust your explanations to each client.

CHECKLIST

- ☐ I understand what is included in a fundamental securities analysis
- ☐ I know how to calculate a company's net worth from balance sheet numbers
- ☐ I understand LIFO and FIFO inventory valuation systems
- ☐ I know what EBIT, EBT, and EAT are
- ☐ I can identify and calculate liquidity, capitalization, profitability, and asset coverage ratios
- ☐ I can calculate EPS, P/E, dividend payout, and current yield
- ☐ I can make a technical security analysis and understand different market analysis theories
- ☐ I know portfolio theory and tools, like diversification and CAPT

SAMPLE QUESTIONS

1. **A fundamental securities analysis looks at:**

   [A] The market as a whole
   [B] The way the market moves in the business cycle
   [C] Data on the health of a corporation, such as balance sheets and income statements.
   [D] The Dow Jones Industrial Average

2. **DEF Corporation has total assets of $1,000,000, and liabilities of $600,000. What is DEF's working capital?**

   [A] $1,000,000
   [B] $400,000
   [C] $600,000
   [D] Unsure; you need to know cash equity to answer this question

3. ABC Corporation sells tractors and holds an inventory of engines. It holds 200 engines in inventory at the end of 2009. Its purchases are recorded as follows:

   January 15: 100 engines at $200 each
   April 15: 150 engines at $225 each
   August 15: 150 engines at $250 each

   ABC Corporation uses the FIFO method for inventory. What is the value of ABC's inventory at the end of 2009?

   [A] $48,750
   [B] $50,000
   [C] $42,500
   [D] $43,750

4. XYZ Corporation paid off a short-term loan of $100,000. What happens to their working capital?

   [A] It is reduced by $100,000
   [B] It increases by $100,000
   [C] Nothing because assets and liabilities are equally affected
   [D] Assets and liabilities are reduced by $50,000 each

5. You are looking at ABC Corporation's balance sheet to determine the current ratio. What do you need to determine this number?

   [A] Cash and bonds
   [B] Assets and liabilities
   [C] Current assets and inventory
   [D] You need an income statement to calculate current ratio

6. Your client is trying to decide between two companies to invest in and needs to know how likely each is to file for bankruptcy. You would use:

   [A] Capitalization ratios
   [B] Liquidity ratios
   [C] Asset coverage ratios
   [D] Tax ratios

7. Technical analysis looks at:

   [A] A corporation's stock
   [B] A corporation's corporate charter
   [C] The market as a whole
   [D] The Fed's policies

8. A market analyst looks at individual sales of fewer than 100 stocks to determine market direction. He bases his analysis on:

   [A] Common theory
   [B] Short-interest theory
   [C] Dow theory
   [D] Odd-lot theory

9. A stock is trading at the following prices: 80, 80.25, 79.75, 80, 80.15, 80.25, 80.50, 80.25, 80, 79.75. What is the resistance level?

   [A] 80
   [B] 80.50
   [C] 79.75
   [D] 80.75

10. A stock's prices are showing an inverted saucer pattern. Your prediction for this stock would be:

    [A] Bearish
    [B] Bullish
    [C] Neutral
    [D] Optimistic

CASE STUDY: LINDA Y. LEITZ, CFP, EA

Pinnacle Financial Concepts, Inc.
7025 Tall Oak Drive, Suite 210
Colorado Springs, CO 90919
(719) 260-9800, extension 6
www.pinnaclefinancialconcepts.com

Linda Leitz is a financial planner for Pinnacle Financial Concepts. Leitz offers fee-only comprehensive financial planning for families, including investment consulting, retirement planning, education funding, estate and tax planning, and financial goal setting. She puts her relationship with her clients first. "I have a positive impact on people's lives," she says of her favorite part of her career as a financial planner. "I love helping my clients meet their goals. I cherish and honor the relationships I have with my clients and the trust they place in me."

Leitz brings this same respect for her clients to the first meeting. "We have a first appointment where we get an overview of the new customer's situation, and discuss some areas where we see we can help. Sometimes we talk on the phone for about 20 minutes or so before making an appointment."

Leitz likes to separate the client's different goals over several meetings. "We have standard appointments to address different areas of the client's financial situation." She finds this helps explain the complex workings of the financial system. "Having different appointments on specific functional areas seems to help. Also, explaining the concepts in the context of their situation makes it more understandable."

During her first year as a financial planner, Leitz built her business by networking through leads groups and networking mixers. "I also met with other professionals," she says, "like CPAs, attorneys, and human resource managers. I told them about the services I offered and asked who they thought I should talk to." Leitz adds that she is a practiced public speaker so she also led seminars and classes to build her business.

Leitz keeps a loyal client base. "We are in regular contact with clients, even if there is not an immediate need for an appointment," she says of her customer retention strategies. "We tell our clients we love working with people like them so we appreciate them sending their friends and family to us."

To keep current on the financial industry, Leitz reads industry publications. "I go to about 40 hours a year of conferences with a heavy continuing education component," she says of her commitment to keep up. "I stay in touch with colleagues around the country. I also listen to some books on the economy on my iPod."

"A financial advisor should be objective, look at as many aspects as possible of each issue – investment return, risk, tax impact, long-term outlook – and have the client's needs as the primary focus," she says of qualities that attributed to her success. Leitz advises aspiring financial advisors to get the necessary training, stay current, and listen to the client. "If you want to make an impact on people's lives, this is an area where that can happen."

CHAPTER 12
Evaluating Your Customer's Financial Needs

So far, this book has covered the markets and different securities you as a registered representative will be dealing with. Your objective in all this is to be able to give your customers the right advice. To do this, you must first analyze their current financial situation: you will have to create a customer profile.

Your Series 7 exam will give you scenarios, expecting you to apply the skills you will learn in this chapter. Customer analysis is a very subjective field, however. If you find you have difficulty with the concepts that follow, practice on your friends, family, or fictional customers to get more accustomed to the process. As a registered representative, you will have to analyze prospective and existing customers daily. Your ability to interpret your client's situation and translate it into a portfolio is crucial to your success so take your time learning the skills and tools in this chapter.

WHAT YOU NEED TO CREATE A CUSTOMER PROFILE

Each individual customer has their own life goals with investment goals to go with them. Your job as a registered representative is to translate those investment goals into investments that are appropriate in risk. You will do this with the customer's stated investment goals, a balance sheet of their assets to determine net worth, and an income statement.

TIP #83

The objective of your Series 7 exam is to ensure you will give your customers the appropriate advice. With each bit of customer information, ask yourself: how does this affect the customer's risk-tolerance?

Investment Objectives

When a customer says, "I want to save for my son's college expenses," what does that actually mean according to their investment? Whether the son is six months or 16 years old will make significant difference in their investment objective (and risk tolerance).

As a customer's advisor, you will need to translate these statements into investment objectives. The following are some of the objectives; comprehending them is enough.

Different types of investment objectives are:

- **Capital growth**: this would mean investing in newer companies where there is a greater possibility for capital growth
- **Current income**: investing in securities that provide cash dividend or interest (bonds, income funds, etc.)
- **Diversification**: investing in different types of securities to offset risk
- **Liquidity**: investing in securities that are easily converted to cash
- **Long-term or short-term**: investing in securities for long-term or short-term gains
- **Preservation of capital**: low-risk investments (like bonds) where capital is preserved

For example, say you are advising 65-year-old Fran Williams who wishes to preserve her retirement capital. Good investment advice would be for her to invest in a government bond (fund) so she does not lose her principal but still earns returns to protect against inflation. With each client's objective, think of how the investment features of the securities you have learned about can benefit him or her.

Determining Net Worth

To recommend investments to a customer, you must first know where their money is right now. The easiest way to determine this is with a simple balance sheet — and you do not need to be an accountant to create one. Simply list a client's **current assets** (like a home, car, or savings), including any securities already held, and **deduct liabilities** (like a mortgage or outstanding loans).

TIP #84

Know how to calculate your client's net worth:

Net worth = current assets - liabilities

Creating an Income Statement

Once you have determined where a client stands financially, you will need to analyze how much they have to invest. An income statement will show income and expenses so you can determine the amount available for investing.

Income statements are particularly helpful in determining how much a client should save for retirement, as it will show their current standard of living. To properly set retirement savings, you must discuss with your client what standard of living he or she expects in retirement and how to achieve this through his or her retirement portfolio.

Beyond the Numbers: Non-Financial Investment Considerations

People are more than their net worth and income statement. Part of your job is to identify other factors that affect your client's investment objectives, like whether the client is a single parent or whether they are close to retirement age. Getting to know your client is an important part of a registered representative's duties; for your exam, you will be given scenarios that include non-financial considerations in investment advice.

For instance, if you have a client whose children have finished college and are independent, certain objectives (like saving for college) are no longer applicable. It is important for you to keep up with your client's life changes to adequately adjust his portfolio to reflect these changes. The most successful registered representatives touch base with clients regularly and understand portfolios are as dynamic as the client's life.

PORTFOLIO ALLOCATION

Once you have decided your customer's risk tolerance, you should be able to make some decisions on portfolio allocation — which securities to invest in. You will base your recommendations on the customer profile you have just created. Portfolio allocation can be split into two types: strategic asset allocation and tactical asset allocation

Strategic Asset Allocation

Strategic asset allocation bases investment choices on the portfolio holder's long-term goals. A simple way to make up a strategic allocation is to subtract your customer's age from 100. That number should be the percentage invested in stock; the rest should be invested in bonds and cash instruments. If you had a 30-year-old customer, this would mean 70 percent in stock, 30 percent in bonds and cash.

This is a very simple way to determine asset allocation; you should look at these numbers as a place to start. If the customer profile indicates your customer is less risk-tolerant, you would adjust their portfolio accordingly.

TIP #85

Calculate a client's baseline asset allocation by subtraction their age from 100; this is the percentage you should invest in stocks. This is a quick way to spread your customer's assets within their portfolio to minimize risk but still have the best chance of returns that outpace inflation.

Tactical Asset Allocation

When making **tactical asset allocations**, you are adjusting a portfolio to market conditions. For instance, if you expect the stock market to fall, you would put more assets in bonds or cash. Tactical asset allocation anticipates market movement by studying the market, with hopes of benefiting from fluctuations.

INVESTMENT STRATEGIES

You have looked at customer profiles and portfolio allocation; investors can use all this information and take on an investment strategy aggressive, defensive, and balanced.

Aggressive, Defensive, and Balanced

When an investor is willing to take great risk in order to acquire larger gains, he or she is said to be **aggressive**. Aggressive investment strategies include investing in volatile stock, put or call options, or buying securities on margin. Aggressive investors tend to be more tactical in their portfolio allocation, hoping to gain from market movement wherever possible.

Defensive investment strategy is focused on maintaining principal while getting interest on that principal. Defensive investors prefer low-risk investments, like stock of established, high-rated companies, AAA-rated or government bonds, and cash investments like money market funds.

Most investors fall somewhere between aggressive and defensive and prefer a **balanced** strategy. A balanced portfolio has a mix of aggressive and defensive stock to offset risk.

TIP #86

Most of your clients will benefit from a defensive strategy; a purely aggressive strategy carries too high a risk for most investors, and a purely defensive strategy incurs high inflation risk.

IDENTIFYING RISK

Once you have decided on your investment strategy, you need to identify types of risk that are associated with different types of investments. One way to identify risk is to look at an investment's benefits, which are easier to identify, and look at the flip side to this benefit. For instance, a money market account may be a safe investment because your client will preserve their capital. However, money market accounts only receive a few percentage points of interest and are at risk of being outpaced by inflation.

Different types of investment risks are:

- **Business**: risk of bad business performance
- **Capital**: risk of losing your principal investment
- **Credit**: risk of not getting paid on time
- **Inflation**: risk of losing purchasing power from inflation
- **Interest**: risk of interest rates outperforming bond rates
- **Legislative**: risk that legislative changes affect the market
- **Market**: risk of market changes reducing an investment's value (all securities are susceptible to this risk)
- **Reinvestment**: risk of having to reinvest returns at a lower rate
- **Sovereign**: a foreign company may change policy that affects investment value

Because the Series 7 exam was created to ensure you are qualified to advise consumers on investments, understanding these risks is crucial to passing your test. Use your logic, and take a look at how the securities this book has covered in previous chapters carry these risks. It will help you answer questions quicker.

TIP #87

You can logically identify types of risks by looking at the adverse consequences of an investment's benefits. The safety of a bond investment, for instance, has the adverse consequence of inflation risk.

PORTFOLIO ANALYSIS AND YOUR CLIENT

As you may have realized, analyzing your client's financial needs is a skill you will use every day and with each new client. As a registered representative, you will need to translate your client's information and investment objectives into suitable recommendations.

Even if you have an investment-savvy client, make sure you do an intricate analysis of his or her financial situation. Make periodic adjustments based on a change in situation or the passage of time. A client who is risk-tolerant when he is single and 30-years-old will be far less risk-tolerant at 40 when he has a wife and young children. Your client's portfolio should be a dynamic package, one you as the registered representative adjusts as time passes.

CHECKLIST

- ☐ I understand how to translate my customer's investment objective by risk tolerance
- ☐ I can identify investment objectives by risk
- ☐ I know how to calculate a customer's net worth
- ☐ I understand the difference between strategic and tactical portfolio allocation
- ☐ I know the difference between aggressive, defensive, and balanced investment strategy
- ☐ I can identify different types of investment risk

SAMPLE QUESTIONS

1. Martha Simmons wants to invest in securities, but does not want to lose her principal. She also wishes to receive returns in cash to supplement her retirement income. What are her investment objectives?

    [A] Capital growth and current income
    [B] Liquidity and preservation of capital
    [C] Diversification and short-term gains
    [D] Preservation of income and current income

2. Chris Jones is 40-years-old and you are making a strategic asset allocation. Without knowing anything else about his objectives, personal situation, or assets, how would you allocate his portfolio?

    [A] 100 percent stock
    [B] 80 percent stock, 20 percent bonds
    [C] 60 percent stock, 40 percent bonds and cash
    [D] 60 percent bonds and cash, 40 percent stock

3. Donna Miller asks you to put together a portfolio for her. She wants to base the allocation on market value of stocks and securities, not on any long-term goals. You would make a:

    [A] Tactical asset allocation
    [B] Strategic asset allocation
    [C] Stock asset allocation
    [D] Bond asset allocation

4. Greg Samuels wants to invest for his retirement, but he also wishes to make short-term gains by "playing" the market. Your portfolio strategy would be:

    [A] Aggressive
    [B] Defensive
    [C] Conservative
    [D] Balanced

5. Your client Henry Zimmerman wants to invest in a C-rated corporate bond. As his registered representative, you would advise him on this risk:

    [A] Inflation risk
    [B] Credit risk
    [C] Legislative risk
    [D] Reinvestment risk

CASE STUDY: JUDY MCNARY

McNary Financial Planning
14597 Benton Street, Suite 200
Broomfield, CO 80020
(303) 410-1745
www.mcnaryfinancial.com

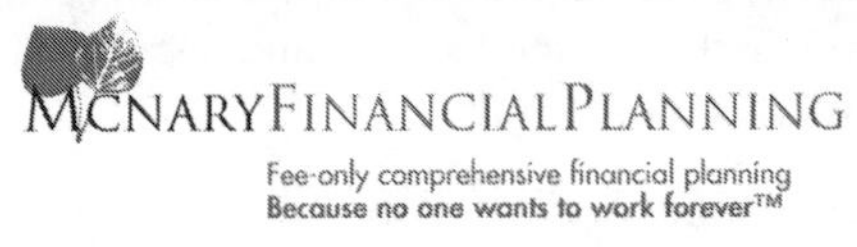

Judy McNary is a fee-only financial planner with a goal-oriented approach to her clients' portfolios. "Clients are families facing the dual challenges of college and retirement planning," she says of McNary Financial Planning services. "They are professional women who want solid retirement plans that don't require compromising current lifestyles and they are entrepreneurs, passionate about creating successful companies from their dreams."

McNary focuses on the client's goals in her investment advice. "Prospective clients embrace the concept that money alone is not enough," she says of her approach. "It must be partnered with one's goals and values to create a rich, fulfilling life." She enjoys helping her clients. "Uncertainty about finances adds stress, so helping clients create a plan and working with them to implement it is really rewarding."

When McNary first opened her practice, she participated in community events to create awareness. "I built my business slowly but surely," she says, adding that National Association of Professional Financial Advisors (NAPFA) referrals have been a significant part of her practice. "Most new clients are referrals from existing clients," she adds.

McNary, like other financial advisors, keeps current by reading financial publications. "Read, read, read," she advises those new to the business. "I have several newsletters I receive daily online." She also attends conferences, takes continuing education classes, and participates in webinars.

When asked what advice she would give those starting out in the financial industry, McNary advises to get organized. "The key is to implement a system that enables you to stay organized," she says. "Without a system, you will work long hours without appropriate compensation for it."

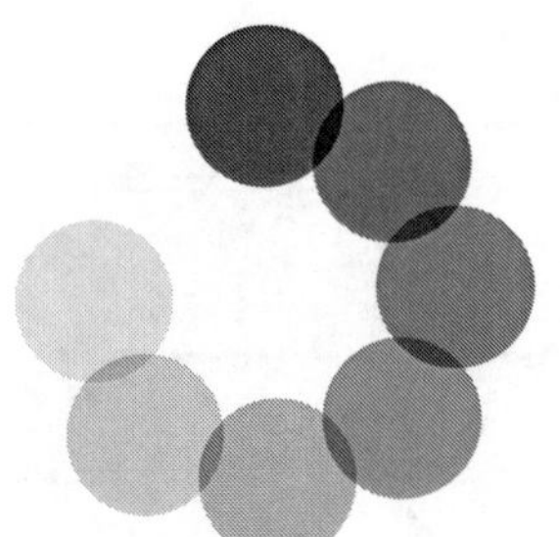

CHAPTER 13
Transactions and Account Management

Once you have established your customer's profile and determined a direction for his or her portfolio, you will need to open an account for your customer. Series 7 includes a fair (and increasing) amount of questions on transactions and account management.

As you will learn in this chapter, the information you gather when opening your client's account can be very revealing and helpful in creating a portfolio. Successful registered representative take a great deal of time with new customers to ensure they get the right portfolio allocation from the start.

OPENING ACCOUNTS

Before you can open an account, you will need some basic information:

- Customer name and address
- Date of birth
- Account type (options, margin, etc.)
- Social Security number
- Occupation and employer
- Citizenship
- Net worth and annual income

- Investment objectives
- Registered representative's and principal's (such as your firm's manager) signature

This information is needed to legally open a new account, but it can also help you assess risk. Is your client young, or near retirement? How secure is his or her employment? What is his or her net worth, and how are his assets currently allocated? This is all information you can derive from your client's information you used to open the account.

Street Name Accounts

Some customers prefer their name not be used on their account, preferring anonymity, and a **street name or numbered account** is used instead. A street name account has an ID number used for trading — all margin accounts trade in this way. These accounts are registered to the broker/dealer but the customer still owns them.

To open a street name account, you need a written statement from your customer confirming their ownership. Customers can choose to change a street name account into a regular account if they wish.

The Patriot Act

In 2001, the **Patriot Act** was created to protect the country against terrorist activity. Broker/dealers now must keep records of customer identification and check customer names against the U.S. Treasury list of known terrorists.

Check with your firm on procedures on opening accounts.

TIP #88

Laws change frequently as changes in presidential administrations mean adjustments of laws and policies. Make sure you are up-to-date on requirements that are part of your new function as a registered representative.

Joint and Single Accounts

A customer can choose to open a single or joint account. Single accounts can only be opened in the customer's name, unless the customer holds a power of attorney, authorizing him to open an account in someone else's name.

Joint Accounts come in two types: **joint with tenants in common (JTIC)**, or **joint tenants with right of survivorship (JTWROS)**. If one of the account holders of a JTIC dies, his or her portion becomes part of his or her estate. In this same situation, a JTWROS account would pass the deceased owner's portion on to the surviving joint holder (usually a spouse).

Custodial Accounts

A customer may open a **custodial account** for a minor (age of a minor is determined by the state). All investment decisions for custodial accounts are made by the custodian (customer). Custodial accounts fall under the **Uniform Gifts to Minors Act (UGMA)** or **Uniform Transfer to Minors Act (UTMA)**.

Series 7 may refer to these accounts as UGMA accounts or UTMA accounts.

To protect minors and avoid abuse of the rights that come with these accounts, custodial accounts have requirements you must know:

- A custodial account can only have one custodian and one minor.
- The account is registered to the custodian, benefiting the minor.
- The account cannot trade on margin (see Chapter 14 on margin accounts) and cannot be held in a street name.
- Any rights associated with the account must be exercised or sold.
- Gifts are irrevocable (cannot be rejected).
- The minor is responsible for taxes.

TIP #89

Once a minor reaches their state's majority age, the account is converted into a single account in his or her name.

Corporate and Partnership Accounts

To open a corporate account, you would need the corporation's tax ID number, and a copy of the **corporate resolution,** which will specify who makes decisions on the account. If that corporation wishes to buy on margin, you will need to make sure the corporate bylaws allow this.

Opening an account for partnerships requires you keep a copy of the **partnership agreement** on file. Partnership agreements, like corporate resolutions, specify who makes decisions on the account.

Discretionary Accounts

When an investor wants you, as their registered representative, to make investment decisions for them, you would open a **discretionary account**. In order to open a discretionary account, you need the investor to sign a written power of attorney.

To protect the investor, there are rules you must follow when placing a discretionary order:

- The investor must periodically review the account to ensure the registered representative is not "**churning**" (trading heavily to generate commissions).
- Orders must be signed by the investor and be marked as discretionary.

ORDERS AND CONFIRMATIONS

When a customer places an order for a trade, you will fill out an order ticket either electronically or on paper. An order ticket must contain certain information, which will be on the Series 7 exam.

Order ticket information:

- Your ID number as a registered representative
- Customer account number and type (cash or margin)
- Securities description and number of shares
- Purchase type (selling long or short)
- Order type (GTC, FOK, etc. — see Chapter 9 on order tickets)
- For option orders, include if the customer is covered/uncovered, opening or closing
- Order time and execution price

TIP #90

You will need to get the principal's (firm manager's) signature the day of the order to be able to execute the order.

Unsolicited Orders

Previously, you have covered how to make investment recommendations based on your customer's profile and investment objectives. Should your customer request an order that is out of line with your recommendations, you are required to advise them of that fact. If the customer wants to complete an order against your recommendations, you would mark it **unsolicited**.

Settlement of Orders

Once an order is placed, it will be traded on the **trade date**. On the **settlement date**, the issuer of the securities will update their records and send certificates to your firm. The buyer then pays for the trade on the **payment date**.

Different securities have different Fed-guided settlement dates, which are listed here:

- U.S. government bonds settle and require payment on one business day after the trade date.
- Municipal bonds settle and require payment three business days after the trade date.
- Stocks and corporate bonds settle after three business days, and require payment five business days after the trade date.
- Options settle after one business day, and require payment five business days after the trade date.

TIP #91

Cash trades trade, settle, and require payment all on the same day.

Trade Confirmation

After each trade, you as a registered representative will send your customer a **trade confirmation.** Trade confirmations include the same information as on the order ticket, as well as these additional items:

- Yield (for bonds), or price of the security, including total dollars paid.
- Committee on Uniform Security Identification Procedures (CUSIP) number (this is a security identification number).
- Commission amount.
- Net amount (amount paid, minus commission).

Good Delivery

As covered in Chapter 2, the transfer agent is responsible for good delivery of certificates. **Good delivery** means the certificates are in good condition (not torn or mangled), endorsed, and for the right type and amount of securities. For good delivery on bearer bonds, the certificates must have attached coupons. Certificates for bonds must come in multiples of $1,000, up to $100,000.

Stock certificates must be issued in lots of 100 with divisors of 1, 2, 4, 5, 10, 25, 50, 100, etc., or in units that make up 100 (you will look at how this works in an example). If a customer makes an odd-lot trade, no good delivery of certificates is required.

EXAMPLE

James Williams receives good delivery on a trade of 640 shares. To follow the rules regarding good delivery, one certificate for 400 shares would be issued and one certificate of 100 shares would be issued. For the remaining shares, he would receive one 60-share certificate plus two 40-share certificates.

The remaining share portions must add up to 100: 40 plus 60 makes 100. Series 7 might give you a question regarding good delivery. Look to see if all shares add up to the total amount sold in the question, then look at denomination of certificates to see if good delivery is met.

ACCOUNT MANAGEMENT

Your responsibilities as a registered representative do not end once a customer receives good delivery. You are required to manage their account, which includes sending statements. The Series 7 exam will not cover this subject much; you should only know your obligations regarding account statements.

Your customers have the right to regular account statements. How often registered representatives must send out statement differs per account, depending on type and account activity. Holders of active accounts must receive a statement for the month in which there was account activity. Mutual fund account holders must receive semi-annual statements, regardless of activity. Inactive accounts must receive at least quarterly statements.

RULES OF CONDUCT REGARDING ACCOUNTS

FINRA's primary concern is to protect investors and has enacted regulations with this purpose. As a registered representative, you should know regulations regarding account transfer, handling complaints, cold-calling, mark-up, and identifying money-laundering activity. This book will cover these rules of conduct in this section.

TIP #92

Know your rules of conduct. The Series 7 exam's purpose is ensuring you will be competent in performing your duties; these regulations are a very important.

Transferring Accounts

Should a customer decide to change brokerage firms, he or she has to fill out a form requesting the transfer. The old broker has three business days to validate the form's information, then another three business days to execute the transfer.

Handling Complaints

In its efforts to protect customers, FINRA has established formal procedures you will have to follow in case a customer wants to file a complaint against you. This is called FINRA's code of procedure, stating complaints must be issued in writing. Complaints are then sent to the **District Business Conduct Committee (DBCC)**, which tries to resolve complaints. If a customer is still dissatisfied, he or she can appeal the DBCC's decision to the **FINRA Board of Governors** and to the Supreme Court, should no resolution be reached.

This court action can be expensive, which is why complaints between FINRA members (like between a broker and a registered representative) are often resolved in arbitration. This code of arbitration reaches binding decisions.

TIP #93

Complaints filed with the SEC can go to civil court and lead to criminal prosecution if applicable.

Cold-Calling Rules

The **Telephone Act of 1991** was enacted to protect consumers from obtrusive sales calls. As a registered representative, you should know rules regarding cold calling — calling potential customers, not existing clients.

Cold calling rules specify you must:

- Give your name, company, company address, and phone number.
- Make calls only between 8 a.m. and 9 p.m. local time.
- Comply if customers request to be put on the do not call list.
- Not fax unsolicited advertisements

Mark-up Rules

FINRA has created guidelines regarding commissions to protect customers from excessive charges by brokerage firms. This is called the **FINRA Mark-up Policy**, which states you should not charge more than 5 percent commission per transaction.

TIP #94

Know this: the FINRA 5 percent mark-up rule is a guideline only and not mandatory.

Certain trades, like sales of securities that are priced too high or foreign market trades, make a broker/dealer's job more difficult, justifying a higher commission.

Trades that are regulated by the FINRA 5 percent rule include:

- Inventory transactions: when a firm buys for or sells inventory securities.
- Broker transactions
- Simultaneous (riskless) transactions: when a firm buys securities to immediately sell to a client.
- Proceed transactions: when the proceeds of a trade fund another trade, a firm cannot charge commission twice.

Anti Money-laundering Rules

As a broker, you are required to look out for possible money-laundering activities. Certain customers could use an account to disguise the fund's origin in illegal activity (arms trading, drug dealing, etc.).

Your Series 7 exam will expect you to identify the three steps of **money laundering**:

1. **Placement**: when funds are deposited.
2. **Layering**: when a customer moves money between accounts to hide its source.
3. **Integration**: when funds from an illegal source are mixed with legitimate business proceeds.

These steps can be difficult to distinguish from legitimate customer transactions. Money-laundering activity is accompanied by other signs, like suspect ID when opening an account, reluctance to reveal information, or

irrational transactions once the account is opened, like transfers without reason. Customers may deposit just below $10,000; cash transactions of $10,000 must be reported on a **Currency Transaction Report (CTR)**.

As a registered representative, you are expected to be vigilant and report transactions more than $5,000 you suspect are money-laundering activity with a **Suspicious Activity Report (SAR)** to the **U.S. Treasury's Financial Crimes Network (FinCEN)**.

Bankruptcy Protection

The government created the **Securities Investor Protection Corporation (SIPC)** to protect investors' assets should their brokerage firm go bankrupt. SIPC protects each customer's assets up to $500,000, including up to $100,000 cash.

Other Rules

In addition to the above-mentioned rules and guidelines, you should be able to identify other types of violations.

Registered representatives should know regulation regarding:

- **Gifts**: you may not give or receive gifts worth more than $100 per customer
- **Painting the tape**: simulating activity, for instance splitting one 20,000-share trade into four 5,000-share trades
- **Marking the open/close**: executing several transactions at open or close, to simulate activity
- **Paying the media**: paying a media securities expert to recommend a security

TIP #95

For your exam, and for your duties ahead as a registered representative, assume any time you are manipulating the price of a security, you are acting illegally.

Your state might employ the **Prudent Man Rule**, which states a representative must act reasonably regarding their customer's investments as a prudent man or woman would. Application of this rule varies by state; check your state's regulations to see if a Prudent Man Rule applies to your business.

ACCOUNT MANAGEMENT AND YOUR CLIENT

The Series 7 exam was created to ensure registered representatives are aware of their responsibilities toward their clients. Your client counts on you to represent him or her in the marketplace. Make sure you keep current on regulations that may affect your actions and your client's investments.

As you have learned in this chapter's portion on money laundering, there are situations when compliance with the law trumps your obligation to your client. Be sure to stay vigilant when it comes to legal compliance as breaking the law can have very serious implications for you, as well as for your client.

CHECKLIST

- ☐ I know the information I need to open a customer account
- ☐ I know what a street name account is
- ☐ I know how I need to comply with the Patriot Act
- ☐ I know how joint and single accounts transfer assets in case a holder dies
- ☐ I understand custodial account requirements
- ☐ I know what is required to open a corporate or partnership account
- ☐ I know what information is on an order ticket
- ☐ I know what an unsolicited order is
- ☐ I can identify settlement dates for trades of different securities
- ☐ I know what information is included on a trade confirmation
- ☐ I can identify good delivery for stock trades
- ☐ I know statement requirements for different types of accounts
- ☐ I can identify different rules regarding the trading of securities

SAMPLE QUESTIONS

1. **Which of the following is not required to open an account?**

   [A] A customer's green card number, if a registered alien
   [B] Customer's occupation
   [C] Annual income
   [D] Tax returns

2. **To comply with the Patriot Act of 2001, registered representatives must keep the following customer information on file:**

   [A] A copy of a customer's identification
   [B] A copy of a customer's last tax return
   [C] A list of all foreign countries the customer has visited
   [D] A list of all foreign corporations a customer does business with

3. **Mary Jones and John Miller opened a JTIC account ten years ago. John Miller passed away; what happens to his share of the account?**

   [A] It passes to Ms. Jones as part of the account agreement
   [B] It becomes part of his estate
   [C] It stays in the account, but Ms. Jones cannot withdraw it
   [D] It depends on the contract the two account holders signed

4. **David Truman opened a custodial account for his daughter Ashley Truman, who has just reached the age of majority in her state. What happens to the custodial account's funds?**

   [A] The funds transfer to his account because he is the custodian
   [B] The account becomes a single account in Ms. Truman's name
   [C] The funds are frozen, and can only be withdrawn at his request
   [D] It depends on the account agreement he signed when he opened the account

5. **Chris Jones and Frank Green are part of a partnership, and have opened a partnership account. Who can make decisions on the account?**

 [A] Only Mr. Jones and Mr. Green together
 [B] Mr. Jones or Mr. Green
 [C] The registered representative
 [D] It depends on who is specified to make decisions in the partnership agreement

6. **Your customer has placed an order for a municipal bond, which you have traded on Friday, April 6. When does this order settle?**

 [A] Monday, April 9
 [B] Tuesday, April 10
 [C] Wednesday, April 11
 [D] Thursday, April 12

7. **Greg Franklin bought 360 shares of ABC stock. Which of the following constitutes good delivery?**

 [A] Two certificates for 100 shares, two certificates for 60 shares, and one certificate for 40 shares
 [B] One certificate for 300 shares, and three certificates for 20 shares
 [C] Three certificates for 100 shares, and three certificates for 20 shares
 [D] One certificate for 360 shares

8. **One of your customers has been involved in what you believe to be money-laundering activity. You have just received a deposit of $7,000. What action should you take?**

 [A] Call the police and report your client
 [B] Talk to your manager about the activity
 [C] Nothing; the transaction is below $10,000, so you do not need to report it
 [D] File a SAR

CASE STUDY: BOB HOWARD

ColdCalling101
1930 E. Rosemeade Parkway, Suite 206
Carrollton, TX 75007
(214) 483-5800

After 25 years managing field and inside sales teams, Bob Howard co-founded ColdCalling101. "We are a telephone prospecting consultancy specializing in the business process of 'dialing for dollars,'" Howard says when asked about ColdCalling101's business focus. "We focus exclusively on helping field sales and internal telemarketing professionals to be more efficient and effective in the pursuit of initial appointments."

Howard recognizes how hard cold calling can be, especially for those new to the process. "Cold calling has tremendous baggage as being painful, because it is – both physically and mentally. Physically, the pain comes from traditional technology to stay organized," he says, referring to the many screens sales people must navigate. "Mentally, the pain is a discomfort from constantly challenging folks on the phone when they say no to your request for an appointment." Howard co-created ColdCalling101's The Prospectors Academy, a packaged sales technique for sales professionals, to meet these challenges. "We teach sales professionals how to move the target into a space where they will speak with them as someone who understands the challenges the target deals with each day."

Howard stresses the importance of separating customer service skills from initial contact or cold calling skills. "Sales agents believe the skills they learn to get the prospects *through* the pipeline will serve them as skills to get folks *into* the pipeline. They are totally different skills," he says of this common misconception among sales professionals.

"Cold calling is a business process, a difficult one, but just a business process that sales professionals must master," Howard says. In his coursework, he hopes to teach student how to set more appointments in less time. He explains that sales professionals can build their business by expanding their marketing territory with warm leads and prospecting territory with cold leads. "Your marketing territory will not generate enough leads to build your practice," he advises Series 7 graduates who are building a new business. "You must use cold calling to supplement. You must be laser-focused on how to make your prospecting territory as large as possible, and as fruitful as possible. This is a combination of your time spent calling, your target mix, the pursuit plan you use, and how fast you execute this plan." He welcomes Series 7 graduates to e-mail him and let ColdCalling101's calculator help determine how many names they should call each year to successfully build their client base.

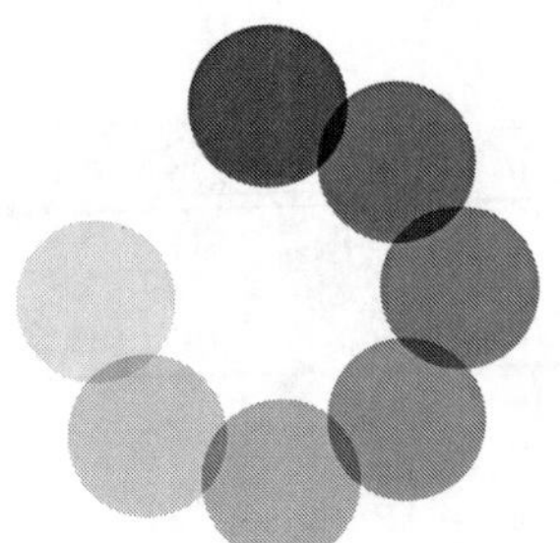

CHAPTER 14
Special Customer Accounts: Margin

When an investor wants to buy or sell securities but does not have the money or securities to fund the transaction, he or she can make use of a margin account. Margin accounts are credit lines with a broker. These accounts allow an investor to buy and sell more securities than they otherwise might be able to afford.

Margin accounts come with a lot of risk because they are created to buy and sell on credit — should the market go a different way than the investor speculates, losses can be great. Because of this high risk, margin accounts are heavily regulated.

Series 7 will test you quite a bit on these accounts, expecting you to make calculations. This book will cover all subjects you should know, including examples of calculations you might be expected to make on your test. This material is difficult, and trips up many test-takers. This book has put margins last so you can build off all your markets knowledge and understand the margin material in its broader context.

THE BASICS: LONG AND SHORT ACCOUNTS

There are two types of margin accounts: long and short.

When a customer wants to buy securities but does not have all the funds to do so, he or she puts down a certain percentage and borrows the rest from the broker. This is a **long margin account**. Long margin account holders are bullish: they speculate the market will go up so they can collect on the increase in market price.

When an investor wants to sell securities he or she does not hold, he or she can borrow those securities from his broker with a **short margin account**. This investor hopes the market will decline so he or she can repurchase the shares at a lower price and repay the lending broker. Short margin account holders hope to profit from a bearish market.

Regulation T

To regulate margin accounts, the Federal Reserve created **Regulation T (Reg. T)**. Reg. T states a customer must back their account with a minimum 50 percent deposit of the total value of the securities they intend to buy or sell; securities firms can demand for this deposit to be higher if they wish.

Reg. T also applies to cash accounts when customers buy securities with cash rather than on margin. When an investor buys securities with cash, there is a window of up to five days during which this investor can pay for the securities bought. To avoid investors taking advantage of this window by buying securities without having funds in their account, Reg. T requires cash buyers to hold at least 50 percent of the value of the securities in their cash accounts.

Another way to meet Reg. T is to have fully paid securities in an account, again at least 50 percent. **When a broker demands this deposit, it is referred to as a margin call**. Series 7 might ask you a question regarding Reg. T and the required deposit. Simple math will do here: investors will have to keep 50 percent, or half, of the purchase or sale amount in their margin account that they hold with their broker.

OPENING ACCOUNTS

Now that you know the basic requirements of Reg. T, you will look at how to open long and short margin accounts for your customers. As you may imagine, the Reg. T is not the only rule you must comply with; this book will cover the exchange rules associated with each account.

To limit risks involved in margin accounts, FINRA and NYSE require at least a $2,000 balance in all margin accounts whether the customer is buying $50 worth of securities or $4,000.

EXAMPLE

John Brown wants to buy $3,000 worth of ABC stock and he is opening a margin account. According to Reg. T, he would have to deposit 50 percent of the purchase price, in this case $1,500. FINRA and NYSE require a deposit of $2,000, which is greater. He would have to make an initial deposit of $2,000 to create a margin account.

TIP #96

Series 7 will phrase questions regarding this margin requirement with "X customer is opening a margin account," or with "initial margin account transaction." This is when you know you will be expected to know and apply these minimum requirements.

EQUITY AND MARGIN ACCOUNTS

The objective to opening a margin account is to profit, or gain equity, from buying or selling securities without having to make the full investment. Series 7 wants you to understand how changes in market value affect the investor's equity and money invested.

Calculating equity for holders of margin accounts can seem complicated, but it is actually quite simple once you apply logic. The biggest mistake test takers make is to confuse short and long margin accounts. This book will look at both in this section so you will not make that mistake on testing day.

Calculating Equity for Long Margin Accounts

After opening a long margin account, the investor hopes the value of his stock will go up. If this happens, he or she will have equity. Because margin accounts include borrowed funds, equity can be complicated to calculate, and a step-by-step approach is crucial to arriving at the right answer on your Series 7 exam.

HOW TO CALCULATE **EQUITY FOR LONG MARGIN ACCOUNTS**:

Equity (EQ) = long market value (LMV) - debit balance (DR)

EXAMPLE

Mary Grey has opened a margin account to buy $5,000 of DEF stock. She has made the minimum deposit of $2,500 (meeting Reg. T and FINRA requirements) when she established this account.

A month later, her stock is trading at $5,500. To calculate her equity, you will take the long market value of $5,500 and deduct the $2,500 she owes her broker to arrive at $3,000 in equity.

Calculating Equity for Short Margin Accounts

For a short account, the calculations work differently. A holder of a short account is selling stocks he or she does not actually hold. As discussed previously, an investor gains from selling short stock on margin if this stock declines, so he or she can buy it back at a lower price. Using this logic, you can conclude an investor's equity rises as the market value of the stock declines. To understand how you might calculate equity for a short margin account, look at an example again.

HOW TO CALCULATE **EQUITY FOR SHORT MARGIN ACCOUNTS**:

EQ = purchase price – short market value (SMV) + margin call

EXAMPLE

Mark Black has opened a short margin account to sell $10,000 worth of XYZ stock. He deposited $5,000 to comply with FINRA rules.

Two months later, the XYZ stock he sold short is trading at $9,000. To calculate his equity you must first take the $10,000 he bought the securities for and deduct the short market value (SMV) then add the margin call amount of $5,000.He has $6,000 in equity.

Calculating Credit Balances for Short Margin Accounts

Short margin accounts have credit balances instead of debit balances because these accounts involve selling stocks not held. Series 7 may ask you to calculate a customer's credit balance. These numbers can feel counter-intuitive, so again look at an example.

HOW TO CALCULATE **CREDIT FOR SHORT MARGIN ACCOUNT**:

Credit (CR) = SMV + margin call

EXAMPLE

Don Williams opened a short margin account to sell $60,000 worth of DEF stock. He had to deposit $30,000 (50 percent for Reg. T). His credit balance is $60,000, plus the $30,000 he deposited, for a total of $90,000.

Credit balances change as the investor makes different short margin sales. To look how credit balances change in existing accounts, continue with the previous example of Don Williams' account.

EXAMPLE

Williams decides to sell XYZ stock worth $30,000. Using his previous credit balance of $90,000, you simply add this short sale to arrive at a new credit balance of $120,000.

TIP #97

Make sure you separate short from long margin account math. Test takers often miss questions on margin accounts because they confuse the formulas.

SPECIAL MEMORANDUM ACCOUNTS (SMAS)

Our examples of equity in long and short margin accounts all ended with a profit for the investor, which means the margin accounts increase in value. When a margin account exceeds Reg. T or FINRA requirements, the excess is called a **special memorandum account (SMA)**. SMAs work like a credit line: the investor can withdraw money from the account, reducing their equity, or simply leave the SMA.

Series 7 likes to ask you questions regarding SMA, or excess equity. Calculating SMA for long and short accounts works differently; this book will cover both in this section.

SMA and Long Margin Accounts

A long margin account gains, or creates, SMA by the increase in stock price. In this example, you can see how you might calculate excess equity in a customer scenario.

HOW TO CALCULATE **SMA**:

SMA = EQ - margin requirement

EXAMPLE

Richard Jones bought 1,000 shares of ABC stock on margin at $100 a share two months ago. The stock now trades at $120 a share.

To calculate his excess equity (SMA), you must first determine what his original debit balance was. To establish the $100,000 long margin position, he had to deposit $50,000 in his margin account. This makes his opening debit balance $50,000. With the increase of market value of ABC stock, he has increased his equity by $20,000 (1,000 × $20 increased stock value).

With this increased stock value, the margin account requirement has also increased; the $120,000 portfolio value needs a margin account balance of $60,000. To calculate Jones' SMA, you need to deduct this extra margin requirement from his total equity, so $70,000 (opening balance + increased equity of $20,000) - $60,000, which leaves $10,000 in SMA.

SMA and Short Margin Accounts

An investor in a short margin account gains, or creates, SMA when the stock they sold loses value. In the following example, you will follow the steps necessary to calculate SMA for short margin accounts.

EXAMPLE

Frank Troy sold 1,000 shares of XYZ stock at $50, opening a short margin account. A month later, the stock traded at $40 a share. First, you must calculate his credit balance: add the SMV of $50,000 to his EQ of $25,000 to arrive at $75,000 CR. With the changed SMV to $40,000, now you will deduct this from his CR to arrive at new EQ of $35,000. This equity makes logical sense too (in case these calculations elude you): he started with $25,000 invested, then gained $10,000 from the market change.

To calculate SMA, you need to take into consideration his margin call has lowered with the decline of XYZ stock. Reg. T would require a minimum balance of 50 percent of the new SMV of $40,000, so $20,000. His SMA is $35,000 - $20,000 = $15,000.

You applied the same formula as above (SMA = EQ - margin requirement), but note how you arrived at equity in a different way. Make sure you take all the steps like in the examples to arrive at SMA.

TIP #98

Use your scrap paper to calculate the right answer for margin accounts. Test takers who try to rush through the steps get the answers wrong; there are no shortcuts in margin math.

SMA as Buying Power

SMA can be cashed out by the investor or it can be used as leverage to buy more securities. This is referred to as **buying power**. Under Reg. T, investors would have twice the buying power of their SMA as SMA can be used to meet the 50 percent requirement of a short or long position.

Series 7 will sometimes change the Reg. T requirement, which makes this calculation a little more difficult to make. Using the following formula, you will get any questions right, regardless of the proposed Reg. T requirement.

HOW TO CALCULATE **BUYING POWER**:

Buying power = SMA ÷ Reg. T

EXAMPLE

Richard Moore has a long margin account with a market value of $30,000. His debit balance is $10,000 with equity at $20,000. His SMA is $4,000 with a Reg. T requirement of 60 percent. To calculate his buying power, you would take his SMA of $4,000, and divide it by 60 percent to arrive at $6,667.

RESTRICTIONS ON MARGIN ACCOUNTS

The markets do not always perform as investors had hoped. Margin accounts in particular expose investors to great potential losses, which is when FINRA and NYSE step in. A margin account that drops below Reg. T requirements becomes **restricted**.

Under a restricted account, investors can still make margin purchases, but must now come up with the new purchase margin requirement. Series 7 will give you questions regarding restricted accounts, expecting you to calculate by how much an account is restricted. Restriction amounts work much like SMA just in the opposite way: instead of excess equity, the investor has negative equity (or loss).

TIP #99

A quick way to remember SMA and restriction: SMA equals profit, and restriction means loss for the investor.

Calculating Restriction for Long Margin Accounts

When an investor buys stock on margin and this stock drops against expectations, the LMV is now lower. Look at the next customer scenario to see how a drop in LMV translates to restriction.

HOW TO CALCULATE **RESTRICTION FOR LONG MARGIN ACCOUNTS**:

Restriction = margin call – EQ

EXAMPLE

Tracy Brown bought 500 shares of XYZ stock at $30 a share using her margin account. XYZ stock dropped to $25 a share, which restricted her account. To calculate how much her account is restricted, you must first take debit balance of $7,500 (Reg. T's 50 percent of $15,000). You then take the new LMV of $12,500 and deduct her debit balance to arrive at $5,000 in equity.

With the reduced LMV, her Reg. T requirement is now 50 percent of $12,500, so $6,250. To calculate her restriction, deduct equity from her margin requirement to arrive at $1,250.

Another way to arrive at a long margin account's restriction is to divide the total losses since purchase by Reg. T's requirement. For the above example, her stock purchase resulted in a loss of $2,500, which she will have to leverage by 50 percent to meet margin account requirements.

Calculating Restriction for Short Margin Accounts

You will use the same formula to calculate restriction for short margin account: restriction = margin call - EQ. To arrive at equity for short margin accounts, you use a different method (as shown earlier in this chapter). This book will use a customer scenario like you will see on Series 7 to show how you would calculate restriction for short margin accounts.

HOW TO CALCULATE **RESTRICTION FOR SHORT MARGIN ACCOUNTS**:

Restriction = margin call - EQ (same as for long margin accounts)

EXAMPLE

Chris Miller used his margin account to sell short 400 shares of ABC stock at $40 a share. ABC's market value went up to $44 a share. To calculate Miller's margin account restriction, you must first calculate his credit balance by taking his original SMV of $16,000 and adding $8,000 in equity he put in to meet Reg. T requirements to arrive at $24,000 CR.

To find Miller's equity after ABC stock went up, you take his credit and deduct the new SMV of $17,600 to arrive at $6,400 in equity. The new margin requirement is $8,800; deduct his equity to arrive at a restriction of $2,400.

MINIMUM MAINTENANCE ON MARGIN ACCOUNTS

A margin account can remain restricted as long as it does not fall below minimum maintenance. A **maintenance call** is issued when a customer must deposit into their margin account right away.

Series 7 will again expect you to calculate for given scenarios; regarding maintenance, you need to know when a maintenance call is issued. You will learn how to calculate minimum maintenance for long and short margin accounts

Maintenance and Long Margin Account

Minimum maintenance for long margin accounts is 25 percent of LMV. As you have learned, LMV changes with the market, so the maintenance call will as well. Look at the following example to see how you might apply calculations to questions on your exam.

HOW TO CALCULATE **MAINTENANCE FOR LONG MARGIN ACCOUNTS**:

Maintenance call = maintenance EQ – EQ

EXAMPLE

Caroline Moore bought 1,000 shares of DEF stock at $55 a share using her margin account. DEF dropped to $35 a share. To calculate when a maintenance call is issued, you must find Moore's current equity. Her purchase price for DEF stock was $55,000, which makes her initial equity and debit value $27,500.

Her current equity is $35,000 (the new LMV) minus her debit value, so $7,500. She should have 25 percent of $35,000 in her margin account, equaling $8,750. Because she has only $7,500 equity, she must add $1,250 to meet the maintenance call.

Maintenance and Short Margin Accounts

The minimum maintenance for short margin accounts is 30 percent of SMV. To calculate maintenance calls on short margin accounts, you will build off previous formulas, just like what you just did for long margin accounts. Again, look at an example to see the steps needed to calculate margin calls for short accounts.

HOW TO CALCULATE **MAINTENANCE FOR SHORT MARGIN ACCOUNTS**:

Maintenance call = maintenance EQ - EQ
(same as for long margin accounts)

EXAMPLE

Janice Adams sold 1,000 shares of ABC stock at $50 a share from her margin account. ABC stock gained to $60 a share. To calculate the maintenance call on her account, you must first find her CR: $50,000 plus her $25,000 Reg. T deposit, so $75,000. Her new SMV is $60,000, making her equity $15,000 ($75,000 - $60,000).

She should have 30 percent of $60,000 in her margin account, which is $18,000. She has equity of $15,000, which puts her maintenance call at $3,000 ($15,000 – $18,000).

TIP #100

Calculating restriction and maintenance is done the same way for both long and short margin accounts.

As you have noticed, you must know many formulas to answer Series 7 questions on margin accounts. Remember that all of these formulas build off each other; as long as you do not rush, you will reach the right answer.

MARGIN ACCOUNTS AND YOUR CLIENT

Investing by use of margin account is only suitable for the most risk-tolerant and knowledgeable investor. If your client expresses interest in margins, make sure you fully explain the risks involved.

The ideal client for margin investing is someone who, independent from your advice as a registered representative, keeps current on the market and the stocks he or she is speculating on. Losses in margin investing can be unlimited, far beyond a client's principal investment, particularly when selling short. Before venturing into margin investing for your client, make sure you both sit down for a thorough portfolio and risk analysis.

CHECKLIST

- ☐ I understand what a long and short margin account is
- ☐ I know Reg. T requirements
- ☐ I know what a margin call is
- ☐ I know FINRA and NYSE requirements
- ☐ I can calculate equity for long and short margin accounts
- ☐ I can calculate credit balances for short margin accounts
- ☐ I can calculate SMA for long and short margin accounts
- ☐ I understand buying power and how to calculate it
- ☐ I know how to calculate restriction for long and short margin accounts
- ☐ I know minimum maintenance levels for long and short accounts and how to calculate them

SAMPLE QUESTIONS

1. Tom Patterson is opening a margin account. According to Reg. T, he must deposit at least:

   [A] $2,000
   [B] 50 percent of the purchase or sale price of the securities
   [C] $1,000
   [D] 60 percent of the purchase or sale price of the securities

2. Barry Jones has bought $50,000 of ABC stock using a long margin account. What is his equity?

   [A] $75,000
   [B] $50,000
   [C] $25,000
   [D] $30,000

3. Jerry Brown has opened a short margin account and wants to sell $100,000 of DEF stock. What is his credit balance?

   [A] $50,000
   [B] $75,000
   [C] $100,000
   [D] $150,000

4. Dave Williams bought 500 shares of XYZ shares on margin at $100 a share. Six months later, XYZ shares trade at $110 a share. What is his SMA?

   [A] $2,500
   [B] $5,000
   [C] $10,000
   [D] $30,000

5. Linda Franklin sold $100,000 of ABC stock on margin. This stock trades at $80,000 three months later. What is her equity?

   [A] $20,000
   [B] $60,000
   [C] $70,000
   [D] $80,000

6. Gary Zimmerman has a long margin account, which has a market value of $50,000. His debit balance is $20,000; his SMA $5,000. What is his buying power?

    [A] $5,000
    [B] $10,000
    [C] $2,500
    [D] $20,000

7. Mary Truman has a short margin account and sold 1,000 shares of DEF stock at $50 a share. DEF now trades at $60 a share. What is her margin restriction?

    [A] $5,000
    [B] $10,000
    [C] $15,000
    [D] $20,000

8. Jacob Carter bought 800 shares of ABC stock at $20 a share using his margin account. ABC stock trades at $10 a share now. What is his maintenance call?

    [A] $2,000
    [B] $4,000
    [C] $8,000
    [D] $10,000

CHAPTER 15
You Passed! Now What?

If you have flipped to these pages after passing your Series 7 exam: Congratulations! Take a moment to pat yourself on the back, celebrate, and thank your family and friends for supporting you while you spent all your free time studying. If you are still studying but anxious to start your career off right, this is a chapter to read closely. Whether you have already passed your exam or are still spending your days studying, you know the hard work is only beginning after passing the test.

You will have to begin acquiring clients, applying what you have learned to real customers, and keeping up with industry news and regulations. The job of a registered representative can be particularly challenging during the first year — which is why this book has added this chapter. This chapter will give you insider tips to make the learning curve a little less steep.

BUILDING YOUR CLIENT BASE

You have covered the cold calling rules for your exam, and you know how to create a customer profile. Now all you need is a customer to profile, which means you will have to pick up the phone and make those dreaded cold calls.

Successful Cold Calling

There is no way around it: you will have to make calls to strangers, or cold calls, to land clients. In your early years as a registered representative, you may be making a few hundred calls a day, only to sign one client every few days. Until you build a client base, this will be your daily task.

The trick to successful cold calling is simply to make a lot of calls. In the beginning, you will still be honing your sales pitch, and it may take some time to get comfortable with the process. By making a lot of calls, you will get practiced in the selling process — and each unsuccessful call will get you closer to the one that lands you a new client.

During these hours on the phone, remember to smile. You will land a new client by making a connection so treat every call with care, remembering that this person on the line may be your next loyal customer. Try to sound friendly, knowledgeable, and not too pushy in that first contact.

If you find these massive cold calls challenging, consider teaming up with another new registered representative. You can cheer each other on, or perhaps bring out the competitive salesperson in each of you. Those hours on the phone can feel lonely at times — find a colleague to keep your spirits up.

Cold calling is often assumed to be a talent, something that comes naturally to some, but not others; this is not the case. Cold calling requires knowledge of the process, just like any other business skill. Look for profiles of cold calling experts in the case studies section and learn from their experience. If you have a mentor available at your firm, ask to listen in on a few phone calls, for cold and warm leads. Watch your mentor's body language, facial expressions, and

listen to how he or she approaches the (prospective) client. The best way to learn is to watch an experienced and successful cold caller in action.

Honing Your Customer Service Skills

As a registered representative, your income will be based on sales. It can be difficult not to get too focused on the numbers and remember the people: your clients. With your client portfolio, keep notes of your client's personal information, like hobbies that emerge during a conversation or favorite vacation spots. Make periodic follow-up calls, especially when the market is down. Your client will feel reassured knowing you are on the job, even when the numbers are not where your client would like them to be.

TIP #101

The most successful and highest-earning sales people know that the secret to success is to take care of your clients. "Know your client," like you learned while studying how to create a customer profile for your Series 7 exam.

It can be tempting to treat your wealthiest client as a king and put the smaller-earning investors on the back burner. Do not make the mistake of dismissing "smaller" clients; often, their situation changes and that client's earnings increase. Sometimes these small investors refer you to their wealthier friend — as long as you do a good job and treat them like you would a "big" client. Treat all your clients as if they are your biggest investor and you will keep them for life.

Setting Goals

After passing your exam, it can be easy to get overwhelmed by the daily challenges your job as a registered representative presents. Between building a new client base, mastering cold calling skills, and setting up your office, you will probably not think too much about what your goals are.

Setting goals is a very important part of a successful career as a registered representative. Ideally, before you even pick up the phone to land that first client, you should first sit down and really think about what you wish to achieve in your career. Where do you want to be in three months, six months, a year, or even five or ten years? Do not be afraid to aim high, but be realistic in what you can achieve. Now ask yourself: what do I need to do to achieve these goals?

Write these goals and objectives down somewhere and reference them every month to chart your progress. Are there any things you did that were particularly fruitful, or not successful? Taking inventory of your goals and accomplishments will ensure you maintain focus, and use your time more efficiently. Discuss your goals with mentors to see if they have any input on how you can achieve them.

KEEPING UP

Your first instinct after passing your Series 7 exam is to immediately let all the knowledge you gained sink to the recesses of your brain. Series 7 would not test you on all these subjects unless you needed them, so keep your study material nearby for reference. You may want to skim the pages periodically as you build your client list to keep your knowledge on securities fresh.

Another way to keep up with industry news is to watch financial investing programs on television or read trade magazines and newspapers like the *Wall Street Journal*. Keeping up with industry news every day is an important part of your job.

Continuing Education

In 1995, FINRA (then NASD) approved **Rule 1120**, specifying requirements for continuing education for securities industry professionals. In order to keep your Series 7 license active, you must complete a computer-based training program within 120 days of your two-year anniversary as a registered representative. After this, you will need to repeat this training every three years. You will need to schedule these exams and pay a fee to take them; check the FINRA Web site when you get close to these dates to get details on current fees and scheduling procedures.

You may also consider increasing your financial skills and experience by obtaining other licenses like the Series 63, 65, or 66. The Series 66, for instance, will qualify you as an investment adviser representative and securities agent. This will allow you to offer investment advice to clients, which could give you an edge over the competition.

FINRA offers many continuing education classes, seminars, and an annual conference, so consider these as a way to keep current on your industry. Universities are also a good place to find finance-related classes; look for your local university course listing, or for online universities for more flexibility. You should also consider taking classes on tax preparation as these will give you more insight on how the IRS treats investments and their earnings. Consider education part of your job as a registered representative; you will be more successful for it.

CHAPTER 16
Conclusion

You may be reading this chapter before or after taking your Series 7 exam. Either way, I hope you found *101 Ways to Score Higher on Your Series 7 Exam* to be a valuable resource during your studies and that it helped you pass the exam and receive your Series 7 license.

This book is intended to be a straightforward guide to prepare you for your Series 7 exam, but it can also assist you in the days beyond the test. You may find it useful to keep it nearby for those times when you want a refresher on municipal bonds or when you need to calculate per-capita debt but can't remember the formula. Moreover, the case studies can provide that bit of expert advice when you are tired of cold calls or simply don't know how to manage the next challenge. The resources in the back will always send you to the right place for those hard-to-answer securities questions.

As a registered representative, you will now be introduced to the exciting, dynamic, and challenging world of finance. I wish you the best of luck in your new career.

APPENDIX A
Formulas

Making calculations is a large component of the Series 7 exam. Without a solid comprehension of the math, you simply will not pass the test.

Before you continue with the full practice exam, I encourage you to go over Chapter 7 on derivatives or options, as well as Chapter 14 on margin accounts. These chapters show you how to solve math problems step-by-step by logically looking at what is happening in each scenario.

To answer math questions, you will have to memorize at least some of the formulas in this book. In order to make your studying time more efficient, all the formulas are gathered here in one easily referenced appendix. A smart way to study these is to write the formulas on index cards and carry them with you for those short bites of studying time throughout the day.

SYNDICATE FORMULAS

HOW TO CALCULATE **THE SYNDICATE'S SPREAD**:

Spread = public offering price – price paid to issuer ($12 - $10 = $2)

HOW TO CALCULATE **THE SYNDICATE'S TAKEDOWN**:

Takedown = spread – management fee ($2 - $.20 = $1.80)

HOW TO CALCULATE **ADDITIONAL TAKEDOWN**:

Additional takedown = takedown – concession ($1.80 - $.50 = $1.30)

STOCK FORMULAS

HOW TO CALCULATE **ISSUED STOCK**:

Issued stock = treasury stock + outstanding stock

HOW TO CALCULATE **THE VALUE OF A RIGHT**:

Value of a right = (market price – subscription price) ÷ (number of rights to purchase one share +1)

BOND FORMULAS

HOW TO CALCULATE **CURRENT YIELD**:

Current yield = annual interest ÷ market price

HOW TO CALCULATE **CONVERSION RATIOS**:

Conversion ratio = par value ÷ conversion price

MUNICIPAL DEBT FORMULAS

HOW TO CALCULATE **PER-CAPITA DEBT**:

Per capita debt = (net. direct debt + overlapping debt) ÷ municipality population

HOW TO CALCULATE **DEBT SERVICE COVERAGE RATIO**:

Debt service coverage ratio: (net revenue ÷ principal) + interest

HOW TO CALCULATE **ACCRUED INTEREST**:

Accrued interest = principal × rate × time

PACKAGED SECURITIES FORMULAS

HOW TO CALCULATE **AVERAGE COST PER SHARE**:

Average cost per share = total dollars invested ÷ shares bought

HOW TO CALCULATE **SALES CHARGE**:

Net asset value (NAV): value of fund's assets ÷ outstanding Shares

Public offering price (POP): net asset value + broker's commission

Sales charge (percent): POP – (NAV ÷ POP)

OPTIONS FORMULAS

HOW TO CALCULATE **TIME VALUE**:

Time value = premium – intrinsic value

HOW TO CALCULATE **THE BREAK-EVEN POINT FOR BUYING A CALL**:

Break-even point = strike price + premium

HOW TO CALCULATE **THE BREAK-EVEN POINT FOR SELLING A CALL**:

Break-even point = strike price – premium

HOW TO CALCULATE **THE BREAK-EVEN POINT FOR BUYING A PUT**:

Break-even point = strike price – premium

HOW TO CALCULATE **BREAK-EVEN FOR SELLING A PUT**:

Break-even = strike price – premium

SECURITIES ANALYSIS FORMULAS

HOW TO CALCULATE **NET WORKING CAPITAL**:

Net working capital = asset – liabilities

(also known as net worth, or stockholders' equity)

LIQUIDITY RATIO FORMULAS

- Current ratio: current assets/current liabilities
- Quick asset ratio: (current assets-inventory)/current liabilities
- Acid test ratio: (cash + marketable securities)/current liabilities

CAPITALIZATION RATIO FORMULAS:

- Long-term capital = long-term liabilities + stockholders' equity
- Bond ratio = bonds par value/long-term capital
- Debt-to-equity ratio = (bonds + preferred stock)/equity

PROFITABILITY RATIO FORMULAS:

Operating profit margin = operating income/net sales

- Net profit ratio = net income/net sales

ASSET COVERAGE RATIO FORMULAS:

- Net asset value per bond = net worth/bonds shares outstanding
- Bond interest coverage = EBT/bond shares outstanding
- Book value per share = (assets - liabilities)/bond shares outstanding

EARNINGS PER SHARE FORMULAS:

- Earnings per common share (EPS) = (net worth - preferred stock)/common shares outstanding (if convertible bonds are included, this is fully diluted EPS)
- Price-earnings ratio (P/E) = market price/earnings per share
- Dividend payout ratio: common dividend/earnings per share

CAPT PRINCIPAL FORMULA:

r = rf + B

r = return of stock

rf = risk-free rate of T-Bills

B = Beta value of stock

MARGIN FORMULAS

HOW TO CALCULATE **EQUITY FOR LONG MARGIN ACCOUNTS**:

Equity (EQ) = long market value (LMV) - debit balance (DR)

HOW TO CALCULATE **EQUITY FOR SHORT MARGIN ACCOUNTS**:

EQ = purchase price – SMV + margin call

HOW TO CALCULATE **CREDIT FOR SHORT MARGIN ACCOUNTS**:

Credit (CR) = SMV + margin call

HOW TO CALCULATE **SMA**:

SMA = EQ - margin requirement

HOW TO CALCULATE **BUYING POWER**:

Buying power = SMA ÷ Reg. T

HOW TO CALCULATE **RESTRICTION FOR LONG MARGIN ACCOUNTS**:

Restriction = margin call – EQ

HOW TO CALCULATE **RESTRICTION FOR SHORT MARGIN ACCOUNTS**:

Restriction = margin call – EQ (same as for long margin accounts)

HOW TO CALCULATE **MAINTENANCE FOR LONG MARGIN ACCOUNTS**:

Maintenance call = maintenance EQ – EQ

HOW TO CALCULATE **MAINTENANCE FOR SHORT MARGIN ACCOUNTS**:

Maintenance call = maintenance EQ – EQ

(same as for long margin accounts)

APPENDIX B
Sample Questions Answer Key

CHAPTER 2

1. **A**
2. **D** – in this Eastern Account, he will have to sell 1/20 of 20,000 remaining shares, so 1,000 shares to fulfill his commitment to the syndicate.
3. **B** – Price paid to issuer ($100) + spread ($20) = $120. The management fee comes out of the spread, and does not factor into this calculation.
4. **D** – Treasury Stocks are shares not sold to the public
5. **B** – Cumulative voting rights allow holders to spread votes any way they please. She holds 4,000 rights.
6. **C** – The split leaves him with 2×100= 200 shares, with stock valued at $10 as a result of the split.
7. **B** – The 15 percent dividend has devalued the stock by 15 percent × $30= $4.50, so $30-$4.50+$25.50.
8. **D**
9. **C**

CHAPTER 3

1. **C**
2. **D**
3. **C**
4. **A**
5. **D** – Current yield=annual interest/ market price, so $60÷1200 = 0.05 (5 percent)
6. **B**
7. **A**
8. **D** – PAC Tranches give a certain amortization rate and carry the least amount of risk
9. **A**
10. **D**

CHAPTER 4

1. **C**
2. **B**
3. **C** – Divide the $2,000,000 (municipal + overlapping debt) by the 500,000 people in the municipality to compute the per capita debt

4. **A**
5. **B** – Divide the net. revenue of $500,000 by principal + interest (500,000+250,000)
6. **A**
7. **D**
8. **C**
9. **B**
10. **A** –The total cost of interest on the bonds is $60,000, times three years, for a total of $180,000

CHAPTER 5

1. **C**
2. **A**
3. **D**
4. **C** – To reach this answer, use the following steps:
    1. Divide for each month the $50 invested by the price per share to find out how many shares he bought, per month
    2. Add the total shares bought (this will equal 18.72)
    3. Divide $200 (the total amount he has invested) by those total shares to arrive at an average cost per share of $10.68
5. **C** – Price per share is $4, so the broker's commission is $0.30/$4.30 = 0.07, or 7 percent
6. **D**
7. **B**
8. **D**

CHAPTER 6

1. **D**
2. **B**
3. **A**
4. **B**

CHAPTER 7

1. **A**
2. **C**
3. **D**
4. **D**
5. **B**
6. **C**
7. **C**
8. **A**
9. **B** – Calculate this by taking the cost of the purchase of the shares (-$40,000), adding the gain from the call premium sold (+$600), and then adding the gains from the sale of the stock (+$42,500). You then deduct the premium paid for the call option ($500), to arrive at a gain of $2,600.
10. **C**
11. **A**
12. **C**
13. **B**

CHAPTER 8

1. **D**
2. **B**
3. **C**
4. **A** – His annual interest income is $60. His annual accretion on this bond is $300÷10 years = $30. This makes for a total annual income of $60 + $30=$90
5. **D** – He receives $100 annually in interest. His $200 premium, amortized over 10 years, gives him a $20 deduction, for an annual income of $100 - $20 = $80
6. **A**
7. **D**

CHAPTER 9

1. **B**
2. **D**
3. **C**
4. **B**
5. **A**
6. **D**
7. **B**
8. **B**
9. **D**
10. **D**

CHAPTER 10

1. **C**
2. **A**
3. **C**
4. **B**
5. **B**
6. **D**

CHAPTER 11

1. **C**
2. **B**
3. **A** – using FIFO, 150 engines were bought at $250 ($37,500), and 50 engines at $225 ($11,250), for a total of 200 engines valued at $37,500 + $11,250 = $48,750
4. **C**
5. **B**
6. **A**
7. **C**
8. **D**
9. **B**
10. **A**

CHAPTER 12

1. **D**
2. **C**
3. **A**
4. **D**
5. **B**

CHAPTER 13

1. **D**
2. **A**
3. **B**
4. **B**
5. **D**
6. **C**
7. **A**
8. **D**

CHAPTER 14

1. **B**
2. **C** – EQ= LMV– DR: $50,000 - $25,000 = $25,000
3. **D** – CR= SMV – margin call: $150,000= $100,000 - $50,000
4. **A** – SMA= EQ – margin requirement: his equity increased from $25,000 to $30,000. Reduce this by the new $27,500 margin requirement for an SMA of $2,500
5. **C** – EQ = Purchase Price – SMV + margin call: $100,000 - $80,000 + $50,000
6. **B** – Assuming a Reg. T requirement of 50 percent, $5,000÷50 percent= $10,000
7. **C** – Her credit balance is $75,000 (SMV + Reg. T). EQ= $75,000-$60,000= $15,000. the margin call is $30,000; $30,000-$15,000= $15,000
8. **A** – His initial equity was $8,000 (50 percent of $16,000). $8,000 (new LMV) - $8,000=0. He needs 25 percent of the LMV to meet the minimum, so $2,000.

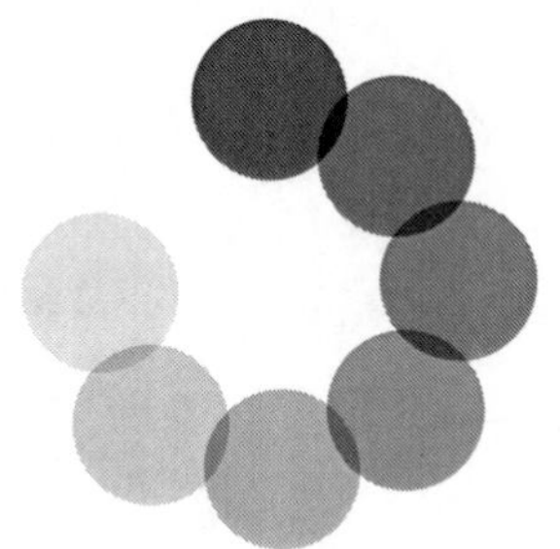

APPENDIX C
Full Series 7 Practice Test

If you have reached this portion, first pat yourself on the back for the studying you have done. The Series 7 material, as you know, is very complex and requires dedication to master.

In this section, you will be able to see if you are truly ready for your Series 7 exam. Appendix C is set up to represent the questions and format you will see on your real testing day. There are two parts, each including 130 questions, just like a Series 7 exam.

To best use this full practice test to see if you are ready, make sure you do the following:

- ☐ **Make sure you have studied the material.** You would not go into your real test unprepared, so do not take this mock exam half-hearted. Taking this exam will give you a chance to see what your score might be on exam day.
- ☐ **Schedule this test just like you scheduled your real Series 7 exam.** You should count on taking seven hours to complete this exam: three hours for each of the two 130-question sections, plus roughly an hour-long break in between. Use this mock test to get an idea of

the physical challenges (like hunger and mental and physical fatigue) your Series 7 exam will impose so you will be prepared.

- ☐ **Be strict with your timing.** The exam officials will not give you an extra minute just to finish up that one question you were not so sure about, so do not allow yourself any extra time when taking the practice exam either.
- ☐ **Supply yourself with a calculator, six sheets of scrap paper, and a pencil.** This is all you will receive on exam day. For this mock exam, give yourself the same limitations.
- ☐ **Resist the urge to take a peek inside this book, or inside your notebook.** You will not be able to during your exam.

This practice exam is a great opportunity to test your knowledge before you sit down for your actual exam. Use the answer key in Appendix C to check your answers with the corresponding chapter and section where each subject is covered and see what subjects you may need to review once more. Good luck!

PRACTICE TEST: PART I

1. At XYZ Corporation, three board of directors positions are up for election. John Miller holds 1,000 shares of common stock. If voting is cumulative, which of the following is/are ways for him to vote?

   I. 1,000 votes to one candidate
   II. 3,000 votes to one candidate
   III. 1,000 votes for each of the three candidates
   IV. 3,000 votes for each of the three candidates

   [A] I, II, and IV only
   [B] II, III, and IV only
   [C] I, II, and III only
   [D] All of the above

2. **Which of the following describes the purpose of Rule 145?**

    [A] Rule 145 limits the commission a broker can charge on a transaction

    [B] Rule 145 states a registered representative must "know the customer"

    [C] Rule 145 requires a 50 percent deposit into margin accounts

    [D] Rule 145 regulates cold calling

3. **Which of the following is true about the par value of common stock?**

    [A] It is the book value a corporation is using

    [B] It represents the value of stock, should the company go bankrupt and have to liquidate its assets to repay investors

    [C] It is the dollar value investors receive should they redeem their shares

    [D] It is the market value of the common stock

4. **Which of the following option investors will receive the dividend if the option is exercised prior to the ex-dividend date?**

    I. **The holder of a call option**
    II. **The holder of a put option**
    III. **The writer of a call option**
    IV. **The writer of a put option**

    [A] I and II

    [B] III and IV

    [C] I and IV

    [D] II and III

5. **In a technical analysis of the market, you find a head and shoulders formation. Which of the following best describes the market?**

    [A] There is a reversal of a bearish trend

    [B] There is a reversal of a bullish trend

    [C] The market is bearish

    [D] The market is bullish

6. Which of the following best describes the objective of dollar cost averaging for mutual fund investors?

    [A] Keeping a fixed total dollar amount invested in mutual funds
    [B] Regularly investing a set dollar amount into a mutual fund
    [C] Buying a fixed number of shares periodically
    [D] None of the above

7. Which of the following is true about ADRs?

    I. The investor does not receive a certificate
    II. The investors will not receive dividend in cash
    III. The share certificates are held by a custodian bank
    IV. They are receipts for U.S. securities that trade in foreign countries

    [A] I and III
    [B] I, II, and IV
    [C] I, III, and IV
    [D] All of the above

8. Which of the following is not a money market instrument?

    [A] ADRs
    [B] CDs
    [C] T-Bills
    [D] Repos

9. Jack Henderson has just opened a margin account. He buys 1,000 shares of DEF stock at $20 a share using his margin account with a Reg. T requirement of 55 percent. What is the loan value?

    [A] $2,000
    [B] $9,000
    [C] $10,000
    [D] $11,000

10. Which of the following statement(s) about variable annuities is true?

    I. The payout to investors depends on the market value of the underlying securities
    II. An investor can claim deductions for the current year, as long as he or she deposits money into the account again the following year
    III. The interest rate always outperforms the S&P 500

IV. An investor should choose life with period certain for the best returns

[A] I
[B] I, II, and III
[C] IV
[D] None of the above

11. XYZ Corporation issues 10,000 shares of 8 percent preferred stock at $100 par value. As a result of this, which of the following will increase?

I. Current assets
II. Quick assets
III. Net worth
IV. Total liabilities

[A] I and III
[B] I and II
[C] I, II, and III
[D] All of the above

12. Which of the following is not considered a leading economic indicator?

[A] M1
[B] Unemployment numbers
[C] Building permits
[D] Industrial production

13. Which of the following is regulated under the Trust Indenture Act of 1939?

[A] Debentures
[B] T-bonds
[C] GO bonds
[D] Revenue bonds

14. Which of the following is true about open-ended investments, but not about closed-ended investments?

I. Investors can redeem their shares
II. The issuer can only issue common stock
III. The purchase price is NAV and a commission
IV. New shares continue to be issued

[A] I and II
[B] I and III

[C] I, II, and IV
[D] II, III, and IV

15. Which of the following is not a reason investors write covered calls?

[A] To hedge a stock position
[B] To increase the yield on his portfolio
[C] To profit from a drop in market value of the underlying security
[D] A and B

16. According to cold-calling rules, which of the following must the caller comply with?

I. Calls must be made between 8 a.m. and 9 p.m. (customer's time zone)
II. Calls must be made between 8 a.m. and 9 p.m. (caller's time zone)
III. The caller has to give his name and firm's name
IV. The caller has to give his firm's telephone number or address

[A] I and III
[B] I, III, and IV
[C] II and III
[D] II, III, and IV

17. George Williams holds the following option positions:

Short 1 ABC Oct 50 call at 3
Write 1 ABC Oct 45 put at 4
He has created a:

[A] Debit spread
[B] Credit spread
[C] Short combination
[D] Short straddle

18. DEF stock is trading at $54. Which of the following options are trading in-the-money?

I. DEF Apr 50 calls
II. DEF Apr 50 puts
III. DEF Apr 60 calls
IV. DEF Apr 60 puts

[A] I and II

[B] III and IV
[C] II and III
[D] I and IV

19. Which of the following securities give its holders ownership of a corporation?

    I. Mortgage bondholders
    II. Convertible bondholders
    III. Preferred stockholders
    IV. Warrant holders

    [A] I and II
    [B] I, II, and IV
    [C] III only
    [D] III and IV

20. Dawn Miller bought $75,000 of DEF stock, using her long margin account. What is her equity?

    [A] $150,000
    [B] $75,000
    [C] $50,000
    [D] $37,500

21. William Smith submits an order to buy 100 shares of DEF stock at 40 stop limit. The ticker of DEF stock reads as follows: 39.75, 40, 40.25, SLD 40, 39.88, 40. When was the order triggered?

    [A] 39.75
    [B] 40
    [C] 40.25
    [D] The order was not triggered at all

22. Which of the following is true about FINRA's 5 percent policy?

    I. The type of security does not matter when it comes to the policy
    II. No-risk transactions are not subject to this policy
    III. Securities sold with a prospectus are exempt from the policy
    IV. The policy is used as a guideline for open-ended security sales

    [A] III only
    [B] I, II, and III

[C] II and IV

[D] I, III, and IV

23. Richard Smith has decided to change brokers and sent you his request form with all the required information. Which of the following statements is true regarding this account transfer?

[A] You must validate the information and execute the transfer in one business day

[B] You have two business days to validate the information, and two business days to transfer the funds to the new broker

[C] You have three business days to validate the information, and three business days to execute the transfer

[D] You can dispute the request through the SEC

24. Henry Jones has purchased an XYZ 8 percent callable bond at 80. The bond matures in ten years. How much does he have to claim on his taxes every year?

[A] $8

[B] $80

[C] $90

[D] $100

25. The Federal Reserve Board controls the money supply by

I. Changing the discount rate
II. Changing the prime rate
III. Engaging in open-market operations
IV. Changing the reserve requirements

[A] I and II

[B] I, III, and IV

[C] All of the above

[D] None of the above

26. Which of the following investments receives interest that is not taxable on a state level?

I. Revenue bonds issued to build toll booths
II. Treasury bonds
III. Bonds issued by the Commonwealth of Puerto Rico
IV. GNMAs

[A] I, II, and III
[B] II and III
[C] II, III, and IV
[D] I, II, and IV

27. You are opening a new account for your customer. Which of the following information do you need to create a customer portfolio?

I. The customer's date of birth
II. The customer's investment objectives
III. The customer's risk tolerance

[A] I and II
[B] I and III
[C] II and III
[D] I, II, and III

28. Who issues and guarantees all listed options?

[A] The OCC
[B] The OAA
[C] The NYSE
[D] The CBOE

29. Which of the following organizations approves OTC stock for margin accounts?

[A] The FRB
[B] FINRA
[C] Any of the exchanges
[D] The state securities commissioner

30. Which of the following does not change the strike price of an option?

[A] A 2-for-1 stock split
[B] A 3-for-1 stock split
[C] A 10 percent stock dividend
[D] A $0.60 dividend

31. ABC Corporation's common stock has a current market price of $60 a share, and the earnings per common shares are $6. ABC Corporation announces a 2-for-1 stock split. Which of the following is true after this split?

    I. The PE ratio is 10
    II. The PE ratio is 5
    III. The EPS remains $6
    IV. The EPS becomes $3

    [A] I and III
    [B] I and IV
    [C] II and III
    [D] II and IV

32. Frank Moore and Jill Truman are part of an oil and gas limited partnership. Which of the following is not an IRS allowed tax deduction for the partnership?

    [A] Principal expenses on a loan
    [B] Interest expenses on a loan
    [C] Depletion
    [D] Depreciation

33. Which of the following two investments do not trade in the secondary market?

    I. Fed Funds
    II. Repurchase agreements
    III. ADRs
    IV. Banker's acceptance

    [A] I and III
    [B] II and IV
    [C] I and II
    [D] III and IV

34. Tom Smith bought 4 XYZ Dec 60 puts for 3 a piece and 400 shares of XYZ stock at $65 a share. Nine months later, XYZ stock trades at $67 a share. He wants to know at what market price per share of XYZ stock he would break even, excluding commission. As his registered representative, what would be your answer?

    [A] $57
    [B] $62

[C] $63
[D] $68

35. Greg Miller heard the Fed is about to announce a very large sale of T-bills. If he wants to profit from this impending Fed sale, what should he do?

I. Buy T-bond yield calls
II. Buy T-bond yield puts
III. Buy T-bond calls
IV. Buy T-bond puts

[A] I and III
[B] I and IV
[C] II and III
[D] II and IV

36. You have just acquired John Henderson as a client, who has an existing portfolio with high liquidity. He has another $30,000 to invest and wants to keep his portfolio liquid, as he is expecting to invest in a business soon. Which of the following investments would you be least likely to recommend?

[A] A long-term bond fund
[B] An oil and gas limited partnership
[C] Blue chip stocks
[D] Zero Coupon bonds

37. Which of these statements about the UGMA are not true?

I. The donor cannot also be the custodian on the account
II. All purchases for the account must be done via a margin account
III. If the account contains stocks with rights, those must be exercised
IV. The custodian must pay all the taxes due on the account

[A] I and III
[B] I, III, and IV
[C] II and III
[D] All of the above

38. Which of the following best describes the reason an investor would write a covered call option?

[A] To increase the return on his investment
[B] To protect against loss in a bear market

[C] To be able to buy shares at a discount, should the market increase
[D] To help lock in market profit on his securities

39. Karen Smith thinks interest rates are going to decrease over the next ten years and wishes to profit from this expected market movement. She asks you, her registered representative, for investment advice. Which of the following bonds are appropriate recommendations?

I. Adjustable rate bonds with ten years to maturity
II. Ten-year, non-callable bonds
III. Bonds maturing at 15 years, but callable at ten
IV. 15-year put bonds, with the option to sell the bonds to the issuer at five years

[A] I and III
[B] II and IV
[C] I, III, and IV
[D] II, III, and IV

40. Your client Barry Miller wants to invest in a DPP for the first time. Knowing the characteristics of the investment, which of the following would you discuss with him?

I. The goals particular to the DPP he wants to invest in
II. The general manager of the DPP and his experience
III. The expected timeframe until the DPP will become profitable
IV. The need for liquidity in his other investments, given the time commitment a DPP requires

[A] I and II
[B] I, II, and IV
[C] I, III, and IV
[D] All of the above

41. Frank Brown is a new customer who wants to invest in mutual funds. When discussing mutual funds with him, you will inform him that the most important thing to consider when deciding between different funds is the fund's

[A] Sales Charge
[B] Investment objectives
[C] Management fees
[D] Redemption fees

42. Which of the statements is true about municipal GO bonds?

    I. GO bonds are issued by the federal government and earnings are federally tax-free
    II. Municipal GO bonds are exempt from SEC registration
    III. GO bonds are issued to fund revenue producing facilities
    IV. GO bonds are largely backed by property taxes

    [A] II and IV
    [B] I, II, and III
    [C] I, II, and IV
    [D] All of the above

43. Chris Williams bought 100 shares of DEF stock at $100 a share. He sold 1 DEF Dec 110 call at 5. He held this position for six months before selling his stock at 109. He closed the DEF Dec 110 call at 4. What is his gain or loss?

    [A] $200
    [B] $800
    [C] $1,000
    [D] $1,200

44. Warren Smith is an accountant, earning $80,000 a year, with no available retirement plan through his employer. He contributes the maximum $5,000 a year to a traditional IRA. How do his IRA contributions affect his taxes?

    [A] His IRA contributions are fully tax-deductable
    [B] His IRA contributions are only partially tax-deductible
    [C] His IRA contributions are not tax-deductable
    [D] His income is too high to allow him to deduct his contributions

45. Troy Brown wants to open a cash account at your firm. He wants to give his sister, Mary Brown, trading authorization. Which of the following is required before you can open the account?

    I. A new account form
    II. A partnership agreement
    III. A limited power of attorney
    IV. A joint account agreement

    [A] I and III
    [B] I, II, and IV

[C] I, III, and IV
[D] All of the above

46. Gary Jones has a margin account with a market value of $30,000 and a debit balance of $12,000. What is his buying power?

[A] $0
[B] $3,000
[C] $6,000
[D] $18,000

47. You have just acquired Norman Miller as a new client. He is 60 years old and you are creating a strategic portfolio asset allocation. Which of the following is the best allocation, without knowing any more about his financial and personal situation?

[A] Allocating 40 percent in stock and 60 percent in bonds
[B] Allocating 60 percent in stock and 40 percent in bonds
[C] Investing 30 percent in bonds, 30 percent in stock, and 40 percent in cash investments
[D] Investing 60 percent in bonds and 40 percent in cash investments

48. Caroline White is a 68-year-old client of yours who you have determined wishes to take a defensive strategy in her portfolio. Which of the following are suitable investments for this client?

I. Blue chip stocks
II. AAA-rated bonds
III. High-yield corporate bonds
IV. Call options

[A] I and II
[B] I and III
[C] II, III, and IV
[D] I, II, and IV

49. Harry Jones has a margin account with a current market value of $27,000 and a debit balance of $15,000. Which of the following statements about his account is true?

I. His account is currently restricted
II. The account has an SMA of $1,500

III. He will receive a margin call for $1,500
IV. He will receive a margin call for $3,000

[A] I, III, and IV
[B] II only
[C] I and III
[D] I and IV

50. The resistance level is

[A] The upper trading level of a security
[B] The lower trading level of a security
[C] The average trading price of a security
[D] None of the above

51. A technical market analyst is looking at the S&P 500 and notices the number of stocks that are increasing versus the number of stocks that are decreasing is beginning to level off. This analyst would conclude that the market

[A] Is oversold
[B] Is overbought
[C] Is volatile
[D] Is stable

52. ABC Corporation is using a syndicate and sold its stock for $8.50 a share. The POP is $9.50 a share, and the manager's fee is $0.15 a share. If the concession is $0.50 a share, what is the additional takedown?

[A] $1.00
[B] $0.85
[C] $0.50
[D] $0.35

53. Chris Truman is part of a syndicate that is offering 2,000,000 total shares to the public. He sold his 300,000 shares allocated by the syndicate; 500,000 shares remain unsold. Which portion of these 500,000 shares is he responsible for selling?

I. 75,000 shares if the syndicate operates as an Eastern account
II. 75,000 shares if the syndicate operates as a Western account
III. 0 shares if the syndicate operates as an Eastern account
IV. 0 shares if the syndicate operates as a Western account

[A] I and II
[B] II and III
[C] I and IV
[D] III and IV

54. Which of these statements are true about callable municipal revenue bonds?

I. Callable bonds tend to have a higher yield than non-callable bonds
II. When interest rates increase, callable bonds will increase in market price more than non-callable bonds
III. The issuer will likely call the bonds when interest rates are increasing
IV. If the bonds are called, call premiums cushion the loss in interest payments that investors would have received had they been able to hold the bond

[A] I and III
[B] I, II, and III
[C] I, II, and IV
[D] All of the above

55. Betsy Jones opens a custodial account for her 6-year-old grandson Tom. Which of the following are true statements about this account?

I. Ms. Jones cannot open this account; she is not Tom's parent
II. Ms. Jones cannot share the custodian job with Tom's parents
III. The account must be a margin account
IV. When Tom reaches majority age for his state, the account will be in his name.

[A] I and III
[B] II and IV
[C] I, III, and IV
[D] II, III, and IV

56. Which of these investments are short-term municipal notes?

I. PNs
II. BANs
III. AONs
IV. RANs

[A] I, II, and III
[B] I, II, and IV

[C] II, III, and IV
[D] II and IV

57. DEF Corporation has announced it is issuing $4,000,000 of convertible mortgage bonds, with a 6.5 percent coupon rate. The bonds are convertible to common stock at $20 and mature in 2026. Which of these statements is true?

I. The bonds are backed by the credit and faith of DEF Corporation
II. The bonds are backed by a DEF Corporation property lien
III. The conversion ratio is 20
IV. The conversion ratio is 50

[A] I and III
[B] I and IV
[C] II and III
[D] II and IV

58. Sarah Smith wants to invest in equity securities but wants to receive dividends as part of her investment objectives. Which of these investments will you be least likely to suggest?

[A] DEF common stock
[B] ABC preferred stock
[C] XYZ warrants
[D] GHI convertible preferred stock

59. Limited partnership with investments in raw land are considered

[A] Conservative investments
[B] Defensive investments
[C] Income-producing investments
[D] Speculative investments

60. Which of the following investors face unlimited loss potential?

[A] An investor who bought a call option and is short the stock
[B] An investor who sold a put option and is short the stock
[C] An investor who sold a call option and is long the stock
[D] An investor who sold a put option and is long the stock

61. As a registered representative, you must send account statements for dormant accounts at least

    [A] Daily
    [B] Weekly
    [C] Monthly
    [D] Quarterly

62. Which of these statements about Roth IRAs are true?

    I. Roth IRA earnings accumulate tax free
    II. Withdrawals from a Roth IRA are tax-free, as long as the investor has held the account for the required time
    III. Contributions to a Roth IRA are made with pre-tax dollars
    IV. Contributions are made from after-tax dollars

    [A] I and III
    [B] I and IV
    [C] I, II, and III
    [D] I, II, and IV

63. Billy Jones holds a long margin account that is currently unrestricted. The market value of his account increased by $2,000. What happens to his SMA?

    [A] It increases by $1,000
    [B] It increases by $2,000
    [C] It decreases by $4,000
    [D] It decreases by $1,000

64. Which of the following is true about a double-barreled municipal bond?

    [A] Double-barreled municipal bonds are automatically exempt from state and federal taxes
    [B] Double-barreled bonds are backed by the municipality's full faith and credit, should revenues of the funded project fall short
    [C] Double-barreled bonds are exempt from state and local taxes only
    [D] Double-barreled bonds are indirectly backed by the federal government

65. Shareholders must vote to approve the following actions:

  I. Split stock
  II. Reverse-split stock
  III. Disburse cash dividend to investors
  IV. Disburse stock dividend to investors

    [A] I and II
    [B] III and IV
    [C] All of the above
    [D] None of the above

66. Which of the following is not a way to invest in annuities?

    [A] Single payment immediate annuity
    [B] Single payment deferred annuity
    [C] Periodic payment deferred annuity
    [D] Periodic payment immediate annuity

67. XYZ municipality is issuing bonds to fund a public park. When analyzing this bond for your client, which of the following characteristics of XYZ municipality would you consider?

  I. Insurance covenants
  II. Ad valorem tax rates
  III. Flow of funds
  IV. Budgetary practices of XYZ

    [A] I and III
    [B] II and IV
    [C] I, II, and III
    [D] All of the above

68. Which of these option combinations is a long combination strategy?

    [A] Sell 1 ABC Dec 50 call; sell 1 ABC Dec 50 put
    [B] Buy 1 ABC Dec 50 call; buy 1 ABC Dec 50 put
    [C] Buy 1 ABC Dec 50 call; buy 1 ABC Dec 40 put
    [D] Buy 1 ABC Dec 50 call; sell 1 ABC Dec 40 put

69. Which of these statements about industrial development revenue bonds is true?

I. The funds raised are used to build a facility for a corporation
II. They are municipal bonds
III. The full faith and credit of the municipality backs these bonds
IV. These bonds are backed by the leasing corporation monthly lease payments

[A] I and III
[B] I and IV
[C] II and III
[D] I, II, and IV

70. Which of these technical theories assumes small investors are usually wrong?

[A] The odd lot theory
[B] The Dow theory
[C] The volume theory
[D] The short interest theory

71. The Fed has just raised reserve requirement for financial institutions. Which of the following responses are you likely to see in the market?

I. Interest rates are increasing
II. Interest rates are decreasing
III. The price of outstanding bonds will decrease
IV. The price of outstanding bonds will increase

[A] I and III
[B] I and IV
[C] II and III
[D] II and IV

72. Joe Miller bought a 10 percent El Paso municipal bond with a sinking fund provision. He bought the bond in the secondary market at 120. If the bond matures in eight years, what is his annual income?

[A] $95
[B] $75
[C] $100
[D] Municipal bonds are not amortized

73. Your firm is sending your client, John Smith, a confirmation after his latest trade of XYZ stock. What information will be included on the confirmation to him?

    I. Trade and settlement date
    II. The capacity in which your firm functioned (agent or principal)
    III. XYZ and how many shares of the stock were traded
    IV. Commission paid, if your firm acted as an agent

    [A] I and III
    [B] I, II, and III
    [C] I, III, and IV
    [D] All of the above

74. In compliance with Blue Sky Laws, DEF Corporation has filed the appropriate documentation with their state. Because XYZ Corporation has issued securities before and filed with the state previously, it has filed by:

    [A] Notification
    [B] Qualification
    [C] Mail
    [D] Coordination

75. As a syndicate member, James Jones has sold his 20,000 shares of the 10-member syndicate's total 200,000 shares. The syndicate has 20,000 shares remaining and operates as a Western Account. How many shares does he still need to sell in order to fulfill his commitment to the syndicate?

    [A] 10,000 shares
    [B] None, he has met his obligation by selling his portion
    [C] 11,000
    [D] 2,000

76. XYZ Corporation wants to issue bonds. To ensure all bonds do not come due at the same time, the corporation needs the bonds to carry staggered maturity. XYZ Corporation will issue:

    [A] Staggered Bonds
    [B] Term Bonds
    [C] Serial Bonds
    [D] Series Bonds

77. Bart Jones wants to buy DEF bonds, but only if he can redeem the bonds at par value whenever he wants. You will recommend:

 [A] Bearer Bonds
 [B] Callable Bonds
 [C] Redeemable Bonds
 [D] Put Bonds

78. XYZ has issued guaranteed bonds. This means the bonds are secured by:

 [A] Their own guarantee to repay
 [B] XYZ's property
 [C] Another firm, usually a parent company
 [D] The government

79. DEF stock is trading at $30 a share. The corporation has decided to issue its stockholders a 15 percent dividend. What is the value of DEF stock on the ex-dividend rate?

 [A] $30
 [B] $25.50
 [C] $34.50
 [D] $24

80. Bill Truman holds 1,000 common stock shares of XYZ stock, with cumulative voting rights. It is time to vote for four board members and he feels strongly about voting for a particular member. He can:

 [A] Put 500 votes per seat
 [B] Put 4,000 votes toward that one seat
 [C] Not vote at all; common stock does not hold voting rights for board seats
 [D] Call XYZ Corporation to buy more votes

81. GHI bonds are rated D by Standard and Poor's. This means the company:

 [A] Is in default
 [B] Nothing; S&P does not have a D rating
 [C] Is speculative
 [D] Has just paid dividends

82. Bill Moore bought a bond at $1,000 with a coupon rate of 6 percent. The bond now trades at $1,200. What is the current yield of his bond?

[A] 6 percent
[B] $200
[C] 8 percent
[D] 5 percent

83. Which of the following factors into assessing a municipality's taxing power?

I. Market value of properties in the municipality
II. Per capita debt
III. Sales tax per capita
IV. Tax base

[A] I, III, and IV
[B] II, III, and IV
[C] All of the above
[D] None of the above

84. George Brown holds shares of preferred GHI stock. GHI Corporation has the right to buy back her preferred stock at any time. What type of preferred stock does he hold?

[A] Straight preferred stock
[B] Adjustable preferred stock
[C] Company preferred stock
[D] Callable preferred stock

85. Dana Lewis bought a 7 percent convertible bond at $1,000. She wants to trade her bond for stock. Her bond carries a conversion price of $40. How many shares will she receive if she converts her bond?

[A] 2,800
[B] 25
[C] 400
[D] 70

86. XYZ's revenue bond funds a toll road and includes a rate covenant. What does this covenant do?

[A] It ensures the municipality will charge enough for use of the toll road to repay its bond investors

[B] It makes sure the bond's interest rates do not drop, so the bond is a safer investment for investors

[C] It makes sure the municipality carries insurance for the project

[D] It makes sure the municipality gives all bond holders the same interest rate

87. A syndicate buys DEF Corporation shares at $100 a share. Their spread is $20, with a management fee of 15 percent. What is the price per share of DEF stock to the public?

[A] $97

[B] $120

[C] $119.55

[D] $132

88. XYZ municipality has finished its toll road, and the road has generated $1,000,000, with $500,000 in operating expenses. The municipality has $500,000 in 5 percent bonds outstanding. What is XYZ's debt service coverage ratio?

[A] $500,000

[B] 95

[C] 100

[D] 200

89. ABC Corporation has issued 2,000,000 shares of common stock. In order to control the stock's value, ABC Corporation has decided to hold 500,000 shares. How many shares of treasury stock does ABC Corporation have?

[A] 2,500,000 shares

[B] 1,500,000 shares

[C] 2,000,000

[D] 500,000

90. XYZ Corporation is splitting their common stock with a forward, 2-for-1 split. Samantha Miller holds 100 shares of ABC stock, with each share valued at $20. How many shares does she hold after the split, and how much is each share worth?

[A] 50 shares at $10 a share

[B] 100 shares at $10 a share

[C] 200 shares at $10 a share
[D] 200 shares at $20 a share

91. Jim Black holds an ADR for ABC Corporation stock. The company is based in the United Kingdom and has just paid dividends. He will receive dividends in:

[A] British pounds
[B] Euros
[C] U.S. dollars
[D] No dividends; foreign investors do not receive stock dividends

92. XYZ municipality wants to issue a bond. The bond counsel has rendered the bond issue unqualified. This means:

[A] The municipality is not qualified to issue the bond
[B] The bond counsel sees no complications to the bond issue
[C] The bond counsel sees issues that would affect the bond's issue
[D] The bond can be sold without a broker

93. Industrial Revenue Bonds are backed by:

[A] The leasing corporation
[B] The tax base of the municipality issuing the bond
[C] The industry's total revenue
[D] The municipality's promise to repay

94. DEF municipality with a population of 500,000 has net direct debt of $1,000,000. There is overlapping debt from other counties of $1,000,000. Your client is considering buying DEF's bonds, and you need to assess the municipality's solvency. What is DEF's per capita debt?

[A] $1,000,000
[B] $2
[C] $4
[D] $40

95. GHI municipality issues a 3-year, 6 percent bond, with total bonds issued at $1,000,000. What is the bond's NIC?

    [A] $180,000
    [B] $1,000,000
    [C] $1,060,000
    [D] $60,000

96. ABC municipality is issuing a bond backed by their good faith, as well as the revenue of the airport the bond is funding. This bond is a:

    [A] Moral obligation bond
    [B] Project note
    [C] Double-barreled bond
    [D] Transportation bond

97. What are the qualifications of a diversified management company?

    I. It has to be open-ended
    II. It cannot hold more than 5 percent of voting stock in one company
    III. It cannot hold more than 10 percent of voting stock in one company
    IV. It must not have more than 5 percent of its assets invested in one company

    [A] I and II
    [B] IV
    [C] III and IV
    [D] All of the above

98. Which of the following is true about LEAPS? LEAPS:

    I. Are long-term options
    II. Are based on the two-to-five-year performance of the underlying security
    III. Are traded on NYSE, Amex, and NASDAQ
    IV. Are always capped to protect investors

    [A] I and IV
    [B] I, II, and III
    [C] All of the above
    [D] None of the above

99. GHI fund carries a fixed amount of shares, which are sold to investors, and then traded in the market. GHI fund is a:

   [A] Closed-ended fund
   [B] Fixed fund
   [C] Open-ended fund
   [D] Mutual fund

100. The seller of a put is:

   [A] Bearish
   [B] Neutral
   [C] Unsure of market direction
   [D] Bullish

101. DEF fund invests in two types of stock to serve combined goals. DEF fund is a

   [A] Specialized fund
   [B] Index fund
   [C] Combined fund
   [D] Dual-purpose fund

102. Which of the following is true about direct participation programs? DPPs:

   I. Pay taxes as a partnership
   II. Investors only receive profits, and do not share any losses
   III. Are usually a short-term investment
   IV. Are a safe investment for any investor

   [A] II
   [B] I and IV
   [C] I, II, and III
   [D] None of the above

103. Gregory Miller bought a 10-year, 10 percent corporate bond at 120. What is his annual income?

   [A] $10
   [B] $100
   [C] $120
   [D] $80

104. Martin Jones deposits $50 a month into ABC fund for four months. Price per share has fluctuated each month:

 January: $10 a share
 February: $11 a share
 March: $12 a share
 April: $10 a share

 What is his average cost per share?

 [A] $11
 [B] $50
 [C] $10.68
 [D] $10.89

105. A limited partnership receives income from leasing trucks. Their leases are short-term, with a steady turnover of equipment. This is a(n):

 [A] Short-Term Lease
 [B] Operating Lease
 [C] Full Pay-Out Lease
 [D] Truck Lease

106. Nancy Griffin bought 1 XYZ Mar 50 call at 4. This is a(n):

 [A] Opening Purchase
 [B] Opening Sale
 [C] Closing Sale
 [D] Call Sale

107. Marcy Brown bought a 6 percent corporate bond at 70, maturing after ten years. What is her annual income?

 [A] $90
 [B] $60
 [C] $360
 [D] $13

108. Which of these officials renders a legal opinion on the issuance of municipal bonds?

 [A] The syndicate manager
 [B] The municipal issuer

[C] The bond counsel
[D] The trustee of the bonds

109. DEF Corporation sells luxury automobiles. In a recession, DEF stock reacts strongly to the market with a significant drop in stock price. DEF stock is

[A] Defensive
[B] Cyclical
[C] Reactive
[D] Counter-cyclical

110. A bank and an insurance company trade securities directly, without the use of a broker/dealer. This is an example of trading in the

[A] First market
[B] Second market
[C] Third market
[D] Fourth market

111. ABC mutual fund has a total asset value of $2,000,000 with 500,000 shares outstanding. The public offering price of one share of DEF fund is $4.30. What is the broker's commission for this fund?

[A] $0.70 per share
[B] $1 per share
[C] 7 percent
[D] 7.5 percent

112. What is the role of the order book official (OBO)?

[A] He orders books for registered representative
[B] He is the exchange bookkeeper
[C] He executes orders immediately
[D] He holds orders that cannot be executed immediately until market conditions are right

113. Karen and Bob Jones opened a JTWROS joint account with your firm years ago. You have just received confirmation of Mrs. Jones' passing. What happens to the account?

[A] The account is transferred to Mr. Jones
[B] Mrs. Jones' half of the account becomes part of her estate

[C] You must look at how much Mrs. Jones invested to determine her share
[D] None of the above

114. Your client Tom Newman worries about his investments being affected by the business cycle. He wants to invest in defensive stocks. Which of the following would you suggest to him?

I. Stocks of large appliance companies
II. Tobacco stock
III. Stock of companies producing alcoholic beverages
IV. Automotive company stock

[A] I and IV
[B] II and III
[C] I, III, and IV
[D] II, III, and IV

115. Mary Miller's margin account has been restricted. Which of these statements about her account is true?

I. She cannot borrow any additional funds from her firm
II. She must deposit money into the account to remove the restricted status
III. She must make all her purchases in cash
IV. The equity of her account has dropped below 50 percent of the LMV

[A] I, III, and IV
[B] I, II, and III
[C] I and II
[D] IV only

116. On the order ticket sell 1 DEF Dec 80 call at 6, 6 stands for the:

[A] Strike price
[B] Amount of days the holder has to exercise the option
[C] Premium the buyer pays for the option
[D] Premium the seller pays to the buyer should the call be exercised

117. Gary Truman invests in a limited partnership, which has given him returns for the year of $20,000. The limited partnership carried a loss of $5,000. What is his income from this investment?

- **[A]** $10,000
- **[B]** $15,000
- **[C]** $20,000
- **[D]** $25,000

118. Frank Henderson has bought a municipal bond at a discount. Which of the following statements is true?

I. He must accrete the discount on his bond
II. The discount on the bond does not need to be accreted
III. He will have to pay capital gains tax if he holds the bond to maturity
IV. He will not have to pay capital gains tax if he holds the bond to maturity

- **[A]** I and III
- **[B]** I and IV
- **[C]** II and III
- **[D]** II and IV

119. Which of the following can a municipal bond trader not do?

- **[A]** Request bids on bonds
- **[B]** Enter offers for a broker/dealer
- **[C]** Rate a bond
- **[D]** Buy bonds for a firm's inventory

120. Nora Franklin bought a 10 percent municipal bond at 105 in the secondary market, with ten years to maturity. Six years into the bond's term, she sells the bond at 102. What is her gain or loss?

- **[A]** $300 capital loss
- **[B]** $200 capital gain
- **[C]** $200 capital loss
- **[D]** $300 capital gain

121. Which of the following statements best defines systematic risk?

- **[A]** The risk of a stock's decline because of negative market conditions
- **[B]** The risk of the issuer's default on its obligation to investors

[C] The risk that a security's earnings will be outpaced by inflation

[D] The risk of a stock's underperformance

122. Frank Patterson bought 5,000 shares of XYZ common stock ten years ago, when the stock traded at $40 a share. He gives his stock to his daughter Jane when the market value of XYZ stock was $50 a share. Which of these statements regarding this gift is true?

I. Frank may be subject to gift tax
II. Jane may be subject to gift tax
III. Frank's cost basis is $40 a share
IV. Jane's cost basis is $50 a share

[A] I and III
[B] I and IV
[C] II and III
[D] II and IV

123. Jeanette Samuels is your client, and she has invested in an oil and gas DPP. When explaining her rights, you will explain the one thing she cannot do is

[A] Participate in managing the limited partnership
[B] Inspect the DPP's books
[C] Invest in other competing oil and gas DPPs
[D] Sue the general partner of the DPP

124. Which of the following is not a way to diversify a municipal bond portfolio?

[A] Buying bonds with different maturities
[B] Buying bonds with a different rating
[C] Buying bonds from different municipalities
[D] Buying a different quantity of bonds

125. Which of the following transactions does not reduce the debit balance of a long margin account?

[A] Cash dividends
[B] Liquidation of long stock
[C] Stock dividends
[D] Cash deposits

126. DEF Corporation's stock is currently trading at $16 a share. DEF has earnings of $4 a share. What is the PE for DEF stock?

 - [A] 4
 - [B] 5
 - [C] 20
 - [D] 30

127. Which of the following securities do not receive interest?

 - [A] Treasury strips
 - [B] Treasury bonds
 - [C] Treasury stock
 - [D] Treasury bills

128. Jerry Williams bought 200 shares of ABC stock at $65 a share. He also bought 2 ABC Dec 60 puts at 7. What is his break-even point?

 - [A] 53
 - [B] 58
 - [C] 67
 - [D] 72

129. Caroline White has a margin account with a $40,000 value and a $14,000 debit balance. If she wants to buy an additional $20,000 of stock, how much does she have to deposit into her margin account?

 - [A] $10,000
 - [B] $4,000
 - [C] $2,000
 - [D] Nothing; her account has sufficient funds already

130. Which of the following is not included in M2 money supply?

 - [A] Time deposits
 - [B] Cash in circulation
 - [C] Checking account funds
 - [D] Jumbo CDs

Take a 30-60 minute break now if you are following the schedule of your real Series 7 exam.

PRACTICE TEST: PART II

1. Which of the following backs an IDR?

   [A] The issuing municipality, should the corporate backer not be able to meet the debt obligation
   [B] The backing corporation only
   [C] The state the facility is located in
   [D] None of the above

2. Jack Vermeer is long 100 shares of DEF stock, which he originally bought at $70 a share. He then wrote a DEF Dec 75 call at 3, when DEF stock was trading at $68 a share. What is his potential maximum loss?

   [A] $300
   [B] $6,500
   [C] $6,700
   [D] $7,800

3. Which of these orders guarantee a certain price or better?

   [A] Buy limits and sell stops
   [B] Sell limits and buy stops
   [C] Buy limits and sell limits
   [D] Buy stops and sell stops

4. Hannah Jones sold short 1,000 shares of ABC stock at $60. ABC stock is now trading at $64 a share. How much is her account restricted?

   [A] $0
   [B] $4,000
   [C] $2,000
   [D] $6,000

5. Which of the following is not a type of state registration for new issues?

   [A] Filing
   [B] Communication
   [C] Coordination
   [D] Qualification

6. Which of the following is not a benefit of a long-term equipment leasing program?

   [A] Capital appreciation
   [B] Regular income
   [C] Deductions for depreciation to offset income
   [D] Deduction of operating expenses to offset revenue

7. Which of the following investments can claim depletion as a deduction?

   [A] Real estate DPPs
   [B] Transportation companies
   [C] Oil and gas DPPs
   [D] Pharmaceutical companies

8. Selling a security with an agreement to repurchase those same securities at a set price and time is called

   [A] Tax exempt commercial paper
   [B] A revenue anticipation note
   [C] A repo
   [D] A reverse repo

9. You are analyzing several companies as investments for one of your clients. Which of the following would indicate a corporation has a high risk of bankruptcy?

   [A] High inventory turnover ratio
   [B] High debt-to-equity ratio
   [C] High current ratio
   [D] Low PE ratio

10. Barry Smith invests in a unit investment trust without a maturation date to his shares. He invests in a:

   [A] Fixed investment trust
   [B] Participating trust
   [C] Variable investment trust
   [D] Open-ended investment trust

11. Your client Vera Williams wants to invest in a limited partnership. Your duty as a registered representative is to:

    [A] Review the subscription agreement to ensure its accuracy
    [B] Fill out and sign the subscription agreement
    [C] Sell the shares for her if she requests it
    [D] Do nothing; limited partnerships are not part of a broker's business

12. Dana Black sold a call for XYZ stock, but does not hold any XYZ stock. She is:

    [A] Neutral
    [B] Bullish
    [C] A naked call writer
    [D] A naked put holder

13. Christine White just bought a bottle of wine and she paid 6 percent sales tax. She paid:

    [A] Excise Tax
    [B] Progressive Tax
    [C] Aggregate Tax
    [D] Regressive Tax

14. Ashley Miller is selling ABC stock to a client from her firm's inventory. She:

    [A] Acts as a broker and will charge a commission
    [B] Acts as a dealer and will charge a mark-up
    [C] Acts as a broker/dealer, violating SEC rules
    [D] Acts as a dealer and will charge a mark-down

15. When it comes to impact by the business cycle, stock in a cruise vacation corporation is considered

    [A] Defensive
    [B] Cyclical
    [C] Recessive
    [D] Leading

16. When index options are exercised, they are paid out in:

    [A] Stock
    [B] Interest in the underlying security
    [C] Cash
    [D] Bonds

17. Your customer Bob Henderson has placed an order for a municipal bond, which you have traded on Friday, May 10. When does this order settle?

    [A] Monday, May 13
    [B] Tuesday, May 14
    [C] Wednesday, May 15
    [D] Thursday, May 16

18. XYZ Corporation has total assets of $2,000,000 and liabilities of $1,200,000. What is XYZ's working capital?

    [A] $1,000,000
    [B] $800,000
    [C] $600,000
    [D] None of the above

19. Mary Newman sold 1 XYZ Apr 100 put at 4. What is her maximum loss?

    [A] $40
    [B] $120
    [C] $400
    [D] $600

20. When the economic growth is slow, bond prices typically

    [A] Fall
    [B] Climb
    [C] Remain Stable
    [D] Stagnate

21. Which of the following is part of the M1 money supply?

    I. Cash in circulation
    II. Demand deposits
    III. Time deposits
    IV. Traveler's Checks

[A] All of the above
[B] I and II
[C] I, II, and III
[D] I, II, and IV

22. On Monday afternoon, ABC stock was trading at its resistance level. The next day, the stock rose eight points. This is called a(n)

[A] Accumulation
[B] Consolidation
[C] Breakout
[D] Re-distribution

23. Which of these statements regarding inventory valuation methods is true?

I. LIFO sells the last goods placed in inventory first
II. FIFO sells the oldest goods in inventory first
III. A company can use both LIFO and FIFO systems
IV. A company must continually use the same inventory method

[A] I, II, and III
[B] I, II, and IV
[C] I only
[D] None of the above

24. Margin accounts must hold securities in

[A] The customer's name
[B] Street name
[C] The stock's name
[D] Segregation

25. Your client Martha Franklin has placed an order for securities at a specific price. The order will remain open until she executes or cancels it. This is a

[A] FOK order
[B] AON order
[C] GTC order
[D] Day order

26. William Brown holds a long margin account with a $100,000 value with equity at $50,000. Should the value of his account fall, how low can the value of his account get before he receives a margin call?

    [A] $42,000
    [B] $40,000
    [C] $33,000
    [D] $25,000

27. The Federal Reserve has just announced it has lowered the reserve requirement. What economic effect does this decision have?

    [A] It increases the requirement of reserve funds for banks
    [B] It increases the funds banks are able to lend
    [C] It decreases available money supply
    [D] It decreases funds available to lend

28. Which of the following government debt securities can be recalled if there is a drop in interest rates?

    I. T-bills
    II. T-notes
    III. T-bonds
    IV. T-Strips

    [A] I only
    [B] II and III
    [C] III only
    [D] IV only

29. Which of these industries is not considered cyclical?

    [A] Appliance manufacturers
    [B] Automobile manufacturers
    [C] Building material manufacturers
    [D] Pharmaceutical manufacturers

30. Martin Zimmerman sold 100 shares of ABC stock short at $58 a share. He also bought 1 ABC Dec 60 call at 4. ABC stock now trades at $72 a share. What is loss or profit on his account?

    [A] $1,800 gain
    [B] $3,200 gain

[C] $200 loss
[D] $600 loss

31. What is the minimum denomination of a T-Bill?

[A] $1,000
[B] $5,000
[C] $10,000
[D] $50,000

32. Which of the following statements about fixed annuities is not true?

[A] A fixed annuity guarantees a certain rate of return
[B] The insurance company carries most of the risk
[C] The annuitant carries all the risk
[D] The annuitant knows what the rate of return is

33. Troy Black bought a 1 DEF Mar 55 call at 4 and sold a 1 DEF Mar 65 call at 2. What is the break-even point for his long call, if DEF trades at $56?

[A] $55
[B] $56
[C] $59
[D] $63

34. Which of these statements best describes legislative risk?

I. The U.S. government has to approve a new securities issue
II. Changes in the tax code can affect a securities issue
III. Foreign securities are not subject to legislative risk
IV. Foreign securities carry more legislative risk because they are affected by both U.S. and foreign legislature

[A] I and III
[B] II only
[C] II and III
[D] II and IV

35. Greg Vernon bought 10 XYZ Oct 45 puts at 3. What is his maximum gain and maximum loss from this transaction?

[A] Maximum gain is $42,000; maximum loss is $3,000
[B] Maximum gain is $4,200; maximum loss is $3,000

[C] Maximum gain is $3,000; maximum loss is $3,000
[D] Maximum gain is unlimited; maximum loss is $3,000

36. Which of the following is included on a customer order ticket?

I. The customer's account number
II. The security and number of shares ordered
III. The registered representative's name
IV. If the trade was solicited

[A] I and II
[B] I and III
[C] I, II, and III
[D] All of the above

37. Wanda Gray has an annual income of $60,000 a year. She has just opened a tax-qualified retirement plan and contributes 5 percent of her income annually. What is her taxable income?

[A] $60,000
[B] $57,000
[C] $55,000
[D] $54,000

38. Bart Miller has bought a corporate bond at a premium. Which of the following statements is correct?

[A] He can accrete the bond
[B] He can amortize the bond
[C] He will be repaid the premium at maturity
[D] He will receive a discount at the bond's maturity

39. Which of the following two positions are bearish strategies?

I. Long call spread
II. Long put spread
III. Short call spread
IV. Short put spread

[A] I and III
[B] I and IV
[C] II and III
[D] II and IV

40. Which of the following statements best describes the objective of a short call option writer?

  [A] The investor hopes the market will rise, so he or she can buy the stock at a lower price
  [B] The investor hopes the market will rise, so the holder of the option will let it expire, and let the writer collect the premium
  [C] The investor hopes the market will drop to he or she can sell the stock at a higher price
  [D] The investor hope the market will drop, so the holder of the option will let it expire, and the writer can collect the premium

41. Cora Stephens has a long margin account with a value of $18,000. The account has a debit balance of $9,000 and an equity of $9,000. What is the minimum maintenance level on her account?

  [A] $12,000
  [B] $9,000
  [C] $6,000
  [D] $4,200

42. Max Jones sold 400 shares of ABC stock short at $59 a share and bought 4 ABC Dec 60 calls at 5. What is his maximum potential loss from this position?

  [A] $100
  [B] $400
  [C] $500
  [D] $600

43. XYZ convertible bonds carry a conversion rate of 20 to 1. Currently, XYZ bonds are trading at 92. In order to trade at parity, at what price must XYZ stock trade?

  [A] $42
  [B] $46
  [C] $50
  [D] $52

44. If a company goes bankrupt, which of the following will have the first claim on liquidated assets?

[A] Options
[B] Warrants
[C] Common stock
[D] Preferred stock

45. In March, John Brown bought a 6 percent corporate bond for $5,000, and sold it six months later for $5,500. Which of the following is true?

[A] He will not be taxed more than 15 percent on the profit he made because he held the bond longer than 61 days
[B] He will be taxed at his bracket for both the interest income and the capital gains from the sale of the bond
[C] He can deduct up to $1,000 from his income
[D] He will not be taxed because he invested in a bond

46. Which of the following orders are placed below the current market price of a stock?

I. Buy stop order
II. Buy limit order
III. Sell stop order
IV. Sell stop limit order

[A] I only
[B] I and II
[C] I, II, and III
[D] II, III, and IV

47. Karen Truman sold 400 shares of ABC stock short at $59 a share and bought 4 ABC Feb 60 calls at 5. At what market price of ABC stock does she break even?

[A] $50
[B] $52
[C] $54
[D] $55

48. If a municipality issues a revenue bond, this means the bond is backed by

   [A] Sales Tax
   [B] Ad Valorem tax
   [C] Project revenues
   [D] Income tax

49. Betty James opened a long margin account to buy 1,000 shares of DEF stock at $57 a share. DEF now trades at $63 a share. What is her equity?

   [A] $31,500
   [B] $34,500
   [C] $57,000
   [D] $63,000

50. Which of the following statements regarding the expansion phase of the business cycle are correct?

   I. Interest rates are high
   II. There is increased production of goods and services
   III. Inflation is low
   IV. Unemployment rates decline

   [A] I and II
   [B] I and III
   [C] I, II, and III
   [D] II, III, and IV

51. Beth Franklin sold 1 XYZ Feb 60 call at 4, and 1 XYZ Feb 60 put at 3. What is her maximum potential gain from this position?

   [A] $700
   [B] $5,700
   [C] $6,700
   [D] Unlimited

52. What is the objective of an annuity investor?

   [A] Investing in the stock market
   [B] Investing in mutual funds
   [C] Securing income for retirement years
   [D] Securing insurance coverage

53. Greg Anderson studies two companies' financial health, using their assets, liabilities, income, and expenses for his analysis. He is a

 [A] Technical analyst
 [B] Fundamental analyst
 [C] Portfolio analyst
 [D] Accounting analyst

54. Which of the following data are considered leading indicators?

 I. Hours logged by manufacturing production workers
 II. Unemployment insurance claims
 III. New building permits issued
 IV. Orders for consumer goods

 [A] I and II
 [B] I, II, and III
 [C] I, III, and IV
 [D] All of the above

55. Denise Keller bought 100 shares of XYZ stock at $44, and 1 XYZ Dec 45 put at 3. XYZ stock now trades at $48. What is her profit or loss from her position?

 [A] Profit of $100
 [B] Loss of $100
 [C] Profit of $400
 [D] Loss of $300

56. JKL firm acted as an OTC dealer, selling a security out of its inventory. JKL will charge a

 [A] Commission
 [B] Nominal spread
 [C] Markdown
 [D] Markup

57. The Federal Reserve has announced a rise in the discount rate. Which of the following is most likely to be an effect of this decision?

 [A] Banks will lower their reserves
 [B] Banks will lend more freely
 [C] Interest rates on loans will rise
 [D] The economy will heat up

58. Barry Griffin bought 1 GHI Oct 70 call at 4, and sold 1 GHI Oct 80 call at 1, to create a long call spread. What is his maximum gain and loss resulting from this position?

    [A] Maximum gain is $700; maximum loss is $300
    [B] Maximum gain is $700; maximum loss is $400
    [C] Maximum gain is $1,000; maximum los is $300
    [D] Maximum gain is $1,200; maximum loss is $700

59. Carrie Henderson has opened a Roth IRA. Which of the following statements about her Roth IRA are correct?

    I. All her contributions are tax-free
    II. All of her contributions are taxable
    III. She can begin withdrawing money tax-free from age 59½
    IV. Gains on the account are taxed

    [A] I, III, and IV
    [B] I and III
    [C] II and III
    [D] I and IV

60. Beth Moore bought 50 ABC Jul 75 puts at 6. At what market price for ABC stock does she break even?

    [A] $69
    [B] $75
    [C] $81
    [D] $85

61. Which of the following statements about preferred stock is correct?

    I. Preferred stock carries limited voting rights
    II. Preferred stockholders have pre-emptive rights
    III. Preferred stock has a greater par value than common stock
    IV. Preferred stock always trades higher than common stock

    [A] I and III
    [B] I and II
    [C] II and IV
    [D] III and IV

62. George Newman is a syndicate member. For each bond he sells, he earns a

[A] management fee
[B] concession
[C] takedown
[D] reallowance

63. What is the minimum maintenance for long and short margin accounts?

[A] 50 percent for both long and short margin accounts
[B] 50 percent for long margin accounts; 150 percent for short margin account
[C] 30 percent for long margin accounts; 25 percent for short margin accounts
[D] 25 percent for long margin accounts; 30 percent for short margin accounts

64. Sam Baker bought a T-Note at 94. What did he actually pay for this investment, in U.S. dollars?

[A] $9,400
[B] $940
[C] $94
[D] $9.40

65. Dawn Black bought 1 ABC Apr 60 call at 5. What can she do with this option?

I. Exercise the option
II. Let the option expire
III. Conduct a closing purchase
IV. Conduct a closing sale

[A] I and II
[B] II and IV
[C] I, II, and III
[D] I, II, and IV

66. Chris Black has invested in an annuity and has just passed away. His wife will receive the payout of this annuity for the rest of her life. This annuity investment is a:

[A] Life Annuity

[B] Life Annuity with Period Certain
[C] Family Annuity
[D] Joint Life with Last Survivor Annuity

67. Samantha Yates made an opening put purchase of XYZ stock. At what point would she realize maximum profit?

[A] XYZ stock soars to a high market price
[B] XYZ stock drops to zero
[C] The market price rises above the strike price
[D] The market price falls below the strike price

68. Which of the following is true about Real Estate Investment Trusts (REITs)? REITs must:

I. Invest in real estate, or real estate related securities
II. Have at least 75 percent of assets invested in real estate
III. Distribute 90 percent or more of income to investors
IV. Pass write-offs to investors

[A] I, II, and III
[B] II and III
[C] II and IV
[D] All of the above

69. Nathan Miller sold a call to ABC stock on the securities market. He is the:

[A] Writer of the call
[B] Manager of XYZ Corporation
[C] Holder of the call
[D] Securities broker

70. On the order ticket Sell 2 GHI Dec 90 call at 5, 90 stands for the:

[A] Strike price
[B] Amount of days the holder has to exercise the option
[C] Premium the buyer pays for the option
[D] Premium the seller pays to the buyer should the call be exercised

71. Veronica Jones bought 1,000 shares of ABC stock at $6 a share. She passes away, and leaves her stock to her cousin Jennifer Jones. The stock now trades at $10. Jennifer Jones has to pay:

[A] The price her aunt paid for the stock, which was $6,000
[B] The difference between the price her aunt paid and the current market value: $4,000
[C] The market value of the stock at the time of her aunt's death: $10,000
[D] Nothing; the estate will pay any taxes incurred by the transfer of assets

72. A broker is buying XYZ stock by phone. XYZ stock is an exchange-listed security. This is an OTC transaction in:

[A] The first market
[B] The second market
[C] The third market
[D] The fourth market

73. Frances Kellerman holds a put option for XYZ stock at 60. XYZ stock is trading at 70. Her option is:

[A] In-the-Money at 10
[B] Out-of-the-Money at 10
[C] Breaking even
[D] Out-of-the-Money at 10, plus her premium paid

74. Chris Black has bought 1 DEF Dec 80 call at 6. What is his break-even point?

[A] 74
[B] $7,400
[C] $8,600
[D] 6

75. Henry James is a broker assigned to handle the IPO of ABC stock. He decides to hold back 50,000 shares to sell when the stock price of ABC has stabilized, and to make sure he gets the best price. He:

[A] Is acting as a broker
[B] Is holding Treasury Stock, a common practice for IPOs

[C] Is bullish
[D] Is free riding, an illegal practice according to SEC rules

76. Joanne Richards has a money market account. Within the market's money supply, this falls under:

[A] M1
[B] M2
[C] M3
[D] L

77. June Williams is placing a sell order for DEF stock, without actually owning any DEF stock. She is:

[A] Bullish and selling long
[B] Bullish and selling short
[C] Bearish and selling long
[D] Bearish and selling short

78. The Federal Reserve is selling Treasury securities with a promise to buy them back again at a future date. This is called a:

[A] Put
[B] T-Sale
[C] Repurchase agreement
[D] Reverse repurchase agreement

79. Martha Simmons wants to invest in securities, but does not want to lose her principal. She also wishes to receive returns in cash to supplement her retirement income. What are her investment objectives?

[A] Capital growth and current income
[B] Liquidity and preservation of capital
[C] Diversification and short-term gains
[D] Preservation of income and current income

80. Mary Valentine bought 500 shares of ABC stock at $80 a share. She sells 1 ABC Mar 100 call at 6. She held this position for a month, and then sold her ABC stock at $85 a share. She closed the outstanding call at 5. What is her gain or loss?

[A] Gain of $1,000

[B] Gain of $2,600
[C] Gain of $5 a share
[D] Loss of $1,000

81. Which of the following is true about Monetarist Theory?

[A] Monetarists believe inflation should be avoided at all cost
[B] Monetarists believe in Keynes' theories
[C] Monetarists believe the key to a healthy economy is a steady growth in money supply
[D] Monetarists believe a government should control the money supply

82. Christine Moore is short XYZ stock, and wants to limit her losses should the market take an undesirable direction. She will likely buy:

[A] XYZ stock to cover her short position
[B] A buy stop order
[C] A sell stop order
[D] A call

83. A Technical analyst looks at:

[A] A corporation's stock
[B] A corporation's corporate charter
[C] The market as a whole
[D] The Fed's policies

84. XYZ stock's market prices are showing an inverted saucer pattern in a graph. Your prediction for this stock would be:

[A] Bearish
[B] Bullish
[C] Neutral
[D] Optimistic

85. When an economy's GDP has been decreasing for a period of 18 months, this is called a:

[A] Recession
[B] Depression
[C] Recovery
[D] Peak

86. Jeffrey Gaines, a market analyst, looks at individual sales of fewer than 100 stocks to determine market direction. He assumes the small investor is usually wrong, and does the opposite. He bases his analysis on the:

   [A] Common Theory
   [B] Short-Interest Theory
   [C] Dow Theory
   [D] Odd-Lot Theory

87. Max Zimmerman places an order to buy 300 shares of DEF stock with his broker, with an FOK order feature. This means his broker:

   [A] Needs to fill his order by the end of the trading day
   [B] Can fill the order later, when the market price could be better
   [C] Needs to fill the entire order of 300 shares, or abandon it altogether
   [D] Needs to fill the order immediately, whole or in part, or it is canceled

88. Sandra Daniels is your client and she is trying to decide between two companies to invest in. She needs to know how likely each is to file for bankruptcy. You would use:

   [A] Capitalization ratios
   [B] Liquidity ratios
   [C] Asset coverage ratios
   [D] Tax ratios

89. Frederic Miller sold a call for XYZ stock at 50, and bought a call for XYZ at 70. His strategy is a:

   [A] Bull call spread
   [B] Bear call spread
   [C] Neutral strategy
   [D] Naked strategy

90. Your client David Patterson has $200,000 in assets, but owes $100,000 on a mortgage and $30,000 in credit card debt. What is his net worth?

   [A] $70,000
   [B] $100,000

[C] $130,000
[D] $200,000

91. Fred Truman opened a custodial account for his son David Truman, who has just reached the age of majority in her state. What happens to the custodial account's funds?

[A] The funds transfer to Fred's account, since he is the custodian
[B] The account becomes a single account in David's name
[C] The funds are frozen and can only be withdrawn at Fred's request
[D] It depends on the account agreement Fred signed when he opened the account

92. A fundamental securities analysis looks at:

[A] The market as a whole
[B] The way the market moves in the business cycle
[C] Data on the health of a corporation, such as balance sheets and income statements.
[D] The Dow Jones Industrial Average

93. One of your customers has been involved in what you believe to be money-laundering activity. You have just received a deposit of $5,400. What action should you take?

[A] Call the police and report your client
[B] Talk to your manager about the activity
[C] Nothing; the transaction is below $10,000, so you do not need to report it
[D] File a SAR

94. Kirsten Davis has opened a short margin account and wants to sell $100,000 of ABC stock. What is her credit balance?

[A] $50,000
[B] $75,000
[C] $100,000
[D] $150,000

95. Zoe Truman has a short margin account and sold 1,000 shares of ABC stock at $50 a share. ABC now trades at $60 a share. What is her margin restriction?

    [A] $5,000
    [B] $10,000
    [C] $15,000
    [D] $20,000

96. Your client Cora Williams wants to invest in fixed annuities for her retirement. As her registered representative, you would advise her on this risk:

    [A] Inflation risk
    [B] Credit risk
    [C] Legislative risk
    [D] Reinvestment

97. Jennifer Jones bought 800 shares of DEF stock at $20 a share using her margin account. DEF stock trades at $10 a share now. What is her maintenance call?

    [A] $4,000
    [B] $6,000
    [C] $8,000
    [D] $10,000

98. ABC Corporation paid off a long-term loan of $200,000. What happens to their working capital?

    [A] It is reduced by $200,000
    [B] It increases by $200,000
    [C] Nothing, because assets and liabilities are equally affected
    [D] Assets and liabilities are reduced by $100,000 each

99. Fred Williams bought 500 shares of DEF shares on margin, at $100 a share. Six months later, DEF shares trade at $110 a share. What is his SMA?

    [A] $2,500
    [B] $5,000
    [C] $10,000
    [D] $30,000

100. Fred Valentine is opening a margin account. According to Reg. T, he must deposit at least:

[A] $2,000
[B] 50 percent of the purchase or sale price of the securities
[C] $1,000
[D] 60 percent of the purchase or sale price of the securities

101. Greg Davis has bought $100,000 of DEF stock, using a long margin account. What is his equity?

[A] $150,000
[B] $50,000
[C] $25,000
[D] $30,000

102. You are looking at ABC Corporation's balance sheet to determine the current ratio. What do you need to determine this number?

[A] Cash and bonds
[B] Assets and liabilities
[C] Current assets and inventory
[D] You need an income statement to calculate current ratio

103. This ticker tape comes across your desk: ABC.X 3K= 62.25^0.25. This is a report of the trade of:

[A] ABC stock
[B] ABC mutual funds
[C] A put of ABC stock
[D] ABC warrants

104. Troy Martin is 20 years old and you are making a strategic asset allocation. Without knowing anything else about his objectives, personal situation, or assets, how would you allocate his portfolio?

[A] 100 percent stock
[B] 80 percent stock, 20 percent bonds
[C] 60 percent stock, 40 percent bonds and cash
[D] 60 percent bonds and cash, 40 percent stock

105. Walter Tannenbaum and Greg Yates are part of a partnership, and have opened a partnership account. Who can make decisions on the account?

 [A] Only Mr. Tannenbaum and Mr. Yates together
 [B] Mr. Tannenbaum or Mr. Yates
 [C] The registered representative
 [D] It depends on who is specified to make decisions in the partnership agreement

106. New home building permits are up, according to *The Conference Board*'s report. This an example of a:

 [A] Leading Indicator
 [B] Lagging Indicator
 [C] Coincident Indicator
 [D] Recovery Indicator

107. Veronica Miller asks you to put together a portfolio for her. She wants to base the allocation her long-term goal of saving for retirement. You would make a:

 [A] Tactical asset allocation
 [B] Strategic asset allocation
 [C] Stock asset allocation
 [D] Bond asset allocation

108. Bob Truman wants to invest in an IRA, but needs for his contributions to be tax-free. You would recommend a:

 [A] Roth IRA
 [B] Traditional IRA
 [C] SEP-IRA
 [D] Coverdell IRA

109. Greg Samuels wants to make short-term gains by "playing" the market, and is not afraid to take losses in the process. You portfolio strategy would be:

 [A] Aggressive
 [B] Defensive
 [C] Conservative
 [D] Balanced

110. As a registered representative, you are looking at an information screen on your computer. It displays bid and ask prices of NASDAQ stock. This is:

[A] NASDAQ Level I information
[B] NASDAQ Level II information
[C] NASDAQ Level III information
[D] NASDAQ Level IV information

111. Frances Davis sold $100,000 of ABC stock on margin. This stock trades at $80,000 three months later. What is her equity?

[A] $20,000
[B] $60,000
[C] $70,000
[D] $80,000

112. Which of the following is not required to open an account?

[A] A customer's green card number, if a registered alien
[B] Customer's occupation
[C] Annual income
[D] Tax returns

113. To comply with the Patriot Act of 2001, registered representatives must keep the following customer information on file:

[A] A copy of a customer's identification
[B] A copy of a customer's last tax return
[C] A list of all foreign countries the customer has visited
[D] A list of all foreign corporations a customer does business with.

114. Tom Jones has a long margin account, which has a market value of $50,000. His debit balance is $20,000; his SMA $5,000. What is his buying power?

[A] $5,000
[B] $10,000
[C] $2,500
[D] $20,000

115. Karen Williams wrote a 10 ABC Oct 50 call at 3. What is her maximum gain on this transaction?

[A] $300
[B] $3,000
[C] $4,700
[D] $5,000

116. Richard Moore sold 1 DEF Jan 50 put at 6 and bought 1 DEF Jan 40 put at 3. This position is called a

[A] Long put debit spread
[B] Long put credit spread
[C] Short put debit spread
[D] Short put credit spread

117. Henry Miller opens a long margin account to buy $3,000 of stock. What is his minimum deposit?

[A] $3,000
[B] $1,500
[C] $2,000
[D] $6,000

118. Which of the following securities does not give its holders dividend?

[A] ADRs
[B] Warrants
[C] Common stock
[D] Preferred stock

119. XYZ Corporation issues convertible 5 percent bonds at par. The bonds are convertible at $40. What is the conversion ratio for XYZ bonds?

[A] 40
[B] 30
[C] 25
[D] 15

120. A market analyst would call which of these investments defensive?

[A] A corporate bond

[B] A blue chip stock
[C] A utility company's common stock
[D] An aerospace company's stock

121. Fred Simmons holds a mutual fund account. He deposits $50 a month into the account. How often does he have to receive a statement?

[A] Bi-weekly
[B] Monthly
[C] Quarterly
[D] Annually

122. Caroline Williams holds 100 shares of XYZ stock at $50 a share. XYZ Corporation announces a 2-for-1 stock split. How many shares does she hold after split, and at what price per share?

[A] 200 shares at $50 a share
[B] 100 shares at $50 a share
[C] 50 shares at $100 a share
[D] 200 shares at $25 a share

123. Fred Samuels has sold short 100 shares of XYZ stock at $60. What is his maximum loss?

[A] $600
[B] $6,000
[C] $12,000
[D] Unlimited

124. The Federal Reserve is trying to revive a sluggish economy, so it

[A] Cuts taxes
[B] Cuts the discount rate
[C] Raises the reserve requirement
[D] Raises taxes

125. The economy is slowing. Bond prices will likely

[A] Climb
[B] Fall
[C] Stabilize
[D] Be unaffected

126. Harry Yates believes the government should utilize fiscal programs to stimulate or slow the economy if needed. He believes in

[A] Monetarist Theory
[B] Keynesian Theory
[C] Government Theory
[D] Federal Theory

127. Martin James bought 1,000 shares of DEF stock on margin at $57 a share. DEF stock now trades at $63 a share. What is the equity in his margin account?

[A] $63,000
[B] $57,000
[C] $34,500
[D] $31,500

128. Frank Henderson has an SMA of $4,000 in his margin account. What is his buying power?

[A] Unlimited
[B] $2,000
[C] $4,000
[D] $8,000

129. Which of the following statements about closed-ended management companies is not true?

[A] They issue a fixed number of shares
[B] They do not redeem their own shares
[C] Shares sell at NAV
[D] Shares sell in the secondary marketplace

130. A bank borrows from its local Federal Reserve Bank at which of the following rates?

[A] Fed funds rate
[B] Call rate
[C] Prime rate
[D] Discount rate

APPENDIX D
Full Test Answer Key

Before you check your answers, eliminate five questions from each part, for ten total questions eliminated. As discussed in the introduction, your Series 7 exam consists of 260 questions, ten of which are test questions FINRA is trying out to see if they are effective and are not scored. Because your real exam will base its score on only 250 of the 260 questions, you should do the same to score your practice test. Pick your ten questions without thinking — do not pick just those answers you know you got wrong, as this will skew your score.

Each answer will list the corresponding chapter and section where you will be able to find the correct answer. Once you finish scoring, look for trends in questions you missed. Did you have trouble with margins or options math, or did you miss the questions on municipal securities? Identifying weak spots will allow you to review the material you need to get those questions right next time and not waste time on concepts you have already grasped.

PRACTICE TEST: PART I ANSWERS

1. **C** – Chapter 2: Voting
2. **B** – Chapter 12: Customer Profile
3. **A** – Chapter 2: Common Stock
4. **A** – Chapter 7: Trading Procedures
5. **B** – Chapter 10: Business Cycle and Markets
6. **B** – Chapter 5: Ways to Invest
7. **A** – Chapter 2: American Depository Receipts (ADRs)
8. **A** – Chapter 3: Other Money-Market Instruments
9. **B** –He bought $20,000 worth of stock, times Reg. T of 55 percent (0.55), to make for $11,000 for his deposit. His loan value (the amount he needs to borrow) is $20,000 - $11,000 = $9,000. For more examples, see Chapter 14: Calculating Equity for Long Margin Accounts.
10. **A** – Chapter 5: Variable Annuities
11. **C** – Chapter 11: Balance Sheet
12. **D** – Chapter 10: Indicators
13. **A** – Chapter 9
14. **C** – Chapter 5: Ways to Invest
15. **C** – Chapter 7: Option Strategies
16. **B** – Chapter 13: Cold-Calling Rules
17. **C** – Chapter 7: Option Strategies
18. **D** – Chapter 7: In-the-Money and Out-of-the-Money
19. **C** – Chapter 2 and Chapter 3
20. **D** – Chapter 14: Calculating Equity for Long Margin Accounts
21. **B** – Chapter 9: Ticker Tape
22. **A** – Chapter 13: Mark-up Rules
23. **C** – Chapter 13: Transferring Accounts
24. **D** – the earnings on these bonds is $80 in annual interest, plus $20 ($200÷10) in annual accretion, to equal $100 in total taxable earnings. For more examples, see Chapter 8: Accretion and Amortization for Bonds.
25. **B** – Chapter 10: The Federal Reserve
26. **B** – Chapter 4: Municipal Securities: Types and Definitions
27. **D** – Chapter 13: Opening Accounts
28. **A** – Chapter 9: Self-Regulatory Organizations (SROs)
29. **A** – Chapter 9: OTC Market Orders
30. **D** – Chapter 2: Dividends and Stock Splits
31. **B** – The shares will now trade at $30 a share, with EPS at $3, due to this 2-for-1 stock split. PE is unchanged, at $30/$3= 10. For more examples, see Chapter 2: Stock Splits.
32. **A** – Chapter 6: Oil and Gas Programs
33. **C** – Chapter 9: The Secondary Marketplace
34. **D** – The math here is simple: add the expense of the put premium of $3 to the price he paid per share XYZ stock: $65 + $3= $68. For more examples, see Chapter 7: Calculating Break-Even.
35. **B** – Chapter 7: Option Strategies
36. **B** – Chapter 12: Identifying Risk
37. **D** – Chapter 13: Custodial Accounts
38. **A** – Chapter 7: Option Strategies
39. **B** – Chapter 12: Identifying Risk and Chapter 3: Types of Bonds
40. **D** – Chapter 6: Basic Characteristics
41. **B** – Chapter 5: Management Investment Companies
42. **A** – Chapter 4: General Obligation (GO) Bonds

43. **C** – He paid $10,000 on ABC stock, and collected $500 for his premium, to make his expense $9,500. He then gained by selling his stock at $10,900, for a gain of $1,400. To close out his call position, he spent $400, for a net gain of $1,000. For more examples, see Chapter 7: Option Strategies.
44. **A** – Chapter 8: Retirement Plans
45. **A** – Chapter 13: Joint and Single Accounts.
46. **C** – Buying power is calculated this way: SMA ($3,000)/Reg. T (0.50) = $6,000. For more examples, see Chapter 14: SMA as Buying Power.
47. **A** – He is 60 years old; deduct this from 100 to arrive at 40, for 40 percent in stock, 60 percent in bonds and cash. For more examples, see Chapter 11: Portfolio Theory.
48. **A** – Chapter 12: Identifying Risk
49. **C** – He has $27,000 - $15,000 = $12,000 in equity. The account has dropped $3,000 in value, which has to be equally split between DR and EQ, so he will receive a margin call for $1,500. For more examples, see Chapter 14: Restrictions on Margin Accounts.
50. **A**–Chapter 10: Business Cycle and Markets
51. **B** – Chapter 11: Market Theories
52. **D** – Concession ($0.50) – manager's fee ($0.15) = additional takedown ($0.35). For more examples, see Chapter 2: Where the Money Goes.
53. **C** – Chapter 2: Syndicate Agreements.
54. **A** – Chapter 4: Municipal Securities: Types and Definitions
55. **B** – Chapter 13: Custodial Accounts
56. **B** – Chapter 4: Municipal Securities: Types and Definitions
57. **D** – Conversion ratio: $1,000/$20 = 50. For more examples, see Chapter 3: Convertible Bonds.
58. **C** – Chapter 12: Identifying Risk
59. **D** – Chapter 6: Real Estate Programs
60. **B** – Chapter 7: Options Strategies
61. **D** – Chapter 13: Account Statements
62. **D** – Chapter 8: Individual Retirement Accounts (IRAs)
63. **A** – Chapter 14: SMA and Long Margin Accounts
64. **B** – Chapter 4: Municipal Bonds: Types and Definitions
65. **A** – Chapter 2: Common Stock
66. **D** – Chapter 5 :Annuity Contracts
67. **B** – Chapter 4
68. **C** – Chapter 7: Option Strategies
69. **D** – Chapter 4 Industrial Revenue Bonds (IDRs)
70. **A** – Chapter 11: Technical Securities Analysis
71. **A** – Chapter 10: The Fed and the Market
72. **B** – He paid a $200 for his bond, which is amortized over eight years, for $25 a year. Deduct this from his annual interest income of $100 a year, for a net income of $75. For more examples, see Chapter 8: Accretion and Amortization for Bonds.
73. **D** – Chapter 13: Orders and Confirmations
74. **A** – Chapter 2: Equity Basics
75. **B** – Chapter 2: Syndicate Agreements
76. **C** – Chapter 3: Types of Bonds
77. **D** – Chapter 3: Types of Bonds
78. **C** – Chapter 3: Risk Analysis: Secured and Unsecured Bonds
79. **B** – Calculate this way: $30 – 15 percent dividend ($4.50) = $25.50. For more examples, see Chapter 2: Dividend Dates
80. **B** – Chapter 2: Voting
81. **A** – Chapter 3: Bond Ratings

82. **D** – Annual dividend ($600)/$1,200 = 5 percent. For more examples, see Chapter 3: Yield
83. **B** – Chapter 4: General Obligation (GO) Bonds
84. **D** – Chapter 2: Types of Preferred Stock
85. **B** – Chapter 3: Convertible Bonds
86. **A** – Chapter 4: Revenue Bonds
87. **B**–A syndicate adds the spread to the price it pays the company, so $20 + $100= $120 POP. For more examples, see Chapter 2: Where the Money Goes.
88. **B** – Net Revenue $500,000/Principal ($500,000) + interest ($25,000) = 95. For more examples, see Chapter 4: Revenue Bonds.
89. **D** – Chapter 2: Common Stock
90. **C** – Chapter 2: Stock Splits
91. **C** – Chapter 2: American Depository Receipts (ADRs)
92. **B** – Chapter 4: Bond Counsel
93. **A** – Chapter 4: IDRs
94. **C** – Total debt of $2,000,000/ population (500,000) = $4. For more examples, see Chapter 4: GO Bonds.
95. **A** – 6 percent × $1,000,000 = $60,000 times 3 years =$180,000. For more examples, see Chapter 4: Buying Municipal Securities.
96. **C** – Chapter 4: Municipal Securities: Types and Definitions
97. **C** – Chapter 5: Management Investment Companies
98. **B** – Chapter 7: LEAPs
99. **A** – Chapter 5: Ways to Invest
100. **D** – Chapter 7: Call and Put Options
101. **D** – Chapter 5: Investment Companies Defined
102. **D** – Chapter 6: Basic Characteristics
103. **D** – His interest income is $100 a year. The bond's $200 premium is amortized at $20 a year, so $100 - $20 = $80 is his annual income. For more examples, see Chapter 8: Accretion and Amortization for Bonds.
104. **C** – To reach this answer, use the following steps:
    1. Divide for each month the $50 invested by the price per share to find out how many shares he bought, per month
    2. Add the total shares bought (18.72)
    3. Divide $200 (the total amount he has invested) by those total shares to arrive at an average cost per share of $10.68. Look at Chapter 5: Ways to Invest for more examples.
105. **B** – Chapter 6: Equipment Leasing Programs
106. **A** – Chapter 7: Opening and Closing Transactions
107. **A** – Her interest income is $60 a year. Accretion of the discount is $300÷10 years=$30 a year, for a total income of $90 annually. For more examples, read Chapter 8: Accretion and Amortization for Bonds.
108. **C** – Chapter 4: Bond Counsel
109. **B** – Chapter 10: Business Cycle and Markets
110. **D** – Chapter 9: OTC Market Orders
111. **C** – The stock was sold for $2,000,000÷500,00 = $4 a share to the broker. The broker's commission is $0.30/$4.30 = 0.07, or 7 percent. For more examples, see Chapter 2: Where the Money Goes.
112. **D** – Chapter 2: Functions
113. **A** – Chapter 5: Annuity Contracts
114. **B** – Chapter 10: Business Cycle and Markets
115. **D** – Chapter 14: Restrictions on Margin Accounts

116. **C** – Chapter 7: Trading Procedures and Officials
117. **B** – Chapter 6: Tax Advantages.
118. **B** – Chapter 8: Accretion and Amortization for bonds.
119. **C** – Chapter 4: Selling Municipal Bonds
120. **D** – She gained 10 percent interest for six years, totaling $600. She paid a $500 premium for the bond, then received a $200 premium when she sold it, so: $600 - $500 + $200 = $300 gain. For more examples, see Chapter 8: Accretion and Amortization for bonds.
121. **A** – Chapter 12: Identifying Risk
122. **A** – Chapter 8: Gifts
123. **A** – Chapter 6: Basic Characteristics
124. **D** – Chapter 11: Portfolio Theory: Diversification
125. **C** – Chapter 14: Calculating Equity for Long Margin Accounts
126. **A** – Calculate this way:$16÷4 = $4. See Chapter 11: Ratios for more examples.
127. **C** – Chapter 3: Treasury Securities
128. **D** – Take the stock price of $65, add the premium of $7, to arrive at a break-even point of $72. See Chapter 7: Calculating Break-Even for more examples.
129. **B** – Chapter 14: Calculating Restriction for Long Margin Accounts
130. **D** – Chapter 10: Money Supply

PRACTICE TEST: PART II ANSWERS

1. **B** – Chapter 4: Industrial Revenue Bonds (IDRs)
2. **C** – His maximum loss is realized if DEF stock loses all its value. He spent $7,000 on the stock, minus his $300 premium collected, for a maximum loss of $6,700. For more examples, go to Chapter 7: Calculating Maximum Loss.
3. **C** – Chapter 7: Call and Put Options
4. **D** – First, you must calculate her credit balance by taking the original SMV of $60,000, and adding $30,000 Reg. T, for a total of $90,000 CR. Now deduct the new SMV of $64,000, to arrive at $26,000 EQ. Her new margin requirement is $32,000 (50 percent of new SMV), so her restriction is $30,000 - $26,000 = $6,000. For more examples, go to Chapter 14: Calculating Restriction on Short Margin Accounts.
5. **B** – Chapter 2: Six Steps to Registering Securities
6. **A** – Chapter 6: Equipment Leasing Programs
7. **C** – Chapter 6: Oil and Gas Programs
8. **C** – Chapter 3: Federal Reserve Repurchase Agreement (Repo)
9. **B** – Chapter 11: Ratios
10. **B** – Chapter 5: Unit Investment Trusts (UITs)
11. **A** – Chapter 6: Formation
12. **C** – Chapter 7: Options Strategies
13. **D** – Chapter 8: Taxation
14. **B** – Chapter 9: Dealers and Brokers
15. **B** – Chapter 10: Business Cycle and Markets
16. **C** – Chapter 7: Index Options
17. **C** – Chapter 13: Settlement of Orders

18. **B** – Use this math: \$2,000,000 - \$1,200,000 = \$800,000 working capital. See Chapter 11: Fundamental Securities Analysis for more information and examples.
19. **C** – The maximum loss here is the \$400 premium. For more examples, see Chapter 7: Calculating Maximum Loss.
20. **B** – Chapter 10: Five Stages of a Business Cycle
21. **D** – Chapter 10: Money Supply
22. **C** – Chapter 11: Charts and Patterns
23. **B** – Chapter 11: Fundamental Securities Analysis
24. **B** – Chapter 13: Street Name Accounts
25. **C** – Chapter 13: Orders and Confirmation
26. **D** – Calculate minimum maintenance by taking 25 percent of \$100,000, equaling \$25,000. For more examples, see Chapter 14: Restrictions on Margin Accounts.
27. **B** – Chapter 10: The Federal Reserve
28. **C** – Chapter 3: U.S. Treasury Securities
29. **D** – Chapter 10: Business Cycle and Markets
30. **D** – He had to exercise his call, resulting in a \$200 loss on the stock price (to meet his short obligation), plus his call premium of \$400, for a total of \$600. For more examples, see Chapter 7: Calculating Break-Even, Maximum Loss, and Maximum Gain
31. **A** – Chapter 3: U.S. Treasury Securities
32. **C** – Chapter 5: Fixed Annuities
33. **C** – You only need to calculate the break-even point of the long call, which is the strike price (\$55), plus premium (\$4), for a total of \$59. Go to Chapter 7: Calculating Break-Even for more examples.
34. **D** – Chapter 12: Identifying Risk
35. **A** – Chapter 7: Calculating Break-Even, Maximum Loss and Maximum Gain
36. **D** – Chapter 13: Orders and Confirmations
37. **B** – Five percent of \$60,000 = \$3,000 is the amount she can deduct from her taxes, bringing her taxable income to \$57,000. For more examples, go to Chapter 10: Individual Retirement Accounts (IRAs).
38. **B** – Chapter 8: Accretion and Amortization of Bonds
39. **C** – Chapter 7: Options Strategies
40. **D** – Chapter 7: Options Strategies
41. **D** – Minimum maintenance on long margin accounts is 25 percent of \$18,000, so \$4,200. For more information, see Chapter 14: Maintenance and Long Margin Accounts.
42. **D** – Maximum loss is realized if he has to exercise his call to meet his short obligation. He would have to buy 400 shares at \$60 a share, and sell them at \$59 a share, for a loss of \$400. Add to this his \$200 premium, for a maximum loss of \$600. For more examples of these types of calculations, see Chapter 7: Calculating Maximum Loss.
43. **B** – The conversion ratio means a \$1,000 bond will convert to 20 \$50 stock shares. At \$920, the conversion ratio of 20 would mean \$920÷20 = \$46 a share. For more information, see Chapter 3: Convertible Bonds
44. **D** – Chapter 2
45. **B** – Chapter 8: Capital Gain/Loss and Taxes
46. **D** – Chapter 7: Call and Put Options
47. **C** – Break-even point is at \$59 - \$5 per share premium = \$54 a share. For more examples of these types of calculations, see Chapter 7: Calculating Break-Even.
48. **C** – Chapter 4: Revenue Bonds

49. **B** – The LMV is $63,000. Her original Reg. T requirement was 50 percent of $57,000, so $28,500. Her equity is $63,000 – 28,500 = $34,500. For more examples of these types of calculations, see Chapter 14: Calculating Equity for Long Margin Accounts.
50. **D** – Chapter 100: Five Stages of a Business Cycle
51. **A** – Her maximum gain is realized when the options she sold are not exercised, so she can collect $400 + $300 = $700 in premiums. For more examples, see Chapter 7: Calculating Maximum Gain.
52. **C** – Chapter 5: Annuity Contracts
53. **B** – Chapter 11: Fundamental Securities Analysis
54. **D** – Chapter 10: Indicators
55. **A** – She gained $400 from the stock's rise in market value, but paid $300 for the option she bought, so $400 - $300 = $100 profit. For more examples of these types of calculations, see Chapter 7: Options Strategies.
56. **D** – Chapter 9: Dealers and Brokers
57. **C** – Chapter 10: The Fed and the Markets
58. **A** – His maximum gain is realized if both options are exercised. He would gain $1,000 on the stock, but would have to deduct net premium cost of $40 - $100 = $300, for a maximum gain of $1,000 - $300 = $700. Maximum loss is realized if the calls expire, at a premium cost of $300. For more examples of these types of calculation, see Chapter 7: Calculating Maximum Loss and Maximum Gain.
59. **B** – Chapter 8: Individual Retirement Accounts (IRAs)
60. **A** – Strike price ($75) – premium ($6) = $69. For more examples of these types of calculations, see Chapter 7: Calculating Break-even, Maximum Loss and Maximum Gain.
61. **A** – Chapter 2: Preferred Stock
62. **C** – Chapter 2: Where the Money Goes
63. **D** – Chapter 13: Minimum Maintenance on Margin Accounts
64. **B** – Chapter 3: U.S. Treasury Securities
65. **D** – Chapter 7: Call and Put Options
66. **D** – Chapter 5: Annuity Contracts
67. **B** – Chapter 7: Calculating Break-Even, Maximum Loss and Maximum Gain
68. **A** – Chapter 6: Real Estate Programs
69. **A** – Chapter 7: Basic Functions
70. **A** – Chapter 7: Trading Procedures and Officials
71. **D** – Chapter 8: Estate Taxes
72. **C** – Chapter 9: OTC Market Orders
73. **B** – Chapter 7: In-the-Money and Out-of-the-Money
74. **C** – His break-even point is at strike price plus premium, so $80 + $6 = $86 a share, or $8,600 total. For more examples of these types of calculations, see Chapter7: Calculating Break-Even, Maximum Loss and Maximum Gain.
75. **D** – Chapter 9: Working in the Primary Marketplace
76. **B** – Chapter 10: Money Supply
77. **D** – Chapter 7: Options Strategies
78. **D** – Chapter 3: Federal Reserve Bank Repurchase Agreement (Repo)
79. **D** – Chapter 12: Investment Objectives
80. **B** – She spent $40,000 on the stock, and gained $600 on the premium of the option she sold. She then gained $42,500 on the sale of the stock, and spent $500 to close out her call position. Calculate it this way: -$40,000 + $600 + $42,500 - $500 + $2,600. For more examples of these types of calculations, go to Chapter 7: Calculating Maximum Loss and Maximum Gain.

81. **C** – Chapter 10: Economic Theories
82. **B** – Chapter 9: Stop Limit Orders
83. **C** – Chapter 11: Technical Securities Analysis
84. **B** – Chapter 11: Charts and Patterns
85. **B** – Chapter 10: The Five Stages of a Business Cycle
86. **D** – Chapter 11: Market Theories
87. **A** – Chapter 10: Market Orders
88. **A** – Chapter 11: Ratios
89. **A** – Chapter 7: Options Strategies
90. **A** – Chapter 12: Determining Net Worth
91. **B** – Chapter 13: Custodial Accounts
92. **C** – Chapter 10: Fundamental Securities Analysis
93. **D** – Chapter 13: Anti Money-Laundering Rules
94. **D** – CR is $100,000 + Reg. T $50,000 = $150,000. For more examples of these types of calculations, see Chapter 14: Calculating Credit Balances for Short Margin Accounts.
95. **C** – Her credit balance was $75,000 ($50,000 + Reg. T). Now deduct the new SMV of $60,000, to arrive at $15,000 in equity. The new margin call is 50 percent of $60,000, so $30,000. Deduct $15,000 to arrive at $15,000 in margin restriction. See Chapter 14: Calculating Restriction for Short Margin Accounts for more examples of how to make these calculations.
96. **A** – Chapter 12: Identifying Risk
97. **A** – The new LMV is $8,000. Her debit balance is $8,000 (50 percent of original LMV of $16,000), which puts her EQ at $8,000 - $8,000 = $0. Her maintenance call is Reg. T 50 percent of $8,000, or $4,000. See Chapter 14: Maintenance and Long Margin Accounts for more examples of these types of calculations.
98. **C** – Chapter 11: Fundamental Securities Analysis
99. **A** – The stock went up $5,000, but this rise also means his Reg. T requirement went up, by 50 percent of this value. His SMA is $2,500. See Chapter 14: SMA and Long Margin Accounts for more examples of these types of calculations.
100. **B** – Chapter 14: Regulation T
101. **B** – 50 percent Reg. T of $100,000 equals $50,000. See Chapter 14: Calculating Equity for Long Margin Accounts for more examples.
102. **B** – Chapter 11: Ratios
103. **B** – Chapter 9: Ticker Tape
104. **B** – Chapter 12: Strategic Asset Allocation
105. **D** – Chapter 13: Corporate and Partnership Accounts
106. **A** – Chapter 10: Indicators
107. **B** – Chapter 12: Portfolio Allocation
108. **B** – Chapter 8: Individual Retirement Accounts (IRAs)
109. **A** – Chapter 12: Investment Strategies
110. **A** – Chapter 9: NASDAQ
111. **C** – He had an original CR of $150,000. With the new SMV of $80,000, his EQ is $150,000 - $80,000 = $70,000. For more examples of how to make these types of calculations, see Chapter 14: Calculating Equity for Short Margin Accounts.
112. **D** – Chapter 13: Opening Accounts
113. **A** – Chapter 13: The Patriot Act
114. **B** – His buying power is SMA $5000, divided by Reg. T 50 percent (0.50), so $10,000. For more examples of how to make these types of calculations, see Chapter 14: SMA as Buying Power.
115. **B** – Her maximum gain is realized if the 10 calls she sold are never realized, and she can collect her premium of $3,000. See Chapter 7: Calculating Maximum Gain for more examples of these types of questions.

116. **D** – Chapter 7: Options Strategies
117. **C** – Chapter 14: Regulation T
118. **B** – Chapter 2
119. **C** – Calculate the conversion ratio this way: $1,000/$40 = 25. See Chapter 3: Convertible Bonds for more information.
120. **C** – Chapter 10: Business Cycle and Markets
121. **C** – Chapter 13: Account Statements
122. **D** – Chapter 2: Stock Splits
123. **D** – Chapter 7: Calculating Maximum Loss
124. **B** – Chapter 10: The Fed and the Market
125. **A** – Chapter 10: The Five Stages of a Business Cycle
126. **B** – Chapter 10: Economic Theories
127. **C** – His long market value is $63,000. Deduct the 50 percent of $57,000 ($28,500) he owes his broker, to arrive at $63,000 - $28,500 = $34,500 in equity. See Chapter 14: Calculating Equity for Long Margin Accounts for more examples of these types of calculations.
128. **D** – Buying power is SMA/ Reg. T, so $4,000÷0.50 = $8,000. See Chapter 14: SMA as Buying Power for more examples of calculations of SMA.
129. **C** – Chapter 5: Ways to Invest
130. **D** – Chapter 10: The Federal Reserve

RESOURCES

Financial Industry Regulatory Authority **(www.finra.org)**

This Web site should be your first stop as a General Securities Representative. You will find information on recent regulation, continuing education, licensing, as well as answers to any questions you may have. The Web site also list information for investors so you could refer your clients to it.

The SEC **(www.sec.gov)**

This Web site contains news and information about SEC filings and links to other resources.

Certified Financial Planner Board of Standards **(www.cfp.net)**

This Web site lists requirements for becoming a Certified Financial Planner (CFP). There are a number of resources, including continuing education for CFPs.

NASDAQ **(www.nasdaq.com)**

This is NASDAQ's Web site, listing current market numbers. The site also includes resources for investors and industry professionals.

***NYSE* (www.nyse.com)**

This is the NYSE Web site, listing current market conditions, and educational reference for investors.

***Chicago Board Options Exchange* (www.cboe.com)**

This Web site provides options trading information, including current data, strategies, and information for financial professionals and institutions.

***Dow Jones Indexes* (www.djindexes.com)**

This Web site lists all the Dow Jones indexes, provides data, news, and other resources.

***The Chicago Board of Trade* (www.cbot.com)**

This Web site gives information on the OTC market, with current market numbers, educational information, and OTC news.

***The Municipal Securities Rulemaking Board (MSRB)* (www.msrb.org)**

This Web site gives information on the MSRB, including board news, rules, and information about forms and procedures.

GLOSSARY

11 Bond Index: Index of 11 bonds of the 20 Bond Index, with at least an AA rating.

20 Bond Index: An Index of 20 General Obligation (GO) bonds with at least an A rating, maturing in 20 years.

40 Bond Index: Index of 40 GO and revenue bonds, listed by price.

403(b) Plan: Allows an employee working for a non-profit with 501(c)(3) classification to make tax-deductible contributions to their retirement account.

Access Levels: Different types of information on trades for NASDAQ.

Accretion: The gains an investor makes from holding a bond.

Accrued Interest: The interest that has not yet been paid by the issuer.

Acid Test Ratio: (Cash + marketable securities)/current liabilities.

Adjustable or Floating Rate Preferred Stock: A type of preferred stock where the dividend rate of stock is reset every six months in line with market interest rates.

Advance-Decline Theory: Compares rising stocks to falling stocks daily to interpret market direction.

Aggressive: Investing in volatile stock, put or call options, or buying securities on margin.

All or None (AON): Order must be filled entirely (can be done in segments) or not at all.

Amortization: Deducting the loss incurred by paying a premium from the interest (or gain) received from the bond

Assets: Include fixed assets (like property and equipment), current assets (like cash, accounts receivable — the more liquid assets), and intangible assets (like copyrights, goodwill, etc.).

At the Close: Order must be filled as close to closing price as possible or is canceled.

At-the-Money: When an option's strike price and the stock market price are the same.

At the Open: Order must be filled at the opening price of a security (can be all or part of the order).

Authorized Stock: The total, maximum number of stock shares a corporation can issue, which is decided under its articles of corporation.

Average Cost Per Share: = Total dollars invested/shares bought.

Balanced Funds: Funds that balance investments between bonds and common and preferred stocks to tamper risk.

Balanced Investments: A mix of aggressive and defensive investments to reduce risk.

Balance of Payments: Contains the balance between import and export activities (current account), as well as the amount of investment either country makes in each other's economy (capital account).

Balance Sheet: A document comparing a company's assets and liabilities.

Banker's Acceptances: A short-term credit investment a bank backs.

Bear Call Spread: The investor buys and sells call options with a different strike price, but with the same expiration month.

Bearer Bonds: These bonds are not registered in anyone's name, and have coupons attached that entitle the bearer to interest payments, which is why they are also known as coupon bonds. Like partially registered bonds, the risk of theft or loss is great, so they are no longer issued. Because bearer bonds still circulate, you must know them for your exam.

Bear Put Spread: The investor buys and sells put options with the same expiration month.

Blue List: Lists all municipal bond offerings alphabetically by state.

Board Broker: Helps with trades for the most active options.

Bond Anticipation Notes (BAN): Notes issued to bridge time when long-term bonds will be issued.

Bond Counsel: A law firm hired by a municipality to navigate the legalities involved in acquiring the funding needed for a project and the corresponding bond issue.

Bond Funds: Invest in bonds; low risk.

Bond Interest Coverage: = EBT/bond shares outstanding.

Bond Ratio: = Bonds par value/long-term capital.

Bonds: Debt instruments that act as loans to the corporation, to be repaid like debt.

Book Entry Certificates: Bonds that are registered electronically.

Book Value per Share: = (Assets - liabilities)/bond shares outstanding.

Breakout: Once a stock breaks through the support or resistance level.

Breakpoint: Hitting the pre-arranged level.

Broker: If a firm makes a trade on securities not in inventory.

Bull Call Spread: An investor would buy a call at a lower strike price, and would sell a call at a higher strike price.

Bull Put Spread: Selling and buying a put with the same expiration month.

Buying Power: SMA can be cashed out by the investor, or it can be used as leverage to buy more securities.

Buy Limit Order: Used if stock is at a price that a customer deems too high, but will be executed if that stock drops to a desired market price.

Buy Stop Order: Is used to protect a customer who is short a stock; when the stock goes up, against expectations, the customer buys it to prevent greater loss.

Callable Bonds: Bonds the issuer has a right to buy back.

Callable Preferred Stock: Gives issuer the right to buy back preferred stock at any time.

Call: Allows the investor to buy a stock at a price determined by the seller of the option.

Call Purchase: A simple way to ensure that when a stock rises, you are able to buy it at the option strike price.

Capital Growth: Investing in newer companies where there is a greater possibility for capital growth.

Capital: Risk of losing your principal investment.

Capped: When index options are limited.

Cash Dividend: The investor receives dividend in cash, which is taxable and decreases the value of the stock.

Certificate of Limited Partnership: Completed by a limited partnership's members and outlines the basic rights and obligations of investors, or limited partners.

Chicago Board Options Exchange (CBOE): Regulates options trading and enforces its rules.

Churning: Trading heavily to generate commissions.

Class: Options of the same type (call or put) of the same underlying security.

Closed-Ended Funds: Also called publicly traded funds, these funds carry a fixed amount of shares, which are sold to investors, and consequently traded in the market.

Closing Purchase/Closing Sale: A transaction opposite to the investor's current position.

Coincident Indicators: These give a picture of the present state of the economy. Examples of coincident indicators are industrial industry production, individual income, and retail sales.

Collateral Trusts: Backed by financial assets the issuer owns, held by a trustee (a financial institution like a bank) in case of insolvency.

Commercial Paper: A corporate investment without collateral, making it a higher risk investment.

Commission: A firm acts as a broker, it charges a commission to act as a middle-man.

Committee on Uniform Security Identification Procedures (CUSIP) Number: A security identification number.

Common Stock Funds: Invest in common stock. These funds are often specialized like growth funds, like blue chip funds investing in blue chip stocks.

Common Stockholder Rights or Access to Corporate Books: A stockholder has the right to see a corporation's balance sheet and income statements.

Companion Tranches: These tranches are created to support the PAC and TAC CMOs and absorb prepayment risk.

Consolidation: A stock is trading within a relatively narrow price range.

Construction Loan Notes (CLN): Issued to fund apartment buildings, these notes provide funding for construction.

Consumer Price Index (CPI): An indicator of inflation or deflation.

Contrarian Theory: Assumes customers trading in small numbers of stocks are usually wrong.

Convertible Bonds: Some bonds carry the option of converting the bond into stocks, aptly named convertible bonds.

Convertible Preferred Stock: Can be traded for common stock at any time. Calculate by using conversion price decided at issue: conversion ratio = par value/conversion price.

Coordination: The issuing company files with the SEC, and the SEC helps the company files with the state.

Corporate Resolution: Specifies who makes decisions on the account.

Coupon Rate: The interest an investor receives on the par value of the bond.

Coverdell IRAs: Savings vehicles for the education of children under 18.

Covered Call: The investor sells call options backed by a holding of the underlying stock.

Covered Put: The investor sells put options on stock he or she holds, expecting the stock to remain (near) stagnant again so he or she can collect the premiums.

Credit: A type of investment risk; the risk of not getting paid on time.

Cum-Rights: A simple formula to calculate the value of this right.

Cumulative Preferred Stock: A type of preferred stock; if dividend is not paid, it accumulates and is owed.

Cumulative Voting: The ability for a stockholder to vote for a board member any way he or she chooses.

Currency Transaction Report (CTR): Where cash money deposits of $10,000 or more are reported to.

Current Income: Investing in securities that provide cash dividend or interest (bonds, income funds, etc.).

Current Ratio: Current assets/current liabilities.

Current Yield: The annual return of an investment based on the market price of the bond.

Custodial Account: For a minor (age of a minor is determined by the state). All investment decisions for custodial accounts are made by the custodian (customer).

Day Order: Order that is only good for that trading day.

Dealer: A firm sells securities from its own account.

Debentures: By agreement, the bond holder receives interest when due and principal at maturity.

Debt Options: Options based on debt instruments, like government or corporate bonds.

Debt Service Coverage Ratio: Net revenue/principal + interest

Debt-to-Equity Ratio: = (Bonds + preferred stock)/equity.

Defensive: Maintaining principal while getting interest on that principal.

Depletion: Limited partnerships are allowed deductions for depletion of resources as a percentage of resources sold.

Direct Participation Programs: Created to form tax shelters by investing in real estate, equipment leasing, and oil and gas programs.

Discount Rate: The rate at which banks can borrow money from the Fed.

Discretionary Account: When an investor wants you, as their registered representative, to make investment decisions for them.

District Business Conduct Committee (DBCC): Where complaints against a registered representative are sent for resolution.

Diversification: Investing in different types of securities to offset risk.

Dividend Payout Ratio: Common dividend/earnings per share.

Double-Barreled: When the good faith and credit of the issuer and the revenue of a project backs a bond.

Dow Jones Municipal Index: Lists weekly averages of state and city bond yields.

Downtrend: When a stock moves down over a long term.

Dual-Purpose Bonds: Investing in two types of stock to serve combined goals, like income and capital.

Early Expansion: Interest rates and inflation are low; consumer confidence, spending, and growth are rising.

Earnings per Common Share (EPS): = (Net worth-preferred stock)/common shares outstanding (if convertible bonds are included, this is fully diluted EPS).

Eastern Accounts: Responsibility of sales is shared between members.

EAT (or Net Income): = EBT - Taxes.

EBIT: = Net Sales - Cost of Goods Sold-Operating Expenses - Depreciation.

EBT: = EBIT - bond interest expense.

Employee Retirement Income Securities Act (ERISA): Signed into law in 1974 to loosen prior retirement plan eligibility and regulate how pension plans are managed.

Employee Stock Ownership Plan (ESOP): Allows an employee to invest in his or her company's stock.

Endorsement: Signing the certificate over to its new holder.

Equipment Trusts: Backed by equipment of the issuer (usually high-priced transportation equipment, like buses, trucks, or airplanes).

Eurodollars: American dollars held at a foreign bank located outside the United States.

Exchange Traded Funds: Funds where stocks are not bought from the issuer, but traded at various exchanges and NASDAQ.

Ex-Dividend Date: The day after the dividend is distributed.

Existing Real Estate: The goal of existing real estate investments is for the limited partnership to gain immediate rental income. Although this is still a lower-risk real estate investment, maintenance and repair costs can eat into the partnership's profits.

Ex-Legal: A bond issued without a legal opinion; needs to be stamped.

Expiration Date: The month an option expires.

Federal Farm Credit Bank: Issues short-term discount notes and interest-bearing bonds with different maturities to fund Banks for Cooperative (COOPS), Federal Land Banks (FLB), and Federal Intermediate Credit Banks (FICB) to fund first mortgages on farm properties.

Federal Home Loan Bank: Makes loans to banks to cover excess credit demand due to market fluctuations.

Federal Home Loan Mortgage Corporation: A subsidiary of the Federal Home Loan Bank (FHLB), it packages different kinds of mortgages, including but not limited to FHA, VA, and FmHA mortgages.

Federal National Mortgage Association (Fannie Mae): Created to make home ownership more affordable, it purchases Federal Housing Association (FHA) mortgages, Farmers Home Administration (FmHA), or Veterans Administration (VA) mortgages.

Federal Reserve Board: Supervises this network, and sets and executes monetary policy for the country.

Fed Fund Rate: The rate at which banks loan/borrow money to meet reserve requirements.

Fill or Kill (FOK): Order must be filled immediately or is canceled.

FINRA Board of Governors: Appeals are sent here if the customer is dissatisfied and wants to appeal a decision regarding a complaint about a registered representative.

FINRA Mark-up Policy: Guidelines regarding commissions to protect customers from excessive charges by brokerage firms.

Fixed Investment Trust: Trust terminates when the investments (usually bonds) mature.

Floor Broker: The broker whose job is to take orders to the trading floor.

Foreign Currency Options: These work like stock options, giving the holder the option to buy or sell the currency at a certain strike price.

Forward Split: Stock is split to create more shares with a decrease in price.

Full Pay-Out Lease: In this scenario, the limited partnership purchases equipment anticipating to lease on a long-term basis, usually to only one user. One contract pays for the equipment.

Fully Registered Bonds: These most common bonds are registered in the investor's name and the investor received interest automatically, without having to submit any coupons.

Fundamental Analysis: An industry risk analysis, which means you will analyze company management, balance sheets, income statements, and any other data on the health of the corporation.

General Obligation Bonds: Created to pay for projects that do not bring in revenue to repay the obligation.

General Partner: A manager in a limited partnership.

Good Delivery: The certificates are in good condition (not torn or mangled), endorsed, and for the right type and amount of securities.

Good until Canceled (GTC): Orders can stay open until filled; specialist will clear his books in April and October so the order would have to be re-entered then.

Government Bond Funds: Invest in Treasury securities only.

Government National Mortgage Association (Ginnie Mae): An agency of the Department of Housing and Urban Development, it backs FHA, VA, and FmHA mortgages traded by securities firms.

Gross Domestic Product: This shows how the production of the entire economy fares, as well as how stable prices are.

Growth Funds: Funds that have capital appreciation (growth) as a goal.

Guaranteed Bonds: A form of secured bonds backed by another firm like a parent company.

Immediate or Cancel (IOC): Order like FOK, but can be partially filled.

Income Bonds: Bonds where principal is paid at maturity but interest is only paid when the issuer's earnings are high enough (very high risk).

Income Funds: Funds that invest in bonds, often higher risk or "junk" bonds, to increase income.

Indenture Agreement: Specifies par value, coupon rate, maturity, collateral, and convertible or callable features.

Index Funds: Invest in funds that mirror an index, like Standard and Poor's. The fund's objective is to have earnings in line with the market.

Index Options: Options based on the performance of an exchange or industry segment, allowing investors to speculate on market movement in these industries or indexes.

Industrial Revenue Bonds: Municipalities issue IDRs, but their repayment comes from corporate lease payment.

Initial Public Offering (IPO): Authorizes a number of shares to be issued to the public.

Insurance Covenants: The municipality must insure the project.

Intangible Drilling Costs (IDCs): Non-tangible expenses, like employee wages and fuel costs, that a limited partnership is allowed to write off.

Integration: When funds from an illegal source are mixed with legitimate business proceeds.

International Funds: Invest in foreign securities. These funds are often used to diversify investment portfolios.

In-the-Money: A term for when an option is profitable for the holder. For a call, it means the stock is trading higher than the strike price; for a put, it means the stock is trading lower than the strike price. If an option is trading in-the-money, it has intrinsic value.

Investment Advisers Act of 1940: Requires all investment advisors to register with the SEC.

Investment Banking Firm: Advises the issuing company and underwrites the issue.

Investment Company Act of 1940: Requires all investment companies to register with the SEC and comply with SEC regulation.

Issued Shares: Stocks sold in the market as part of an IPO.

Joint Life with Last Survivor Annuity: This annuity pays two investors for both their lifetimes; pays both portions to the survivor (usually a spouse) until their death.

Joint Tenants With Right of Survivorship (JTWROS): JTWROS account would pass the deceased owner's portion on to the surviving joint holder (usually a spouse).

Joint With Tenants in Common (JTIC): If one of the account holders of a JTIC dies, his or her portion becomes part of his or her estate.

Keynesian Theory: It believes governments should intervene for an economy to remain balanced.

Lagging Indicators: Changes after the economy has already moved to the next stage in the business cycle. Lagging indicators are prime interest rates, ratio of consumer debt to income, and the consumer price.

Late Expansion: Consumer demand grows and begins to outpace supply, causing inflation and a rise in interest rates.

Layering: When a customer moves money between accounts to hide its source.

Leading Indicators: Numbers that change before the economy by large changes — they give us a taste of what is to come. Examples are first filings for unemployment, new building permits issued, and the index of consumer expectation.

Letter of Intent (LOI): The investor has to meet the share requirement in this document within 13 months; the agreement can be backdated up to 90 days; and shares are kept in an escrow account until the LOI obligation is met.

Level I: Created for registered representatives, this computer screen displays bid and ask prices for several hundred NASDAQ stocks.

Level II: For traders, this screen displays asking prices of each market maker (principal or dealer).

Level III: Most complete information for market makers, allowing them to enter and change quotes.

Life Annuity: This investment pays out only for the life of the investor and stops paying when the investor dies.

Life Annuity with Period Certain: This annuity gives a payout for a specified time (20 years for example) with survivor benefits should the investor die before the term is up.

Limited Life: Where a corporation aims to exist forever, a limited partnership must have a maturity date or goal.

Limit Order: Is also a conditional order: The customer wants to buy or sell a security at a certain market price, to increase profit.

Liquidity: Investing in securities that are easily converted to cash.

L: M3, plus T-Bills, savings bonds, commercial paper, banker's acceptances, and U.S.-held term Eurodollars.

Locked Investment: Limited partners cannot sell or transfer their investments like stock.

Long-Term Anticipation Securities (LEAPS): Speculate on the long-term, two-to-five year performance of an underlying security, and are traded on NYSE, Amex, and NASDAQ.

Long-Term Capital: = Long-term liabilities + stockholders' equity.

Long-Term or Short-Term: Investing in securities for long-term or short-term gains.

M1: Most liquid: cash in circulation, demand deposits, and traveler's checks.

M2: M1, plus time deposits < $100k, individual money market accounts, overnight repurchase agreements, and overnight Eurodollars.

M3: M2, plus time deposits >$100k, institutional money market accounts, and term repurchase agreements.

Maintenance Call: Issued when a customer must deposit into their margin account right away.

Maintenance Covenants: Ensure the municipality takes care of the property (or facility and equipment).

Managing or Lead Underwriter: Underwriter who puts a syndicate together.

Margin Call: When a broker demands this deposit.

Mark-down: Charged when a dealer sells securities for a customer; it is taken out of the customer's profit.

Market Maker: Broker registered to trade specific options for their own account.

Marking the Open/Close: Executing several transactions at open or close, to simulate activity.

Mark-Up: A dealer buys securities for a customer; it charges a (sales charge) to the customer.

Monetarist Theory: A gradual growth in money supply, not government intervention, leads to a stable economy.

Money Market Funds: Invest in short-term money market investments.

Money Supply: Broken into categories named M1, M2, M3, and L. Each of these categories is separated by their ease of use: how easy it is to access this money supply and spend it.

Moral Obligations: Issued when only a source outside the municipality's tax base or other revenue backs a bond. These bonds are considered high risk.

Mortgage Bonds: Backed by property owned by the issuer.

Municipal Bond Funds: Invest in municipal bonds only, often limited by state.

Municipal Securities Rulemaking Board (MSRB): The MSRB was created to develop regulation regarding municipal securities transactions by banks. MSRB makes rules for these transactions, but does not actually enforce them — nor does it enforce SEC rules.

Negotiable Certificates of Deposit (CDs): Negotiable time deposits with a higher interest rate due to the investment required ($100,000 is the minimum).

Net Asset Value (NAV): Value of Funds Assets/Outstanding Shares.

Net Asset Value per Bond: = Net worth/ bonds shares outstanding.

Net Interest Cost (NIC): Total cost of interest payments a municipality will make until a bond's maturity.

Net Profit Ratio: = Net income/net sales.

Net Revenue Pledge: Guarantees that the municipality has the funds to repay bondholder obligations with generated revenue after paying operating expenses.

New Construction: The limited partnership purchases land to build homes, which it then hopes to sell at a profit. New construction is considered less risky than land investment.

New York Stock Exchange (NYSE): The largest and oldest exchange market in the United States, the NYSE lists securities, sets exchange policies, and enforces them.

Nominal Yield: The interest of a bond at issuance, also called coupon rate.

Non-Marketable Savings Bonds: A U.S. Treasury security that is non-negotiable, meaning they are not re-sold in the marketplace.

Non-Qualified Plans: A retirement plan that takes contributions from after-tax dollars. Gains are tax-deferred under non-qualified plans, and when the investor draws from the account at retirement, the contributions are not taxed again.

Not Held (NH): Order allowing broker to fill it later if a better market price is expected.

Notification: Established companies who have filed with a state for previous securities offering(s) can simply renew their application.

Odd-Lot Theory: Looks at customers trading in odd-lot numbers of stocks (1-99 shares), with the assumption these customers are usually wrong.

Open-Ended Funds: Best known as a mutual fund, these funds have an unlimited amount of shares available – new investors are always welcome. A prospectus needs to be available to investors.

Opening Purchase: When an investor first buys a call or put.

Opening Sale: When an investor sells a call or put.

Operating Lease: The limited partnership leases equipment for a short term. The partnership needs several lease contracts before the equipment and financing is paid for.

Operating Profit Margin: = Operating income/net sales.

Options Clearing Corporation (OCC): Issues all options contracts; is co-owned by the exchanges and regulated by the SEC. It keeps track of sellers and buyers, ensuring both meet the options contract obligations.

Options: Also known as derivatives, or derivative instruments; contracts based on the value of an underlying investment, most often a company's stock.

Order Book Official: Holds the order until market conditions are right.

Original Issue Discount (OID) Bonds: These bonds are issued at a discount and reach par value at maturity. OID bonds also receive interest, which is non-taxable.

Out-of-the-Money: A term for when an option is not profitable for the holder. For a call, it means the stock is trading lower than the exercise price; for a put, it means a stock is trading higher than the strike price.

Outstanding Stocks: Remaining stocks in the marketplace.

Oversold: When the index is declining, but individual stocks show an uptrend.

Painting the Tape: Simulating activity; for instance, splitting one 20,000-share trade into four 5,000-share trades.

Partially Registered Bonds: These bonds only register the par value in the investor's name, not the interest. Also known as registered coupon bonds, these are no longer issued but still circulate in trading (and are therefore part of the Series 7 Exam).

Participating Preferred Stock: A form of preferred stock, where the investor receives common stock dividend.

Participating Trust: A type of unit investment trust that invests in set mutual funds shares, with no set maturation.

Partnership Agreement: Specifies who makes decisions on the account.

Patriot Act: Created to protect the country against terrorist activity.

Payment Date: When the buyer pays for the trade.

Peak: Part of the economic cycle where growth is at its highest and begins to decline. Reduced spending by businesses and consumers follows.

Placement: When funds are deposited.

Planned Amortization Class (PAC) Tranches: CMO tranche with the most certain amortization date and therefore the least risk (and corresponding return).

Pollution Control Mutual Bond: Bonds issued to fund construction of pollution control facilities. Like with Industrial Revenue Bonds (IDRs), the value of the bond is rated by the solvency of the future lessee of the facility.

Preemptive Rights: Right to buy shares before it is offered to others.

Preferred Stockholders: These stockholders are repaid their investment before common stockholders, should the issuing company go bankrupt.

Preferred Stock: Works much like common stock in the sense that it gives the investor ownership in a company. Preferred stock was created because investors often have different risk tolerance, tax needs, and financial objectives.

Preservation of Capital: Low-risk investments (like bonds) where capital is preserved.

Price-Earnings Ratio (P/E): = market price/earnings per share.

Primary Offerings: When Treasury stock is sold to the public.

Prior or Senior Preferred Stock: Investor receives money before other preferred stockholders in case of bankruptcy of issuer.

Progressive Taxes: Cover income tax and gift and estate taxes — progressive taxes affect higher-income customers more.

Project Notes (PN): Notes used to fund low-income or subsidized housing projects.

Public Offering Price (POP): Net asset value + broker's commission.

Public or Government-Assisted Housing: This limited partnership investment derives its income from rental payments and tax credits. This is the least risky of real estate investments because the government backing these programs compensates for any payments tenants miss.

Put: Allows the investor to sell a stock at a price determined by the seller of the option

Put Bonds: Bonds the holder has the right to redeem (or put back) with the issuer at par value.

Put Purchase: A simple way for an investor to protect himself against a drop in stock.

Qualification: When a security is exempt from filing with the SEC but must still file with the state.

Qualified: The bond counsel sees issues, or qualifiers, that affect the bond issue.

Quick Asset Ratio: (Current assets - inventory)/current liabilities.

Rate Covenant: A municipality must charge enough for use of facility to ensure principal and interest can be repaid to the investor.

Recession: Marked by reduced consumer demand, unemployment, and lowering inflation are all signs of this stage in the business cycle. If this downturn continues beyond 18 months, it is called a depression.

Record Date: When a company declares dividends.

Recovery: Part of the economic cycle indicated by a rise in consumer and/or business spending, which leads to the beginning of a new business cycle.

Refunding Bonds: These bonds are issued to refund outstanding bonds, often if there has been a significant drop in market interest rates. The issuer saves money by issuing these lower-interest Refunding Bonds. Sometimes called Advanced Refunding Bonds.

Registrar: Ensures there is no over-issuance of stock.

Regressive Taxes: Set taxes on payroll, sales, property, etc. Regressive taxes are set at the same rate for everyone, regardless of income.

Regular Account: The investor simply buys a certain amount of shares.

Regulation T (Reg. T): This rule states a customer must back their account with a minimum 50 percent deposit of the total value of the securities they intend to buy or sell; securities firms can demand for this deposit to be higher if they wish.

Reinvestment: A type of investment risk of having to reinvest returns at a lower rate.

Repurchase Agreements: The Fed buys Treasury securities so it can temporarily inject money into the system, only to agree to sell them again according to the agreement.

Resistance Level: A stock's highest trading price.

Restricted: A margin account that drops below Reg. T requirements.

REVDEX 25: Index of 25 revenue bonds, rated A or better and maturing in 30 years, based on yield.

Revenue Anticipation Notes (RAN): Notes issued to fund operations in anticipation of a municipality's expected revenue.

Revenue Bonds: Created to fund projects that will generate the revenue to pay the obligation back.

Reverse Repurchase Agreement: The Fed can sell Treasury securities to reduce the money supply.

Reverse Split: Stock is combined to increase price and decrease shares.

Roth IRA: Individual retirement account in which contributions are not tax-deductible.

Rule 1120: Specifies requirements for continuing education for securities industry professional. In order to keep your Series 7 license active, you must complete a computer-based training program within 120 days of your two-year anniversary as a registered representative. After this, you will need to repeat this training every three years. You will need to schedule these exams and pay a fee to take them; check the FINRA Web site when you get close to these dates to get details on current fees and scheduling procedures.

Sales Charge (%): POP-NAV/POP.

Secondary Marketplace (or Aftermarket): Has four components: the first (or auction) market, second (or OTC) market, third market, and fourth market.

Section 529 Plans: Allow investors to save for higher education.

Self-Regulatory Organization (SRO.): Can enforce their rules by fining, reprimanding, or suspending violating members; SROs do not have the authority to criminally prosecute violators of its rules.

Sell a "Naked" Put: The investor expects the underlying security to rise. Even though someone does not hold the stock, he or she expects the stock to rise and the option not to be exercised. He or she will collect the option premium as profit but risks having to buy the stock, should it drop low enough for the option to be exercised.

Selling a "Naked" Call: The investor expects the stock to drop (bearish expectations), and therefore speculates the call is never exercised so he or she can collect the premium.

Selling Group: A brokerage firm the syndicate hires to help sell securities.

Sell Limit Order: Used by a customer who holds a stock and wants to sell it once it reaches a certain market price or higher.

Sell Stop Order: Is used to protect a customer who is long a stock; by selling before stock drops too much, the customer limits losses.

Serial Bonds: Bonds that carry different maturity dates.

Series Bonds: These bonds are issued in different years, but mature at the same time.

Series: Options of the same strike price, same class, and same expiration month.

Settlement Date: The issuer of the securities will update their records and send certificates to your firm.

Short-Interest (or Cushion) Theory: Looks at short sellers' actions to determine market direction. It also takes a contrarian position: this theory assumes a rise in short sales actually means the market will rise.

Short Straddle Strategy: Selling both a call and a put option at the same strike price and with the same expiration date.

Simplified Employee Pensions (SEP): Retirement plans for self-employed individuals, or those working for small-business employers without traditional retirement plans.

Sovereign: A type of investment risk where a foreign company may change policy that affects investment value.

Specialized Funds: Invest in a particular industry, companies in the same area, etc. These funds are speculating on out of the ordinary growth in a particular investment segment.

Special Memorandum Account (SMA): When a margin account exceeds Reg. T or FINRA requirements.

Standard and Poor's Composite Index: Similar to the Dow Jones in its composition. S&P's uses 400 industrial, 20 transportation, 40 utility, and 40 financial stocks for its index of the market.

Stated Value: Assigned by the company for bookkeeping purposes to protect stockholder in case of great losses.

Statutory Voting: When a stockholder has to vote evenly, not any way they choose. (See Cumulative voting.)

Stock: A form of ownership, or equity, in a company in the form of shares.

Stock Dividend: The investor receives their dividends in stocks, which is non-taxable.

Stop Limit Order: A combination of the stop and limit order.

Stop Order: A conditional order: The customer wants to buy or sell a security, should it reach a certain market price to limit losses.

Straight Preferred Stock: Receives no accumulation of dividend if issuer does not pay.

Strategic Asset Allocation: Bases investment choices on the portfolio holder's long-term goals.

Street Name Accounts: An ID number used for trading — all margin accounts trade in this way.

Strike Price: The price at which an option is exercised.

Student Loan Marketing Association (Sallie Mae): Owned by its participants, it guarantees student loans.

Subscription Agreement: Details annual income and net worth, much like credit application.

Subscription Price: Number of rights to purchase one share.

Support: The bracket that the stock trades in (lowest trading price).

Suspicious Activity Report (SAR): A report of suspicious transactions of more than $5,000.

Syndicate Agreement: Indicates who gets paid what and the responsibility each member has to the shares the syndicate commits to as a whole.

Syndicate: Group of underwriters, each responsible for selling a portion of the securities.

Tactical Asset Allocations: Adjusting a portfolio to market conditions.

Tangible Drilling Costs (TDCs): Deductions allowed for depreciation of salvage-able assets over several years.

Targeted Amortization Class (TAC) Tranches: CMO tranche with less certain payment schedule and higher risk and return.

T**ax Anticipation Bills (TAB):** Geared toward corporate tax-paying investors and issued at a discount to mature at par, usually a few days after corporate tax dates.

Tax Anticipation Notes (TAN): Notes a municipality's anticipated taxes will finance.

Tax-qualified plans: Allows the investor to use pre-tax dollars to invest, therefore deducting the contributions from his income.

Telephone Act of 1991: Created to protect consumers from obtrusive sales calls.

Term Bonds: Bonds that are issued at the same time and mature at the same time.

The Conference Board: Publishes a report on the state of the most important economic indicators.

The Dow Theory: Theory argues if the market as a whole declines, so will individual stocks, regardless of their position or rating.

The Multiplier Effect: An example is when people were worried about not having their jobs, which led to a lower propensity to consume and an in-crease in savings; Keynesian theorists believe it leads to a recession or even depression in an economic cycle.

The Prudent Man Rule: A representative must act reasonably regarding their customer's investments, as a prudent man or woman would.

The Securities Act of 1933 (also known as the Truth in Securities Act): Requires registration and disclosure of securities in a prospectus.

The Securities and Exchange Act of 1934: Assigned enforcement responsibilities of the 1933 act.

The Securities Investor Protection Corporation (SIPC): Protects investors' assets should their brokerage firm go bankrupt.

The Trust Indenture Act of 1939: Required all securities issued must be filed with an indenture agreement, specifying a trustee free of conflict-of-interest.

The Wash Sale Rule: Investors cannot buy or sell the same security 30 days before or after claiming a loss on the sale of that same security.

Time Value: = Premium – Intrinsic Value

Trade Confirmation: Confirmations include the same information as on the order ticket.

Trade Date: Date when the order is placed.

Traditional IRA: An individual retirement account where contributions are tax-qualified.

Tranches: Portions of CMOs, or collateralized mortgage obligations

Transfer Agent: Typically is a commercial bank, but sometimes an issuing corporation that records the holders of the stocks that have been sold.

Treasury Bills (T-Bills): Issued at a discount to mature at par; carry an initial maturity of 4, 13, and 26 weeks.

Treasury Bonds (T-Bonds): Pay interest every 6 months; mature at 10 to 30 years.

Treasury Inflation-Indexed Securities (TIPS): Pay market interest every six months, and par value adjusts to market inflation or deflation.

Treasury Notes (T-Notes): Pay interest every six months; mature at two, three, five, and ten years.

Treasury Stock: Stocks a company issues then buys back.

Trendline: Charting data.

True Interest Cost (TIC): Net interest cost (NIC) plus the time value of money.

Undersold: A market that will show an index incline but decline in individually sold stocks.

Underwriter: A broker dealer who helps the issuer brings securities to prospective buyers.

Unqualified: The bond counsel sees no complications in the bond issue.

Unsecured Bonds: A riskier investment because they are not backed by a security and generally carry a corresponding higher yield.

Unsolicited Orders: When the customer wants to complete an order against your recommendations.

Uptrend: When a stock moves up over a long term.

U.S. Treasury's Financial Crimes Network (FinCEN): Where Suspicious Activity Report (SAR) is sent.

U.S. Treasury Strips (T-Strips): Issued at a discount to mature at par; mature after 6 months to 30 years.

Variable Annuities: Work like mutual funds and must be sold with a prospectus.

Voluntary Accumulation Plan: The investor limits price fluctuation risk by investing periodically, or using dollar cost averaging.

Warrant: The right to buy a stock at a certain price.

Western Accounts: Each member is only responsible for their portion of assigned syndicate shares.

Yield: A return on an investment.

Z-Tranches: These tranches are created as support until the CMO retires. Z-tranches are the last tranches remaining in a CMO. These tranches do not receive interest, but are bought at a discount and reach their full value at maturity.

BIBLIOGRAPHY

Curley, Michael T. and Joseph A. Walker, *Stockbroker Examination: Series 7*, Barron's Educational Series, New York, 2007.

Downes, John, A.B. and Jordan Elliot Goodman, A.B., M.A., *Dictionary of Finance and Investment Terms*, Barron's Financial Guides, New York, 2006.

Majka, Richard P., *EXAM CRAM Series 7 Securities Licensing Review*, Que Publishing, Indianapolis, IN, 2006.

N/A, *Test-Taking Power Strategies*, LearningExpress, New York, 2007.

Rice, Steven M., *Series 7 Exam for Dummies*, Wiley Publishing, Hoboken, NJ, 2007.

Walker, Robert, *Pass the 7: A Training Guide for the NASD Series 7 Exam*, First Books, Portland, OR, 2007.

www.finra.org, Financial Industry Regulatory Authority – Content Outline for Test Series 7 (.pdf)

AUTHOR BIOGRAPHY

Claire Bradley spent many years working in the finance industry, starting as a teller and working and studying her way to financial consultant. She lives in Colorado with her husband and two daughters.

INDEX